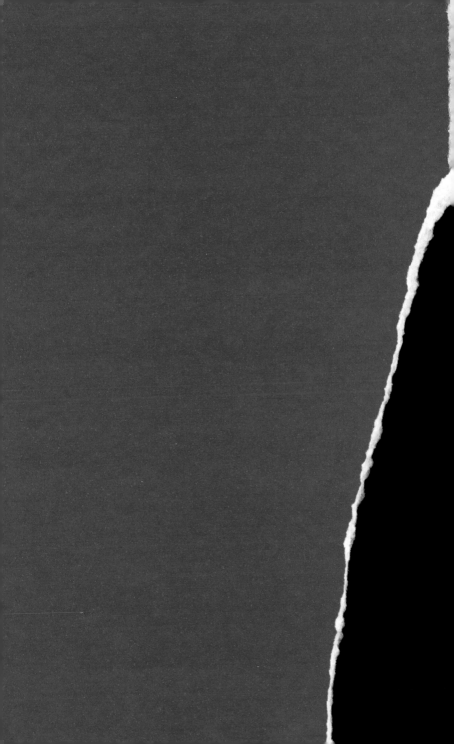

# Praise for *The Invisible Majority*

'An excellent panoramic perspective on India's disability sector… I am sure this well-researched and deeply engaging book will enable policy makers and practitioners to serve the cause of divyangjans more effectively.' – **M. Venkaiah Naidu, Vice President of India**

'One cannot read this book without conceiving enormous admiration for the empathy the authors evoke for people with disabilities. Readers will find their constructive perspective refreshing and persuasive. You will come away with a deep appreciation for life seen through others' eyes.' – **Vint Cerf, vice president and chief internet evangelist, Google**

'The book is timely since the focus must now shift to leveraging all workers as society opens up after the pandemic. I have personally seen the passion that Ferose brings to the issues of inclusion and how it affects not just people with disabilities but the people around them. The book will change your perspective on the disabled and how you can support this cause for creating a better society for all.' – **Kris Gopalakrishnan, vice chairman, Infosys**

'*The Invisible Majority* is a comprehensive and fascinating account of the story of Persons with Disabilities. I found it to be well-written, in many places even charmingly so, with endless amounts of original information. The book opened new vistas that broadened my knowledge and imagination of this universal issue.' – **Philip Zimbardo, Professor Emeritus in psychology, Stanford University, and founder, Heroic Imagination Project**

'This book is a substantial contribution to the disability sector since it is packed with information on what is contemporary and exciting in this field. The wide range of innovations and entrepreneurs documented is simply breathtaking. Indeed the book gives one much hope and optimism for the possibilities of enrichment and inclusion. A must-read.' – **Poonam Natarajan, former chairperson, National Trust, Government of India**

'This book provides a clear and accessible overview of disability and inclusion. While it focuses on India, its message is global in every way. With a sense of cautious optimism for the future, it explores how attitudes have shifted over the years and the challenges that still lie before all of us to create a truly inclusive society.' – **Christian Klein, CEO, SAP**

'Each sentence in this generous book expresses the Inclusivity of the Heart – the largest inclusivity of all.' – **Gary Zukav, author of *The Seat of the Soul* and *Universal Human***

'An absorbing, transforming and inspiring read from start to finish. Every chapter is infused with stories from people, movements, and organizations. Anecdotal and illustrative, it is thoroughly grounded in research and offers ideas for an inclusive future. A much-needed book, a timely book, a book we cannot be without.' – **Pradeep Sebastian, author**

'It is richly comprehensive. I also like the "tell it like it is" tone of the writing. Both the format and the content lend themselves to a general reader audience as well as people who are themselves dealing with disabilities and their caregivers.' – **Rajni Bakshi, author and Gandhi scholar**

'The book reads so wonderfully, like an engaging travelogue with so many stories of the "travel" that persons with disabilities and their families have to (perforce) undertake.' – **Shekhar Seshadri, psychiatrist and professor, National Institute of Mental Health and Neurosciences**

'This book is an eye-opening narrative of an often-overlooked part of our lives and society. It allows us to enter the lives of the disabled and instils in us a deep respect for those who have forged their experiences into weapons of empowerment.' – **Malvika Iyer, disability activist**

# THE INVISIBLE MAJORITY

## INDIA'S ABLED DISABLED

C.K. MEENA
AND
V.R. FEROSE

First published in 2021 by Hachette India
(Registered name: Hachette Book Publishing India Pvt. Ltd)
An Hachette UK company
www.hachetteindia.com

1

Cover design by Tanya Pradhan

ISBN 978-93-91028-67-1

Hachette Book Publishing India Pvt. Ltd
4th & 5th Floors, Corporate Centre,
Plot No. 94, Sector 44, Gurugram 122003, India

Typeset in Minion Pro 10/13.5
by R. Ajith Kumar, New Delhi

Printed and bound in India
by Thomson Press India Ltd.

*To the memory of Javed Abidi,*
*pioneering disability campaigner*

# CONTENTS

# FOREWORD

The most precious asset we human beings possess is our unique intelligence. To make full use of its extraordinary potential, it is essential that it be accompanied by a compassionate attitude towards all others.

Though we may differ from one another in minor ways, fundamentally we are all human beings who aspire to lead happy, meaningful lives. We must therefore work to cultivate a sense of the oneness of humanity and include all within our sphere of concern, irrespective of their religion, nationality, or race.

It is crucial that we recognize the capabilities of those with some form of disability. We must make effort to facilitate their proper education in order to include them in the workforce. For those who are completely dependent on others, we must show our concern both mentally and by our actions.

*The Invisible Majority*, by C.K. Meena and V.R. Ferose, addresses a range of issues that concern our fellow brothers and sisters experiencing a variety of challenges. I commend the authors for their hard work; I hope this book will give insight into the needs of so many of them and thereby help in providing them with our support.

30 September 2021

# PREFACE

*THIS IS A BOOK ABOUT DISABILITY. WHICH MEANS THIS IS A book about all of us.*

According to the World Health Organization (WHO), Persons with Disabilities (PwDs) form the largest minority in the world – close to 1.3 billion or 15 per cent of the global population. But the numbers conceal a cold, hard fact that few of us have considered: Even if we have no disability today, we will almost inevitably acquire one tomorrow. All we have to do is live long enough.

If that sounds unbelievable to you, perhaps it's time for a rethink. You might have to shed the stock, negative images that fill your brain when you hear the term 'disability', and try to fully grasp its meaning.

To understand why we say this, it's important to first understand the meaning of the term 'disability'. There is no single definition of disability. It is 'an evolving concept' according to the Convention on the Rights of Persons with Disabilities (CRPD) adopted by the United Nations (UN) in 2006. If we were born without a sense of smell, does that mean we may park our vehicle in the 'disabled' slot? Perhaps not. If one is unable to read without glasses, is that a disability? It appears to be so.

Simply put, we are disabled if our inability to carry out daily activities hinders us from participating fully in society. Disability covers everything from stuttering to schizophrenia; it can be mild, moderate or severe, a temporary or long-term impairment; it may be physical, mental, intellectual or sensory, the result of old age, an accident, illness, a communicable disease or a rare genetic disorder.

So now perhaps you may see the point we are trying to make: In one way or another, at some point or the other, disability touches us all. If you haven't been a PwD and aren't a caregiver of one, you may have at least known of or interacted with one. Just look around you. Your colleague has depression, your boss survived cancer, your neighbour is due for a cataract operation, the gardener in your block of flats is hearing impaired (HI), there's a woman with dwarfism who sits begging on the pavement down your street, your friend's cousin uses a wheelchair after a nasty fall, and oh, wasn't your mother's uncle what they called an 'idiot' in the previous century?

*We believe that persons with disabilities form an 'invisible majority'.*

PwDs are rendered invisible because the fear of public humiliation keeps them indoors, or because an inaccessible environment forces even those who wish to venture out to remain locked in. They are also invisible when their disability is not physical. Society does not see the millions affected by 'invisible disabilities' – impairments and illnesses of the mind.

But PwDs are the majority because every one of us is liable to join their ranks. And also because we must include those whose lives are radically impacted and altered by being caregivers. If we assume that there are at least three family members for each PwD, 60 per cent of the world's population is directly affected by disability – an absolute majority. Besides, every seventh person on this planet has a disability! PwDs come from every class, gender, race, religion, community and nationality. And yet we often fail to grasp the magnitude of the invisible majority.

Since disability is such an impartial benefactor, shouldn't it be shocking that the world hasn't recognized its worth? Far from it. Even though millions of PwDs have proudly united in their refusal to consider disability a curse, mainstream society's mindset hasn't changed.

But PwDs remain undeterred and have successfully created a thriving global community that claims its rights in no uncertain terms. The community insists on being represented in all decisions made about its interests. 'Nothing about us without us' is the slogan of the global disability movement.

Unfortunately, India does not yet have a cohesive group of PwDs – a sizeable 'us' who can forge a mass movement. Nonetheless, there are many individuals here who are asserting their identities – PwDs who have heaved aside mountainous obstacles to carve out a track for themselves and for others like them.

*This book will introduce you to some of these empowered and empowering individuals with disabilities.*

While introducing you to them, we refuse to parrot the Indian media's pet clichés about them – warriors, champions, brave-hearts and so on. We will also resolutely avoid the word 'inspiring'. Most PwDs we spoke to are tired of being 'inspirational', of being held up as exemplars for other PwDs as well as the 'able-bodied' and of hearing: 'If even they can do it, why can't you?'

But we request their permission to slip in an 'incredible' or an 'astounding' once in a while. Because what they have overcome, achieved and continue to live through can sometimes appear beyond belief. Their stories will pierce the core of your being.

As we read their stories, we must remember that it wasn't too long ago when the world's citizens with disabilities were considered less than human. They were hidden from public view; if they did venture outside their house or asylum, they were spurned, feared, ridiculed, demonized and even killed. It has been a gruelling, protracted journey from recognition to acceptance, integration and finally inclusion.

*This is a book about disability and inclusion in India.*

We tried to reach out to PwDs from as many regions of India as we could through the individuals and organizations that one of us (V.R. Ferose) had judiciously connected with, over 10 years of working towards inclusion in the country. Mostly, we were able to interview people in or from the national capital, and the capitals of Kerala, Karnataka, Tamil Nadu, Andhra Pradesh, Maharashtra, Gujarat and Rajasthan. One of us (C.K. Meena) did the work of conducting a total of 64 interviews, either in person or over the telephone, between November 2018 and December 2020. These conversations held in homes, offices, schools, parks, restaurants and hotels inevitably left her feeling hopeful and energized, and opened up a whole new universe for her. As we try to make sense of disability and inclusion in India, we hope to amplify the voices of many of these individuals, but before we do that perhaps it will help to get some key facts and figures in order.

India's PwDs form 2.2 per cent of its population, according to the latest census – a grossly underestimated figure by all accounts. Of course, D&I (Diversity and Inclusion) has recently become a buzzword in the Indian corporate space and 'Universal Design' is on many people's lips. But, as a country, we are far behind Western nations; for example, the United States has taken giant strides since its government passed the Americans with Disabilities Act (ADA) in 1990. One must keep in mind though that disability rights activists in that country kick-started the movement six decades ago. India was still speaking the language of sympathy when disability activists, such as the remarkable (late) Javed Abidi, introduced the language of rights. Indubitably, it was the fierce thrust of activism that pushed the Indian government to pass the

Persons With Disabilities (Equal Opportunities, Protection of Rights and Full Participation) Act, 1995, which finally led to the current Rights of Persons with Disabilities (RPwD) Act, 2016.

*This is a book about the changing attitudes towards disability in India.*

While we will not gloss over the persisting myths, prejudices and superstitions about disability (many of which make us wonder whether to laugh or cry!), we will shine a light on the signposts of hope. We will mark the trends and make sense of how the disability sector is moving from a charity-based approach to a rights-based approach. We will track how the discourse has shifted from the medical model, which seeks a 'cure' for disability, to the social model, where society and the environment are seen as the hurdles to inclusion.

Another change we've noticed is that Indian companies are gradually waking up to the disability advantage. It is dawning on them that a PwD is not a liability and, if given the right skills-training, can become a priceless asset. Indian business is also growing aware that PwDs constitute a huge untapped consumer base. Globally, together with their friends and families, they control over $13 trillion in annual disposable income![1] Their purchasing power alone should motivate big businesses to support inclusion.

*This book examines each of the seven pillars that support the foundation of an inclusive society (advocacy, awareness, prevention/ diagnosis, education, employment, lifestyle and assisted living) and seeks to assess where India stands in relation to them.*

---

[1] Rich Donovan, *Return on Disability – 2020 Annual Report: The Global Economics of Disability* (Toronto: The Return on Disability Group, 2020).

There are countless non-governmental organizations (NGOs) operating in the disability sector and innumerable government initiatives channelled towards inclusion. But they are far away from achieving their goals. It will take a long time to remove every barrier – physical, social and attitudinal – for PwDs in India to enjoy full and equal participation in society. The RPwD Act mandates accessibility, inclusive education and job reservations, and mentions a long list of such laudable targets. On paper everything sounds hunky-dory. But when it comes to acting on the directives of the Act, much is found wanting.

*This book features some of the pioneering and committed individuals and organizations that strive to bring out the abilities of those with disabilities and enrich their lives.*

Their objectives, if collated, provide a cradle-to-grave vision for PwDs where they are enabled to complete their academic goals, be gainfully employed, form nourishing relationships, enjoy flourishing social lives and be assisted to live independently or inter-dependently till the end of their days.

*This book also features young entrepreneurs who are finding imaginative ways to aid PwDs' autonomy and bring about inclusion.*

There is a crop of young social entrepreneurs who are contributing to the building blocks of the seven pillars. A few of the many creative projects that this generation of Indians have come up with include: inclusive art shows, inclusive sports programmes, films on disability, dolls with physical disabilities, driving lessons for wheelchair users, inclusive parks, tourism for PwDs, devices to enable people to learn Braille themselves, blind-friendly railway stations, and websites that foreground the emotional and sexual needs of PwDs. It gives us hope that their future rests in thoughtful and caring hands.

*This book does not forget the caregivers.*

We salute those who are directly and emotionally connected to PwDs – parents, siblings and others who often shift their own moorings to anchor the lives of their loved ones. They have known denial, anger, sorrow, frustration and guilt, and they have trekked the long road to acceptance.

*A word about terminology.*

New terms crop up every day in line with the latest wave of political correctness. For example, in the LGBTQIA+ (lesbian, gay, bisexual, transgender, queer, intersex and asexual plus) space the initialism has kept expanding over the last couple of decade. It is now recognized that there could be further additions, hence the plus sign. Similarly, labels for disability have changed over the centuries.

In the early twentieth century, 'idiot', 'moron' and 'imbecile' were not offensive terms but actual medical classifications of degrees of intellectual capacity. As time passed, they began to be used as insults. Similarly, 'mentally retarded (MR)' and 'spastic' were legitimate medical descriptions that later came to be used pejoratively.

Harvard linguist Steven Pinker coined the term 'euphemism treadmill' for this phenomenon. The moment you invent a polite term for something, 'the euphemism becomes tainted by association and the new one that must be found acquires its own negative connotations', Pinker wrote in his 1994 piece in the Op-ed page of the *New York Times*.[2]

Terminology for disability has shifted from 'handicapped' to 'disabled', then to 'challenged' and 'special' respectively, and finally

---

[2] Steven Pinker, 'The Game of the Name', the *New York Times*, 5 April 1994.

now the acceptable term is 'persons with disability'. 'People-first language' is the current norm: one must put the person before the disability, as in 'student with dyslexia' or 'person with autism' and not 'dyslexic student' or 'autistic person'. The label of 'differently abled', though popular in the media, is rejected by many PwDs who point out that everybody has different abilities and so the expression is meaningless. In fact, many today have had enough of mainstream society's pussyfooting around the subject and actually prefer to baldly call themselves 'disabled'. After all they do live in a disabling environment, and they own their disability with pride.

Since any attempt to get off the euphemism treadmill is futile, we will decide on our own choice of terminology, presuming that PwDs know we are well-meaning. When we quote them we will of course respect each individual's self-definition of their identity. What we will NOT use is 'normal'; instead, it will be 'average', 'typical' or 'neurotypical' (NT) and occasionally, where syntax demands it, 'non-disabled'. We will mainly use 'PwD' and sometimes 'disabled' and try not to use 'differently abled'. The self-appointed guardians of political correctness can look the other way.

*This book will offer suggestions from PwDs and those working in the disability sector on how we could build a movement that would lead to an inclusive India.*

You cannot clump PwDs into a single homogenous entity. They have diverse and strong opinions, and you will hear them all. There are those who demand that the world change to suit their lives, and those who change their lives to suit the world because they don't expect it to change. You will see or hear a multitude of voices – lively, sardonic, angry, defensive, witty, resigned, pragmatic, serene and wise. What you will not get is a faceless crowd defined by the label of disability.

While we promise that our book will spark in you several 'wow,

I didn't know that' and 'oh, I hadn't thought of that' moments, we hope it will also give you pause to think about our collective future.

Because disability, which will touch all of our lives sooner or later, should be of concern to us all.

# 1

# THE FICTION OF NORMALCY

THE COVID-19 PANDEMIC HAS SPAWNED THE TERM 'THE new normal'. But what was the 'old normal' like, if indeed it ever existed?

Before we speak about disability, we must banish the spectre of the 'normal'. It seeps into our language; it haunts our daily lives. If we stopped to think for a moment, we would know it doesn't really exist.

The norm is what is accepted by 'most people'. It is the standard to which we are expected to conform. But do 'most people' look, behave or live the same way? Human beings differ widely from one another in their appearance, sexual orientation, behaviour, attitudes and belief systems. And yet, society prescribes an entire catalogue of social customs, practices, and codes of behaviour and morality, to which 'normal' people must adhere. Physical appearance also comes into the picture. Apparently, there is a prototype into which we must all fit. Any deviation results in varying degrees of exclusion.

But while the ideal of beauty and perfection (and normalcy) seems to be written in stone, there is an exquisite concept that runs contrary to it. It is *wabi-sabi*, the Japanese aesthetic notion of finding beauty in what is deemed imperfect. The Japanese treasure aged, cracked and well-worn objects; they consider them beautiful because such objects remind us of life's impermanence and induce in us a melancholic joy.

Why can't we expand the notion of *wabi-sabi* to embrace all manner of humanity – young and old? Why not find beauty in shortened bodies, reduced limbs, sightless eyes, contorted torsos, hunched backs, twitches and spasms, wrinkles and gummy smiles? In a rolling gait and a dragging foot, in a closed, expressionless face and a frenetically mobile one?

A child is born. You inspect her – check fingers and toes, all correct and present. She is 'normal'. As she grows, day after day and month after month, you check the signs periodically. She can hear; she can speak. She is 'normal'. Now all that remains is for her to go to a 'regular' school, get 'acceptable' marks in college, get a 'regular' job, marry an 'acceptable' man and have 'normal' children.

You can immediately see how problematic the terms 'normal', 'regular,' and 'acceptable' are – not to mention, how dreadfully boring they sound and how easy it is to be labelled 'abnormal'. The one per cent is held up as the ideal to which the rest must aspire. If your newborn is missing a body part, if you discover that she can't hear or speak, if her mind is wired differently, if she drops out of college, if she works as a long-distance lorry driver, if she doesn't marry or marries but refuses to have children, or if she marries a woman or transitions into a man, will you have the heart to brand her 'abnormal'? It is those who represent the fabulous diversity of the human race and the wealth of human experience that are dubbed 'not normal' if not 'abnormal'.

PwDs will tell you they are just like everyone else. No less, no more.

# 2

# MYTHS AND MISCONCEPTIONS

THE RPWD ACT BLITHELY SPEAKS OF CREATING AN 'ACCESSIBLE' and 'barrier-free' environment, but even before PwDs can overcome physical barriers they have to cross an even more daunting one: the attitudinal barrier. That is, persistent negative attitudes of society towards disability.

## 'Let's Fix It'

In December 2019, villagers in some districts of Karnataka buried their children with physical disabilities neck deep in compost pits during a solar eclipse, hoping it would 'cure' them.[3] When we sent a link of a news report on this to Prarthana and Prateek Kaul of GiftAbled foundation, which works for PwD empowerment, livelihood and inclusion, they sent us a 'gift' in return: a message from a stranger who suggested 'moon phase education' for the blind so that they could 'have some redemption'. We never figured out what exactly this pedagogic method entailed but one thing was clear: whether it be the sun, moon or stars, every celestial object seems to hold out a false promise for parents hankering after that elusive 'cure' for their child's disability.

---

[3] 'Karnataka: Kids buried in dirt to cure disability', *Deccan Herald*, 26 December 2019.

No surprises here. Because, unfortunately, disability is seen as a problem to be fixed.

Fervent appeals are sent up to the heavens – to visible bodies and invisible beings alike – to 'repair', to put it bluntly, the 'damaged goods' delivered to them. Most of society's attitudes towards PwDs are rooted in misconceptions. There's the ever popular karma connection – the belief that the 'curse' of disability results from sins committed in one's previous birth. Superstitions exert a rigid hold on the vulnerable.[4]

The hunger for cures drives parents to try alternative forms of medicine, offer prayers at temples and *dargah*s across the country, and approach assorted gurus, quacks and 'godmen'. Hoping against hope that their child can become 'normal', they clutch at every straw however flimsy. The most frantic are often the parents of children with developmental disabilities (DD) such as autism, Intellectual Disability (ID), Cerebral Palsy (CP, 'spastic'), Learning Disorders (LD, 'slow learner') and Attention-Deficit/Hyperactivity Disorder (ADHD).

Gitanjali Sarangan, founder of the Snehadhara organization that uses Arts-Based Therapy (ABT) for children and adults with DD, takes a sympathetic and non-judgmental approach to such parents. 'Parents are resorting to so many things [like this]. There's a Babaji who tells them what to do. He tells them black magic is why your child is like this.' Gitanjali tells us that there was one mother who sent a *laddoo* every day with instructions that it be fed to her daughter at 12 o'clock. When a puzzled Gitanjali asked why the insistence on that particular time, the mother replied: 'Do you notice how calm she becomes after she eats it?' Later she confessed

---

[4] By the way, superstitions are thoughtlessly referred to as 'blind beliefs', which is not exactly complimentary to the blind and the visually impaired! But then again the English language is ridden with idiomatic expressions that 'unwittingly' dishonour PwDs ('turn a deaf ear or a blind eye to', 'not have a leg to stand on' etc.), so let's not step into that minefield.

that the sweets were spiked with marijuana! She was using it as a substitute for anti-psychotic drugs.

A young mother, who doesn't want to be identified, speaks of how distressed she was when her parents-in-law started pointing fingers at her after her son was diagnosed with autism. In her presence they would discuss amongst themselves the possible reasons for the boy's 'abnormality'. Was the caesarean delivery conducted at an inauspicious time (during *rahu kaalam*)? Perhaps the autism was hereditary and there was someone on her side of the family with a similar 'problem'. Or maybe, they speculated, it was the result of bad parenting: she may not have paid enough attention to him and had focussed only on her neurotypical children. Her in-laws actually suggested that she take her son with autism with her to stay permanently with her parents, leaving the rest of her family behind; they feared that if she devoted time to him she wouldn't be able to 'look after' their precious son, and they believed that as a result of this his job would be at risk!

'Every parent first asks: is there a cure?' says Prachi Deo who started Nayi Disha, which provides information resources to parents of kids with disabilities. 'Especially for autism, when they are suddenly told the child who is apparently normally developing has autism at 15–18 months, they want to know if it can be "corrected". They want to know what can make it "normal". In this hunt for a cure they end up going to quacks. Like you have *jhola chhaap* doctors (quacks) you also have *jhola chhaap* therapists,' says Prachi.

'You'll find people trying HBOT – hyperbaric oxygen therapy, where you put the child into an oxygen chamber. Or else, stem cell therapy. It's not just those who have low education or poor economic background who do this, but those who have resources. Not only do they lose out on money, but also on valuable time for the child; the same time could have been spent on the right therapy for the child,' she adds.

Priyanka Malhotra tried out many treatments all over the country for her son Nipun. He was born in Bombay (since renamed Mumbai) with the rare disease arthrogryposis, which stunted the development of the muscles in his limbs. She even consulted a doctor in Kashmir. When she took him to Jaipur for the corrective surgery of one of his hands, which 'had a few muscles that could be saved', they manufactured a contraption to make him stand. Watching the little fellow struggle with the device she said to herself: 'Why am I making him go through all this pain?' Instead of 'correcting' him, she felt he should make the most of what he already had.

Priyanka had instinctively made a wise decision that parents rarely do. Instead of forcing her child into the straitjacket of 'normalcy', she had accepted his disability. She started focussing on what he *could* do, instead of what he couldn't.

And going by the Nipun Malhotra you meet today, he could do plenty! An alumnus of St. Stephen's and of the Delhi School of Economics, this 33-year-old who 'sits up' for his rights has taken the government to court multiple times over accessibility issues. Besides being on various boards and committees, he is the chief executive officer of Nipman Foundation – which works towards the 'health, dignity and happiness' of PwDs.

When we reflect on the tremendous amount of time, energy and money that many parents have poured into the enterprise of striving to make their children 'normal', we can only say with a sigh: 'Such a pity.'

Unfortunately, it is the disability and not this futile effort that is looked upon with pity by society.

## Pity, Rejection, Shame

Pity and avoidance are the two primary responses of Indian society to PwDs. The sight of a person with a physical disability elicits (depending on the region) an '*ayyo paavam*' or a '*hai bechaara*' (both of which mean 'poor thing'), while the 'abnormal' behaviour of a person with DD is generally met with averted eyes and hurried footsteps.

Disability carries such a strong social stigma that many parents either neglect their children with disabilities, believing them to be 'useless', or they hide them from public view. Out-and-out rejection is not unusual, especially in rural and underprivileged contexts. When the man realizes that his newborn child – particularly if it is a girl – has a disability, he disowns her and abandons his wife. The maternal instinct usually kicks in, and the mother bears the responsibility of bringing up the child. We use the term 'bringing up' loosely for oftentimes it involves nothing more than fulfilling bare minimum needs.

One of the most extreme cases of this kind was reported in July 2019 when Bengaluru police arrested a daily-wage labourer for hiring a man to kill his five-year-old son. The labourer had four children and allegedly wanted to get rid of his youngest, who was speech and hearing impaired. He had reportedly hired an assassin who succeeded in strangling the boy. According to the police, he said he couldn't afford the medical treatment for the boy and therefore decided to have him murdered.[5]

Geetha Sridhar, principal of Sahas, the opportunity school of Bharatiya Vidya Bhavan Kodagu Vidyalaya in Madikeri (Karnataka), recounts the story of a former student – a girl with profound hearing loss. Her father, a police constable, used to beat her mother with his lathi. He would only acknowledge his NT son and rejected his daughter outright. Before he went to work every day, he used to lock up his wife and daughter. The determined mother would somehow sneak out through the window with her

---

[5] 'Bengaluru man hires supari killer to murder five-year-old differently abled son', *New Indian Express*, 19 July 2019.

daughter and bring her to Sahas, making sure to return before her husband got home. In this way, she got her daughter educated. 'The day she [the daughter] uttered her first word *baa* (come), the mother held my hand and cried,' says Geetha, her voice trembling with emotion. When the girl's father died, her mother got a government job in his place as a Class IV employee. She raised her children on her own. In the end, her daughter finished twelve years of schooling and got a diploma from JSS Polytechnic, Mysuru.

It's not only 'poor and ignorant villagers' who behave in this manner. The urban and 'educated' are equally capable of walking out of a marriage the moment they find out that there's 'something wrong' with their child. Prachi Deo has found that in most middle class families of children with disabilities, it is the mother who faces the pressure: 'Many times mothers find themselves alone on the journey. Either the father is too busy with the job, saying he is earning for the family, and is not involved at all, so everything falls on the mother, or the father checks out – gets out of the marriage.'

Ignorance about disability cuts across classes. Neither a substantial bank balance nor a college degree makes a difference to people's limited understanding and bizarre notions of disability. According to Manjula Kalyan, founder of Swayamkrushi in Hyderabad, which rehabilitates girls and women with ID, once an IAS (Indian Administrative Services) officer she was speaking to voiced his disturbing and completely unfounded opinion about those who are severely impaired and low functioning: 'I believe they kill people!'

Gagandeep Singh Chandok, who has the genetic blood disorder Beta-Thalassaemia Major, works for the welfare of thalassaemics ('thals' as they colloquially refer to themselves). He says that people believe the disability is infectious: 'The public is scared; they think it's contagious, it will spread like HIV (human immunodeficiency virus)!' He knows of many marriage proposals for siblings of thalassaemics that have fallen through because of this misconception. 'I know of a father who abandoned the mother after the child was diagnosed. Divorce has taken place because of this. There are many 'thals' who don't even tell their grandparents or their relatives about their condition. Sisters have been told not to tell their in-laws that they have 'thal' brothers,' he tells us.

Marriage proposals get stymied at the tiniest whiff of any type of disability. What if the 'defect' is passed on to the next generation? The family tree is minutely examined and friends-turned-sleuths volunteer to scout for 'relevant' information. It doesn't even need to be a sibling who has a disability for weddings to be called off; it could be some remote dead relative who was known to have had epilepsy or asthma.

Naturally then, a person with a visible physical disability faces the toughest resistance from potential in-laws. In 1993, when 22-year-old Sumathy told her parents she wanted to marry 27-year-old Suresh Vaidyanathan, they wouldn't hear of it. It was of no consequence to them that Suresh was already a well-known ghatam artist, having played with stalwarts of Carnatic music at international concerts. His polio was the only scale by which they measured him. 'Ours was a love marriage,' says Ghatam Suresh (as he is popularly known). He met the 'beautiful, intelligent' Sumathy at the Life Insurance Corporation office where he was then employed. Suresh gallantly offered to switch seats with newbie Sumathy who was struggling to cope with her overbearing boss in the claims department. She was quite impressed by how he skilfully convinced her boss to take him in by professing a keen interest in learning the nitty-gritty of claims. An 'office romance' bloomed, and they tied the knot despite her parents' disapproval.

Disability has so much shame and ridicule attached to it. Mockery is something that many PwDs have experienced, particularly during childhood. Suresh remembers going out with his mother and hearing passers-by calling him rude names. In a voice laden with emotion he relates how his (late) mother would furiously confront the perpetrators, regardless of who they were, and shower them with the choicest abuses. When they got home she would tenderly embrace him, caress his head and tell him: 'God has given you this disability because he knows you are strong enough to handle it.'

Not all mothers are as doughty as Suresh's. Society's responses often induce a sense of shame in parents for having produced a child with a disability. As if that were not enough, they have to deal with anxiety about the myriad pinpricks and humiliations the child might face in the future. Which of us hasn't seen, at one time or the other, a person with disabilities such as ID or dwarfism being teased or derided by strangers? It is such a common occurrence in our country that the RPwD Act makes a point of mentioning it. Besides punishment for abuse, violence and exploitation of PwDs, it specifies: 'Whoever intentionally insults or intimidates with intent to humiliate a person with disability in any place within public view...shall be punishable with imprisonment for a term which shall not be less than six months but which may extend to five years and with fine.'[6]

There are many cases, though, where such an 'intention' to humiliate or insult is not there, or is hard to establish, but that does not take away from the hurt PwDs have to go through in such instances. Janaki Narayan who teaches at Brindavan Education Trust for children with LD has a son with autism, Siddharth (also known as Sid). 'The curious and unrelenting stares are still there when we step out with Sid,' she says. 'Small children point and giggle, and we hear them ask: "What's wrong with that *anna* (brother)?" Parents learn to swallow the hurt and move on.'

Some parents want to avoid the hurt altogether by hiding away their children with disabilities, never bringing them out in public. Mini Menon of Endeavor ELS, which runs the Special Education

---

[6] RPwD Act, Chapter XVI, Section 92 (a).

department of Deens Academy in Bengaluru, tells us about a student with Down Syndrome (DS) who lives with his brother and parents in a gated community. The boy's brother is NT and a high achiever. Mini discovered that the couple had hidden their child with DS so thoroughly that even neighbours didn't know of his existence! When the residents of the gated community held a dance night, the boy was predictably left behind at home. And Mini knows, from the activity sessions held at school, that he simply loves to dance. She says sorrowfully, 'If only they'd taken him to the dance night... How he would have enjoyed himself!'

Prachi Deo has seen how social stigma plays a role in parental behaviour. 'They feel isolated, not being able to go to social events,' she says. Her own parents were the polar opposite. They took her brother Pranjan everywhere. Because they were comfortable with his diagnosis as a child with DS, she was too; their attitudes percolated down to her. 'I never saw the need to cover up; I was never ashamed. Anyone who came to my house to meet me would interact with my brother. A lot of that comes from what my parents taught me,' she adds.

Similarly, Smrithy Rajesh who is the mother of Advaith – a child with autism and ADHD says, 'We take Addu (short for Advaith) everywhere. The restaurants near our house – they all know us. They take our orders first and give him his food first since he can't wait! No one has said: Don't make noise here. Some people stare, but when they see us laughing and enjoying ourselves, they look at us and smile.'

But not all parents are like Smrithy. The classic 'what will people think?' dreadfully familiar to every Indian is uppermost in the minds of many parents of kids with disabilities. And children with DD are often at the receiving end of the cruellest isolation.

People often behave as if they can't even bear the sight of them. Manjula Kalyan, who pioneered the concept of independent living in a 'group home' as opposed to the 'institution' model in 1991, recalls the first apartment she rented for women with ID. The woman in the flat downstairs complained that they were using the common stairwell of the apartment block. And the problem was…? The 'girls' were going up and down the stairs in the presence of her kids. The woman had demanded that they avoid using the staircase whenever her children were in view! Attitudes did change after Manjula's determined efforts to build awareness among the residents, but that's a story we'll save for later.

When Gitanjali started Snehadhara in JP Nagar (the centre has since shifted to another locality), Bengaluru, too the neighbours were against it. It wasn't that the kids at the centre were creating a ruckus. The neighbours were offended by the very sight of a house full of 'abnormal' kids. Gitanjali went from door to door to talk to residents. One cited the karma theory; another asked her why she wanted to get into 'all this', and why she couldn't start a beauty parlour instead. A senior citizen said, 'It is a nuisance for us; we can't be seeing them every day.' After the first year, she went around with a box of sweets to each house. When she spoke to the senior citizen, she came to know that his wife was bedridden, and he had lost a son to cancer. Disability was entrenched in his own life, and that should have made him empathetic. But no, he didn't want to 'add to his suffering' by witnessing what he assumed was more suffering that the children were going through. 'Apartment complexes are also driving out families of Children with Special Needs [CWSN],' says Gitanjali. 'In two or three cases we had to intervene.' And this is happening today in the 'IT (Information Technology) City' of Bengaluru!

## Crushing Ignorance

Society is ignorant of what PwDs are actually capable of. It robs them of opportunities to extend themselves to their full potential. First, society does not know the nature of each disability – what its characteristics are, and what exactly it entails. Second, it makes assumptions that restrict what a PwD can do.

Smrithy Rajesh, who conducts workshops for mothers of children with DD, tells us about the mother of a 'boy' with DS; the 'boy' is actually a 26-year-old man. All he has ever done in his life is sit on the sofa in his living room, eat and sleep. Smrithy is appalled by the wasted years and the missed opportunities that the right intervention at the right time could have prevented.

Shanti Raghavan who is the co-founder of Enable India (EI), which works towards the economic independence of PwDs, says that a man once told her about his two blind sisters. 'What do they do?' she asked him, presuming they had some kind of job. 'They sing,' he replied. That's the only thing they did the livelong day: sit in their house, open their mouths, and sing.

Ignorance leads to assumptions, and these assumptions can sometimes take a comic turn. In the United States Immigration Services (USIS) Programme Charcha-Cast hosted by Nick Novak, activist and blind comedian Nidhi Goyal describes a hilarious incident. Her blind friend was waiting for her by the side of the road when a 'helpful' stranger grabbed him by the arm and led him to the other side. He waited till they'd crossed the road and then he told her, 'Now please take me back to the other side because I was waiting for someone there!'

Tiffany Brar, a National Award-winning community-service worker who is blind, recalls how she was waiting at a bus-stand in Kerala's capital. An old woman selling a basket of vegetables got up, walked across to her and gave her a tenner! Despite Tiffany assuring her she was well-to-do, the vendor refused to take it back saying, 'It will bring me *punya* (merit).' She believed that charity towards a blind person, who must surely be poor and helpless as well, would earn her an extra share of divine blessings.

Pavithra Y.S. who is the founder of Vindhya e-Infomedia, which employs hundreds of PwDs, tells us about one of her staff members who used to commute to work by bus. 'He had a master's degree. He also had 90 per cent disability; polio had affected both his legs. He said that when he waited in the bus-stop, people would drop money near him!'

His experience bears a striking similarity to that of a prominent disability rights activist in the United States whom journalist Joseph P. Shapiro mentions in his book, *No Pity: People with Disabilities Forging a New Civil Rights Movement*. Mary Lou Breslin was sitting in her wheelchair and sipping a cup of coffee placed by her side. A passing woman threw a coin into the cup and it splashed all over Mary's business suit! It didn't matter how she was dressed. A PwD with a cup beside her meant only one thing.[7]

Change can only come about with awareness. Unless society becomes aware of what PwDs can do, and stops assuming what they can't do, PwDs themselves will be hindered from visualizing how far they can go and grow.

---

[7] Joseph P. Shapiro, *No Pity: People with Disabilities Forging a New Civil Rights Movement* (New York: Three Rivers Press, 1993), p. 19.

# 3

# THE ABC OF DISABILITY

AWARENESS, LIKE CHARITY, BEGINS AT HOME. IF SOCIETY needs to be aware of disability to change its behaviour and attitudes towards PwDs, doesn't 'society' include you, the reader – particularly the non-disabled reader?

You've probably heard this colloquial expression before, usually spoken in an irritated tone when someone is airing an opinion about a matter they know little about: 'They don't even know the ABC of it, and just listen to them talk!' Well, we too didn't know the ABC of disability before we started researching about it. (One of us had a ten-year head-start over the other though.) How about we pass on some basic *gyaan* (gen) to you so that you don't make the mistakes many well-meaning others do, and so the next time someone reveals their ignorance, you know how to put them right?

## Use and Invite Others to Use Correct Terminology

For a start, avoid expressions that imply a state of helplessness such as victim, sufferer or afflicted with. It's not 'wheelchair-*bound*' or '*confined* to a wheelchair', but 'wheelchair *user*'. Those who have lost their vision completely are blind; those who have 100 per cent loss of hearing are deaf; others have low vision, or are visually impaired, hearing impaired, hard of hearing or speech and hearing impaired. Government data and documents use the initials LV, VI, HI, HOH and SHI respectively.

Never say 'dumb' because of its pejorative association, use 'mute' instead; it's not 'deaf and dumb' but 'deaf-mute'. However, there is a difference between 'deaf' with a capital 'D' and with a lower case 'd'. The latter is used when you're referring to deaf individuals; the former refers to the group of persons who are deaf, HI or SHI who communicate only through Sign language; they belong to the extremely tightly knit Deaf community. The Deaf say to the rest of the world: If you want to speak to us, learn our language. And this could be American Sign Language (ASL), British Sign Language (BSL) or – what is most in use in our country – Indian Sign Language (ISL).

The disability comes after the person. For example: it is a person with dwarfism – not dwarf or midget, a person with epilepsy and not an epileptic, a person with autism or Autism Spectrum Disorder (ASD) – and not an autistic person. But this usage comes with a rider, so try not to get confused. PwDs might use several other epithets to self-identify. Just as the LGBTQIA+ community reclaimed the insult 'queer', people with physical disabilities in the United States for example claimed 'crip' which stands for cripple. There are those with ASD who say they are 'autistic' and use it as a badge of honour. But that doesn't give others the right to use these terms to their face. Ground rule: always find out how a PwD would like to be addressed as or referred to, and go by their preference.

One thing is for certain: No PwD wishes to be called Your Divine Highness! This is no joke. In December 2015, Prime Minister Narendra Modi spoke of the 'divine qualities' of PwDs in his monthly *Mann Ki Baat* radio programme. In May 2016, the Indian government officially changed the Hindi translation of the Department of Empowerment of Persons with Disabilities

(DEPD), substituting '*Divyangjan*' or 'persons with divine abilities' for the earlier '*Viklang*' (handicapped).

There was uproar in the community. PwDs said they found the term 'patronizing' and described it as 'reverse stereotyping' – from PwDs being seen as 'sub-normal', they were forced into being 'super-normal'. The National Platform for Disability Rights, which had sent a letter to the prime minister after his radio broadcast objecting to his description of the 'divine qualities' of PwDs, now sent another letter in which it urged the government of India to withdraw the notification about the name-change of the DEPD. In fact in September 2019, the United Nations Convention on the Rights of Persons with Disabilities (UNCRPD) itself said the term 'divyangjan' was 'controversial' and equated it to other 'derogatory' terms that had to be repealed.

## Offer and Take Lessons on How to Behave Towards PwDs

Condescension is widespread. People often infantilize PwDs, talking down to adults with intellectual or physical disabilities as if they were children who couldn't think for themselves. They 'help' them, unasked, in order to feel good about themselves. This 'help' is often misplaced.

The worst thing you can do is to lift and heave a wheelchair user without their consent, as if they were a sack of rice. Also, everyone should realize that *a wheelchair is an extension of the user's body just as a cane is an extension of the blind person's arm*. Don't touch it without permission. Don't treat the wheelchair like an obstruction in your path and push or tug at it carelessly. If (and only if) a blind person asks you to help them cross the street, never grab their hand and take away their cane. Instead, offer your arm for them to grip and match your pace to theirs as they tap/feel their way across.

Let's say you're at a public function during a lunch buffet and you see a blind person looking rather lost. Filled with the do-gooder spirit you offer to bring them a plate of food. Vegetarian or meat? That's the only question you deem important. Off you go to the buffet table and pile the plate higgledy-piggledy with every dish you see. You convey the plate to where they are seated, even remembering to get a glass of water on the way. With halo firmly affixed to your head, you go back to get your own lunch.

Good deed done? No way! The blind person has no clue what's in front of them. Do you expect them to finger, smell and sample each item? And what about the dishes they didn't want, wanted less of or more of? What you should have done is led them to the buffet table with an empty plate, serving only what and how much they wished to eat after having named and described the items to them one by one. Oh, and don't forget the dessert later!

When you're speaking to a deaf person through an interpreter, make eye contact with and address the person – not the interpreter. A seasoned interpreter will simultaneously and fluidly turn their Sign into speech; your speech will be similarly transmitted into Sign, which the deaf person will absorb through quick glances at the interpreter. The conversation between you two will flow as seamlessly as if both of you were hearing each other.

## Ignorance Springs from Rarely Being Conscious of Disability Despite Its Omnipresence

Generally speaking, disability is not a topic most people think about every day or idly browse online – until it impacts their kith and kin. As Prachi Deo remarks, 'Invariably every parent [of a child with disability] I spoke to said, "I heard the word 'autism' or 'Down Syndrome' for the first time [when I discovered mine had it]."' Of course it is not possible to know or even have heard of every type of disability, particularly when it comes to DD – an umbrella term for a diverse group of disorders caused by mental and physical impairments, of which a new variety seems to be diagnosed every day. No one, besides the person affected, would be greatly disadvantaged if they didn't know what Crouzon Syndrome or Ehlers-Danlos Syndromes is, or that Charcot-Marie-Tooth is a form of muscular dystrophy (MD).

The RPwD Act lists 21 disabilities, where the Persons with Disabilities (PwD) Act 1995 had just seven. But merely adding the names of disabilities is a futile and endless exercise. Instead of keeping on expanding the list, it would be much wiser to go by the simple definition of disability in the ADA: 'a physical or mental impairment that limits one or more major life activities'. The ADA provides no exclusive list of disabilities, but broadly identifies the impairments and the medical conditions that would lead to them.

The disadvantage of listing can be clearly seen in how DS got entangled in classic Indian red tape. Just because DS hasn't been cited in the Act, it was becoming difficult to get a disability certificate from state governments. The Down Syndrome Federation of India (DSFI) had to approach the Indian government to fix this discrepancy. The Ministry of Social Justice and Empowerment (MSJE) finally issued a notice on 15 October 2019 clarifying that DS fell within the broad category of ID, which was on the list of 21. At this rate, government will have to repeatedly issue notices each time persons with a non-listed disability fail to obtain a certificate!

## Acquire a General Understanding of At Least a Few Disabilities

Here's how the RPwD Act defines a PwD: 'a person with long-term physical, mental, intellectual or sensory impairment which, in interaction with barriers, hinders his full and effective participation in society equally with others'. Among the list of 21 – besides the more well-known conditions such as blindness, deafness, dwarfism, Parkinson's, leprosy cured and acid attack –

there are CP, ASD, MD, Multiple Sclerosis (MS), haemophilia and thalassaemia.

Muscular dystrophy is a hereditary genetic condition in which muscles progressively weaken and waste away. MS attacks the central nervous system, resulting in a whole range of physical and mental problems. Haemophilia and thalassaemia are both inherited blood disorders that are rare diseases: the former is characterized by poor blood clotting ability and the latter by low haemoglobin – necessitating continual blood transfusions.

In India, CP occurs in roughly two of every 1,000 births. It is a syndrome (i.e., a group of conditions) caused by damage in areas of the brain during pregnancy, at birth or shortly after. The most common type of CP involves spasticity, which makes muscles stiff, and can cause uncontrollable movements that make it difficult to walk. Growth retardation is common, and so are intellectual disabilities, and difficulties with speech and swallowing. Hearing and sensory impairments may be present. The person with CP is prone to sleep disturbances and seizures, for which drugs may be prescribed.

Let's say a lay person looks at someone with CP, notices their unfocussed eyes, hears their slurred speech and observes that their body hasn't grown to average proportions. He may immediately think, 'Oh, mental.' This slur (and its equivalent in local languages) is applied to anyone who fits the popular imagination of a 'mentally retarded' person (i.e., a person with ID). People are not aware that unless CP is accompanied by ID, that dancing body might contain a keen and sparkling mind.

'Mental' is a catchall term that the ignoramus also applies to someone with a mental disability. There is a difference between a mental disability and an intellectual one. We say a person has a mental disability when a psychiatric illness/mental illness interferes with their daily activities. Depression, to give a common example.

Mental disability falls in the category of *invisible disability* because it is not visible from the outside. Because persons with invisible disabilities 'look normal' they are the most misunderstood. Invisible disabilities could be physical, mental or neurological (including diabetes, chronic pain or fatigue, Irritable Bowel Syndrome (IBS), MS, personality and psychiatric disorders, and many, many more).

CP, DS and ID are all examples of DD. DS is a genetic irregularity caused by an extra chromosome. Persons with DS have varying degrees of ID. Way back in the nineteenth century, the medical term for a person with DS was 'mongoloid' because the English physician who described the condition was under the impression that 'mongolism' was a reversal of evolution since the 'mongoloids' of the Caucasian race had the facial features of the 'inferior' Oriental (Mongol) race!

Of all the developmental disabilities, the invisible disability ASD is perhaps the one that confuses a lay person the most. Autism has, of late, received much attention in the Indian media and hence has entered the public consciousness, but recognizing the word doesn't mean comprehending its scope. The medical definition sounds deceptively simple. The American Psychiatric Association's Diagnostic and Statistical Manual of Mental Disorders (DSM) is the global standard and DSM-V (DSM's fifth edition) describes ASD's criteria as: deficits in social interaction and communication, and restricted, repetitive patterns of behaviour, interests or activities. However, these criteria do not add up to a clear-cut array of 'symptoms'. We cannot pigeonhole people with autism because – and this is important to understand – *behaviour differs from individual to individual.*

Noted American professor with ASD, Temple Grandin, points out in *The Autistic Brain: Thinking across the Spectrum*, the book she co-wrote with science author Richard Panek, that a person with autism could exhibit sensory-seeking behaviour, such as repetitive movement, but they could also be either over-responsive to sensory stimuli (hate noise and light, for example) or underresponsive (shut down completely). They could be oversensitive to touch, smell or taste.[8] They literally live in an 'alternate sensory reality', she says, clarifying that autism is not a by-product of 'bad' wiring in the brain, but the product of wiring. Period – there's no good or bad to it.

But enough of describing disabilities. We only wanted to give you a glimpse of their vast range. You can find out more about these and myriad others through an internet search. Besides, is diagnosis really the be all and end all?

## Many Reject the 'Medical Model of Disability' in Favour of the Social Model

In the medical model, disability is seen as the result of a 'problem' that belongs to the individual; defining the 'problem' and identifying the impairments becomes the primary focus. In the social model, the problem lies with the social and environmental barriers that disable the individual.

Only by removing barriers and providing 'reasonable accommodations' (as the UNCRPD defines it) – making 'necessary and appropriate modification and adjustments' – can PwDs enjoy equal rights. Pinpointing their impairments and rating them as mild, moderate or severe is not more crucial than knowing what their challenges are and figuring out how to accommodate them. Reasonable accommodation paves the way towards inclusion.

## Learn the Difference between Integration and Inclusion

Integrating a child with disabilities into a classroom, or an adult into a workplace, would mean providing special facilities to help

---

[8] Temple Grandin and Richard Panek, *The Autistic Brain: Thinking across the Spectrum* (New York: Houghton Mifflin Harcourt, 2013), p. 70.

them fit in – in other words, helping them adapt to the mainstream environment. In an integrated classroom, for instance, they would sit alongside typical pupils but would have a separate curriculum.

In inclusion, you change the mainstream environment because the facilities you provide PwDs will benefit everyone else too. The underlying principle: Everyone is different, whether you call them disabled or non-disabled. Therefore in an inclusive workplace, you build a culture that is sensitive to everyone's needs, where everyone's strengths are brought out, and everyone is heard and valued. In an inclusive classroom, 'special education' is merged with 'regular' education (although the terms 'Special Ed.' and 'Children with Special Needs' remain in vogue) so that all children have full access to the same curriculum.

Temple Grandin and Richard Panek write in *The Autistic Brain: Thinking across the Spectrum*, 'If you really want to prepare kids to participate in the mainstream of life, then you have to do more than accommodate their deficits. You have to figure out ways to exploit their strengths.'[9] Some of these strengths are what Chally Grundwag and his research team have called 'coolability'.

## Disability Can Give Rise to Special Ability

Independent researchers Chally Grundwag and David Nordfors in California along with Nurit Yirmiya of The Hebrew University of Jerusalem's Department of Psychology coined the word 'coolability'[10] for the ability of a PwD to be better at a task than the average person precisely because the trait that disables them in one context helps them excel in another.

---

[9] Temple Grandin and Richard Panek, *The Autistic Brain: Thinking across the Spectrum* (New York: Houghton Mifflin Harcourt, 2013), p. 184.

[10] Chally Grundwag and David Nordfors, '"Coolabilities" – The Generalized Concept of Enhanced Abilities in Disabling Conditions', working paper, ResearchGate.net, January 2017.

Now, it is important to know what coolability is not. It is NOT the ability of a PwD to perform some task that is touted as 'brave' and 'inspiring'. It is not 'inspiration porn' – a neologism coined in 2012 by disability rights activist and comedian Stella Young in an article in an Australian newspaper, which she later used in her TEDx talk. Inspiration porn is 'objectifying disabled people for the sake of non-disabled people', Stella said in her talk. It is using the images of PwDs – for example, a girl with no hands drawing with a pencil in her mouth or a child running on artificial legs – to 'motivate' the non-disabled although 'they are not doing anything out of the ordinary'. She said, 'I want to live in a world where we don't have such low expectations of disabled people that we are congratulated for getting out of bed and remembering our own names in the morning.'

Coolabilities, on the other hand, are 'disabling' traits that become valuable when you change the context. They could be abilities amplified to compensate for the loss of other abilities (missing limbs or eyesight for instance), or special abilities in an individual with specific cognitive or physical traits that are rarely found or absent in an average person.

The acute hearing ability of the blind can become their coolability. Mohan Sundaram, executive team member of the Artilab Foundation, gave us an instance from a branch of Ernst and Young that takes on legal processing/transcribing work from overseas. One employee who was blind achieved 40 per cent more productivity than her co-workers. Everyone wore headphones, but she was the only one who never needed to hit 'replay'. As an experiment, the company asked all the employees to wear blindfolds while they worked. The overall productivity went up by 25 per cent.

The rise in total productivity can be attributed to increased concentration in the absence of visual distractions. But what explains the blind employee's superior performance? Research has shown that blind persons can hear speech as fast as 25 syllables a second – mere garbled noise to non-disabled ears. R. Douglas Fields writes in the *Scientific American* that researchers from the University of Tubingen in Germany found scientific evidence for how the blind compensate for their lost vision. Through MRI (Magnetic Resonance Imaging) brain scans, they discovered that 'in blind people the part of the cerebral cortex that normally responds to vision was responding to speech'.[11]

Through a stroke of inspiration, one of us – V.R. Ferose – hit upon the coolability of an employee of SAP Labs in Bengaluru. On one of his regular rounds of the campus with his facilities manager, both of them descended into the air-conditioned office basement where the power plant was creating its usual ear-splitting racket. The manager explained to Ferose that it was impossible to find an employee who could stick on in such a cold and noisy environment. Working with local resources, Ferose was able to identify a deaf employee who was a native of a cold region of India. He fit right in.

We need to find the hidden coolabilities in every PwD so that we become an inclusive society. Disability awareness is only the first step but surely a crucial one. Even as the government takes baby steps to spread awareness in wider society, it is vital for families of PwDs too to gain extensive knowledge of the subject, and equally vital for PwDs themselves to be able to gauge their own strengths and test their own limits.

---

[11] R. Douglas Fields, 'Why Can Some Blind People Process Speech Far Faster than Sighted Persons', *The Scientific American*, 13 December 2010.

# 4

# THE HISTORY OF DISABILITY RIGHTS

WE DON'T HAVE TO LOOK TOO FAR BACK TO FIND A TIME when PwDs were considered 'abnormal' and less than human. They were seen as punishments for sins and as burdens to be endured if not discarded, incarcerated or eliminated.

In the West, it was World War I that brought disability to the forefront when thousands of wounded soldiers had to be accommodated in civil society. The disability rights movement started picking up pace in the United States in the 1960s. Disability activists learnt from the black civil rights movement, and used the same tactics of sit-ins and marches to get the ADA passed, which finally happened in 1990. The United Kingdom passed its Disability Discrimination Act (DDA) in 1995, making it unlawful to discriminate against PwDs in education, employment, transport, and goods and services.

In India, the government woke up to the issue of disability in the late 1970s. The government started setting up National Institutes across the country to undertake research, and promote education and rehabilitation of PwDs.[12] The government also set

---

[12] They were the National Institute for the Physically Handicapped (NIPH) in Delhi, for Orthopedically Handicapped (NIOH) in Kolkata, for Visually Handicapped (NIVH) in Dehradun, for Hearing Handicapped

up Composite Regional Centres (CRCs) to provide rehabilitation services, and a National Handicapped Finance and Development Corporation (NHFDC) that gives loans to PwDs for self-employment. To regulate and monitor the training of rehabilitation professionals the government set up the Rehabilitation Council of India (RCI) as a registered society in 1986. It became a statutory body in 1993 after the RCI Act was passed; the Act was amended in 2000 to make it more broad-based.

Disability was under the Ministry of Welfare, which was changed to the MSJE in 1998. In 2012, a separate department of disability affairs was created under the MSJE. It is now known as the Department of Empowerment of Persons with Disabilities.

In 1999, a statutory body of the MSJE was set up under the National Trust for the Welfare of Persons with Autism, Cerebral Palsy, Mental Retardation and Multiple Disabilities Act. The National Trust mainly addresses the concerns of parents of PwDs with intellectual and developmental disabilities, and their niggling 'after me, what?' question – that is, their anxiety about what will happen to their children after they died. It works towards providing opportunities for PwDs, fulfilling their rights and creating an enabling environment. Its activities include training, shelter, caregiving and empowerment.

The key initialisms to keep in mind as we proceed, which we will continually refer to, are MSJE, DEPD and RCI.

Among the disabilities, mental illness was the first to be recognized all over the world – perhaps predictably since some of them are more 'in your face', palpably impacting and intruding into 'civil society'. Until the British colonized India, we had never

(NIHH) in Mumbai, for Mentally Handicapped (NIMH) in Hyderabad, for Rehabilitation Training and Research (NIRTAR) in Cuttack and for Empowerment of Persons with Multiple Disabilities (NIEPMD) in Chennai. Only a few of them have amended their names to conform to terminology acceptable to PwDs.

systematically incarcerated the mentally ill en masse. The colonizers introduced the Western practice of confining and chaining the 'insane' in jails and 'lunatic asylums'. The Indian Lunacy Act of 1912 was in effect even up until 1987, when the Mental Healthcare Act was finally passed in its stead.

As modern psychiatry took root in India, we progressed from 'asylum' to 'hospital' and then to 'institution', from 'mad' to 'mentally ill', and from the notion of mental illness to that of mental health and mental healthcare. The All India Institute of Mental Health was established in Bangalore (now known as Bengaluru) in the old state of Mysore (now renamed Mysuru) in 1954; it merged with the mental hospital there in 1974 to form the National Institute of Mental Health and Neurosciences (NIMHANS). Today, NIMHANS is an autonomous and pioneering body in the country in the areas of patient care and research.

The Mental Healthcare Act 2017, which superseded the 1987 Act, recognizes the agency of persons with mental illness and aims to 'protect, promote and fulfil' their rights. They are no longer passive recipients of mental health 'services', but individuals with the right to make decisions about their health – within the bounds of their ability and knowledge. Additionally, the new Act restricts the use of electroconvulsive therapy, aims to decriminalize suicide and rules that medical insurance must cover mental illness.

## From Welfare to Rights

It goes without saying that the countries of the North, and especially a wealthy country like the United States, would be miles ahead of the South when it comes to disability welfare. But it wasn't prosperity alone that effected changes in the law for PwDs in the country. The changes were more due to concerted action by the PwD community and their families. And because the movement was championed entirely by PwDs – a crucial factor indeed.

A special set of circumstances propelled the disability movement in the United States, as Joseph P. Shapiro describes in his book *No Pity: People with Disabilities Forging a New Civil Rights Movement*[13] on the history of the movement. Rehabilitation became a priority with the return of World War I veterans in the 1930s. The country had a PwD president – although he took great pains to downplay it; polio-struck Franklin D. Roosevelt kept his 'weakness' hidden by never appearing in public, or even in photos, in a wheelchair. In the 1940s and 1950s, parents of children with disabilities rallied to fight for funding for special education. The historic protest in 1988 by the deaf students of Gallaudet University gave a powerful fillip to the movement.

And then there was a fortuitous slip of the pen. Shapiro writes about the unknown hand that added a section to the Rehabilitation Act of 1973: Section 504.[14] The Act had mainly to do with spending money, but 504 made it illegal to discriminate on the grounds of 'handicap'. Activists pounced on this section and used it to assert their prerogative to be included in every aspect of daily living. The government faced a groundswell of protest in a decades-long battle with many ups and downs, fought by PwD activists, students, teachers, parents, lawyers and likeminded politicians.

The United States disability movement has had many PwDs such as Ed Roberts, Judy Heumann, Bob Burgdorf and Bob Kafka as leading lights, but as Shapiro points out it was 'without one visible leader'. He describes it as 'a mosaic movement' with hundreds of groups of different disabilities, and with diversity as its central characteristic.[15] 'The ADA brought this fragmented population together in a fight against discrimination.'[16]

---

[13] Joseph P. Shapiro, *No Pity: People with Disabilities Forging a New Civil Rights Movement* (New York: Three Rivers Press, 1993), pp. 58-64.

[14] Ibid., pp. 64-65.

[15] Ibid., p. 11.

[16] Ibid., p. 126.

India has yet to have a cohesive disability movement. It has an Act but is short on action.

There are literally thousands of government and voluntary organizations working in the Indian disability sector. Many were founded by the non-disabled with the intention of providing services and securing benefits for PwDs. But as PwDs themselves started to lead from the front, their calls for the recognition of their human rights began to echo in the corridors of power – forcing the government to change its tune.

There were two major triggers for the government's proactive measures on disability. They were: India being a signatory to UN/ international conventions and proclamations, and pressure from Indian disability rights activists.

India signed a Proclamation in Beijing in 1992 on the Full Participation and Equality of People with Disabilities in the Asia and the Pacific region. Having signed it, the country was now obliged to enact legislation. It passed the PwD Act in 1995 – but not without a vigorous push from disability groups.

If you speak to people in the disability sector you will inevitably hear of Javed *bhai* (brother). Javed Abidi, who died at 53 of a chest infection in 2018, was one of the most outspoken and combative advocates for the rights of PwDs. Born with spina bifida (a congenital defect of the spine), he was a wheelchair user from the age of 15. His parents moved to the United States and he completed his education there with a degree in journalism but could not pursue it as a career. Inspired by his experiences with disability on university campuses, he moved to India at 24 and plunged into disability awareness building.

Sonia Gandhi invited Abidi to create the Rajiv Gandhi Foundation's disabilities unit, which led to the birth of the National Centre for Promotion of Employment for Disabled People (NCPEDP). He served as director of NCPEDP since 1997. In the meanwhile, he joined and gave momentum to the Disability Rights

Group. The firebrand Abidi often kicked the butt of the sluggish government into moving forward; while working with ministry officials, he also filed petitions in the Supreme Court and led protests on the streets.

Arman Ali, one of Abidi's protégés and the current director of NCPEDP, remembers him as 'a hard taskmaster and a no-nonsense type'. He recounts an incident that typifies his radical approach: 'I remember going for a meeting with him to the ministry, and the washroom was not accessible. He went out and came back into the room where senior officers were. He said, "Can I get a bottle?" And he told them what it was for!' He had bluntly announced that he wanted a bottle to piss into. The shamefaced officers quickly called off the meeting and searched for an accessible venue to reschedule it.

One of Abidi's pioneering efforts was his attempt at creating a cross-disability movement in India, encouraging people with different disabilities to work together for collective solutions. He also strove to involve other movements, such as the trade union and women's movements, in the struggle for disability rights. The PwD Act was passed three days after he led a huge protest before the Parliament. Among his numerous pathbreaking initiatives in disability rights advocacy are the inclusion of disability as a separate category in the national census and mandating accessible polling booths. A staunch believer in 'nothing about us without us', he pushed for PwD representation in all decision-making bodies that dealt with disability. He was elected world chair of the Disabled People's International in 2011.

Abidi's activism contributed to India signing the UNCRPD of 2006 in the following year. The process of negotiating the CRPD at the UN was unique. One-third of the seats in the working group, which saw the participation of a record number of civil society representatives, were reserved for PwDs. For the first time, PwDs from around the world and from different impairment groups had a common platform. Till then, they were working in silos. Here they realized that instead of conducting separate negotiations, they could find strength in unity. They abandoned their 'scarcity mindset' and formed a coalition. What emerged from the process was the International Disability Alliance (IDA). IDA now has a secretariat in New York and in Geneva, which negotiates with all of the treaty bodies and UN development organizations for the inclusion of PwDs.

IDA helps national organizations present alternative reports to the UN. In fact after India presented its first report on the status of disability in the country to the CRPD in 2015, a coalition of thirty-odd Indian disability groups got together to prepare a response. In February 2019, they submitted an alternative report on behalf of the National Coalition towards the CRPD Parallel Report, which was read out at the UN.

Abidi was at the forefront of the movement that engendered the RPwD Act. It took India almost a decade to pass the RPwD Act in compliance with the CRPD it had signed in 2007. Most people in the disability sector concur that it is comparable to the best in the world. However, its ambitious objectives must have capable hands to execute them. It is as if a moped rider were asked to sit behind the wheel of a sports car. They have to learn how to handle the surge in power and steer it towards the finish line.

With 17 chapters and 102 sections, the RPwD Act is comprehensive; it covers in minute detail every conceivable aspect of disability to ensure PwDs' equality, non-discrimination and full inclusion in society. Funds for disability, healthcare, inclusive education, job reservation, total accessibility, independent living, legal rights, right to recreational activities... you name it, the Act has it – on paper.

Four years on, as we write this, India is still trundling towards its disability goals which are supposed to be in keeping with the

UN's Sustainable Development Goals (SDGs). Disability features prominently in the SDGs for 2030.

You might wonder: 'How can we possibly dream of making India inclusive by 2030?' In response, allow us to introduce you to some of those who are working towards this seemingly unreachable target, those who are behind the wheel of that sports car.

The flag-off is over. We are waiting at the finish line, not yet ready to give up hope.

# 5

# TRAVELLING WITH THE CAREGIVERS

WHEN A CHILD IS BORN WITH A DISABILITY OR ACQUIRES one in early childhood, the universal initial reaction of the parents is distress. Perhaps you are one such parent. Perhaps you've just been dealt the sucker punch. Or maybe while still reeling from the blow you've begun to feel you've stumbled into a fog.

Fortunately, there are beacons to guide you. But these didn't just emerge out of thin air. In all but a few instances, those who can light your path were themselves in the spot where you now stand. And they had no one to turn to in their time. They are caregivers who, having fought their way through the murkiness, decided to go back and lead other stranded souls towards a shelter of peace.

It takes more than guts to do what they have done. To not collapse into victimhood and despair, to pick themselves up after many a fall…and then after finding their own answers, not sit back and take that well-deserved rest but open their hearts and hands to others in distress.

———

'My son would have been 40 this year,' Poonam Natarajan says calmly while narrating the story of how she founded Vidya Sagar. There is a framed pencil sketch on the wall behind her – a portrait of her son Ishwar. She lost Ishoo (short for Ishwar) in 2001 when he was 22. Born with CP, he was the seed that brought Vidya Sagar into fruition – the now famous Chennai organization for children and adults with neurological disabilities.

Poonam had married her Jawaharlal Nehru University (JNU) classmate Natarajan and was doing her PhD in the field of population geography when they decided to have a child. Back in 1979, when Ishoo was born prematurely, the state of medicine in India was such that when his developmental milestones were delayed, doctors simply said he was 'slow'. Years passed before he was diagnosed, and then 'everyone said, nothing can be done'. Therapists and parent support groups were yet to become a reality.

'There was no way to find out what to do with your child unless you yourself got trained,' so Poonam went to Bombay, where her dad was posted, to do a year-long course offered by the Spastics Society of India (SSI) for Special Ed. teachers. She 'just loved this field'. So she dropped her plan to complete her PhD and joined SSI where she worked for three years, shifting to Madras (since renamed Chennai) when Natarajan was posted there.

No school was prepared to admit Ishoo, who was six and severely disabled. Therefore, in 1985, Poonam opened a branch of SSI in Madras, and started a parent training programme in her garage. This was the origin of what would become Vidya Sagar, the 'ocean of knowledge', which grew organically to provide various services as and when the needs of children, their families and communities arose.

Just six months before Ishoo died, Poonam had lost her husband. Two catastrophes in a row would have brought a lesser person to their knees, but she managed to steady her faltering steps and continue striding towards her larger goal. She was called upon to be chairperson of the MSJE's National Trust in 2005, a post she held for over eight years, after she passed the baton to her team at Vidya Sagar. As the National Trust Chair, she initiated several pathbreaking schemes to create support systems for PwDs whose parents have died. After returning to Chennai from Delhi, she got busy planning a pilot project to enable PwDs to live independently in the community.

'In my time, there was no knowledge – no one to explain what was happening, [or] who to go to. You had to fight your own battles,' she says.

———

G. Vijayaraghavan, or GVR as he is known, was an engineer who worked with the government companies Keltron and Centre for Development of Advanced Computing (C-DAC) before being sent on deputation to set up the Techno Park in Thiruvananthapuram. His wife Rema had done her master's in zoology and was qualified to teach at the postgraduate level. The couple already had a son when Rema became pregnant with triplets. They were born premature; one didn't survive, but the twins did. They were taken for regular check-ups and everything seemed okay, but when Lekshmy and Parvathy were two-and-a-half neither had spoken a word.

When the parents, who by now had started having doubts, asked the doctors about it, they treated the matter casually, saying that some children take time to begin talking. Finally, GVR and Rema went to an audiologist at Thiruvananthapuram Medical College who said that they didn't have the facilities to conduct hearing tests for children this young. They had an audiometer but it required the subject to raise her hand when she heard a sound. That was the state of technology in a major government hospital in a state capital in the 1990s.

The audiologist, who had qualified at the All India Institute of

Speech and Hearing (AIISH) in Mysore, suggested they take their daughters there to confirm their doubts. Since Rema was doing a course at the Central Sericultural Research and Training Institute in Mysore at the time, they found it convenient to take the twins to AIISH. Both were diagnosed as deaf. In Thiruvananthapuram, Lekshmy and Parvathy were given speech therapy sessions at the Sree Chitra Tirunal Institute of Medical Sciences. Education at a school for the deaf followed, and the twins went on to study in the United States. They were the first girls from India to study in Gallaudet, a reputed university for the Deaf in Washington DC which is run and taught by the Deaf.[17]

GVR set up the National Institute of Speech and Hearing (NISH) in Kerala's capital, serving as its honorary director for twenty years. We know NISH today as a premier institute in the state, which educates and rehabilitates those with speech, language and hearing impairments, but it had humble beginnings. GVR started it in a rented building with an initial team consisting of a parent (Dr Pavitran) who handled the technology side, and a few speech therapists. The first thing they did was introduce a testing facility which had, besides an audiologist and an audiometer, technology that the twins had lacked in their infancy: Brainstem Evoked Response Audiometry (BERA). Today BERA is a standard test that is widely used across the country. In GVR's words: 'Today a one-day-old child can be tested for hearing in any maternity hospital anywhere in Kerala.'

———

There are countless such organizations in India, big and small, which were started by parents or siblings of children with

---

[17] The historic protest at Gallaudet in 1988, which resulted in the university having its first deaf president, was a watershed moment for the disability movement in the United States.

disabilities. There are livewires like Shanti Raghavan in Bengaluru who co-founded Enable India with her husband Dipesh Sutariya after her brother started going blind around 1991, and pioneers like Uma Tuli in Delhi – founder of the Amar Jyoti Charitable Trust – whose brother lost a leg in an accident in 1965.

They all began small. Shanti quit her job as a software programmer and started conducting workshops in her home in 2004, offering computer training for the blind because that's what she'd done for her brother. Uma, who taught at a college, had been saving money from her salary ever since her brother's accident with the idea of starting a project to fight against 'the attitudinal barrier of *hai bechaara* (poor thing)'. In 1981, when the concept of inclusion didn't exist in India, Uma started a nursery with 30 children sitting under a tree – 15 of them with, and 15 without, disability.

———

Now, you might feel somewhat daunted by these narratives and may say to yourself, 'These are exceptional personalities. What can I as an ordinary parent do for others when I am struggling with my own child's disability?' Our response to you is: Hey, no pressure! This isn't the 'parents version' of inspiration porn. There are other 'ordinary parents' like you who have gone through the same struggles. And they have benefitted from what is known as 'disability gain'.

The modern term 'disability gain' refers to the advantages that would never have arisen without that disability. Just like the PwD's coolabilities we spoke about earlier, good can come out of their disability for their caregivers too. There are 'ordinary parents' whose lives have changed for the better, who have experienced personal growth, *because* of their children with disabilities.

Smrithy Rajesh is a native of Padinjare Vemballur, a village near

Kodungallur in Kerala's Thrissur district. She was once a sheltered girl with little knowledge of the outside world, so the sudden move to a metro after her marriage unsettled her. 'I was a girl brought up in a village. I had no idea how to interact with city folk,' she tells us (speaking in Malayalam, in which she is more at home). She didn't think beyond keeping house and looking after her family.

Aditya was born in 2006, and two years later Advaith. Till he was a year old, Advaith seemed like any other charming, playful baby. Then Smrithy and Rajesh observed changes in him: he wouldn't make eye contact; he would sit and play alone, and was obsessed with the cartoons that Aditya used to watch – to the extent that he'd want them on all the time. Smrithy remembers it clearly – the day she realized that something was wrong. Addu (as she calls him) was one-and-a-half when one afternoon the power went off, and so did the TV. He started crying. And crying. He cried non-stop until he dropped off to sleep from sheer tiredness.

From that day on, she noticed that he would cry whenever there was even a slight change in his surroundings. Every little change would set him off. She recalls, 'He would not speak. He was constantly restless, getting up at 4 a.m. and going to bed only at 11 p.m. When we told the paediatrician this, he said, "You are comparing him to your older son who is very smart, that's why you think there's a problem with him."'

When she admitted him to the local pre-school the crying continued, and a teacher told her to get him evaluated. A speech therapist at a private hospital immediately told them to take him to NIMHANS. At the over-stretched NIMHANS, which caters to thousands every day, Smrithy had to spend long hours each day with a restless Addu waiting for their turn to meet the general physician, the paediatrician or the neurologist. They had to shuttle frequently between the neurology and the speech departments. Advaith was two years and some months old when NIMHANS confirmed that he had ADHD. Then they asked her: 'Do you know what autism is?' They were not sure if he had ASD, so they put a question mark on the evaluation sheet.

The neurologist gave them an appointment for a month and a half later but he said, 'Don't wait for the diagnosis; start intervention at the earliest.' The pre-school teacher advised Smrithy to go to a centre that taught ABA (Applied Behaviour Analysis), a controversial teaching method for autism that involves punitive action. 'At that stage I wasn't in the frame of mind to accept that he had autism. Today I can say it – that he is severely autistic,' she explains. With ABA Addu started vocalizing in the initial six to seven months, but his parents' hopes were dashed when the crying resumed. They decided to get an assessment done. 'The psychiatrist told me, "I can tell you without doing any assessment that this child is in the autism spectrum." When he said this coolly, right to my face, I became upset and started feeling terribly depressed,' she says.

Smrithy tried home-schooling him at first, using the only method she knew – ABA – in coordination with the therapist. 'After four or five months of this I went crazy.' Now she had to take care of Aditya as well, who had developed regular bouts of vomiting. The paediatrician said it was a psychological issue; Aditya was feeling neglected since she had focussed all her attention on Advaith. Smrithy's depression too was in full flow. She was in tears constantly, and in no mood to do anything.

Bubbles, a school for kids with autism, was recommended to them. But the school was 40 km away from their home. Smrithy realized she had no option but to learn driving. Her mother came to stay and looked after Addu while Smrithy went for driving lessons. After she got her licence, each morning she would tentatively drive her Tata Nano onto the highway. 'The engine would get turned off at signals and people would honk. It would take me one and a half hours to get to Bubbles, and Addu wasn't toilet trained then,' she recollects. One day she saw people staring into the car, and pointing and laughing. Advaith, in the back seat, had removed his trousers and was pissing. So from then on she would park on the roadside wherever she found space and let him pee before carrying on.

Bubbles initially put Advaith in an after-school programme from 2–3 p.m. Aditya finished school at 3 p.m. every day. She therefore requested his classmate's mother – who lived near the school – to take him home with her, so that she could pick him up from there after Addu's session. A year later, Addu joined the regular morning class and Smrithy enrolled in their one-year course of Special Ed. in autism. From Monday to Friday she did her practical work (two case studies), and on Saturdays she attended a theory class at the opposite end of town.

That was when Rajesh, who had been a mere provider thus far, started pitching in after realizing the tremendous effort Smrithy had been putting in. She had course work to do and assignments to submit, and he offered to type them for her. As he typed, the subjects and their content impressed itself on his mind too, and he started to understand a lot more about ASD. Adi (short for Aditya) and Rajesh helped with Addu's learning, and 'the four of us became a team'. Besides taking him to speech therapy and occupational therapy, they put Addu through a spate of physical activities to help assuage his hyperactivity – swimming, cycling, horse riding, roller-skating, badminton and basketball.

'Instead of focussing on what he couldn't do, I started looking for what capabilities lay hidden inside him, and focussed on what he could do,' says Smrithy who was inspired by Temple Grandin's ideas in *The Austistic Brain*.[18] Advaith is a champion skater now, even winning a silver medal (in the special category since he was underage) at the Special Olympics in Chikkamagaluru organized

---

[18] Temple Grandin and Richard Panek, *The Autistic Brain: Thinking across the Spectrum* (New York: Houghton Mifflin Harcourt, 2013), p. 184.

by the Karnataka state disability department. Smrithy also hit upon a method of putting his stimming (repetitive movements) to good use. He would keep poking things with a piece of thread. She had the brainwave and decided to channel his stimming into making jewellery with beads, wire and thread. 'Addu's Creations' are now sold online to customers across the globe.

One day, a team from Avaz Inc. held a workshop at Bubbles and announced that their app could be downloaded for free. The Avaz app, invented by Ajit Narayanan who won the National Award for Empowerment of PwDs in 2010, is India's first Augmentative and Alternative Communication (AAC) device for children who have speech and language difficulties. Smrithy had no clue about technology, but when she told Rajesh about the free app, he immediately downloaded it. Smrithy uploaded all the Picture Exchange Communication System (PECS) pictures that Addu, who couldn't vocalize, would point to when he wanted to say something. Now when he touched the pictures, related sounds emerged. He looked at Smrithy's face with such an eager expression that she instinctively knew this could be used to develop his skills.

Smrithy decided to create her own original pictures in the place of Avaz's symbols. She conceived and made the material herself, painstakingly cutting out easily recognizable images from magazines and other literature. She made a video of how she used Avaz to help Addu vocalize and put it up on social media where it gained traction immediately. 'Then Avaz came searching for me! They put my videos on their website; it got a lot of publicity, and many parents are using Avaz now.' The combination of words, sounds and pictures made Addu try to speak, and he was finally able to do so.

Her only intention was to train Addu, but Rajesh said, 'Why not start a YouTube channel? You will also help other parents.' Since she was short on time, he put up videos of her teaching Advaith words, and progressing from nouns and prepositions to forming sentences. She then started him on typing with the colourful, adaptive Clevy keyboard that had big keys. He slowly graduated to the laptop and with his improved typing skills, he now adeptly operates it. When she started blogging and later joined Facebook, parents began to contact her. A group of around 15 mothers of non-vocal kids from Hyderabad called and asked if she would train them in the use of Avaz. She naively charged them only for the flight, because all she wanted was to get back to her family the same day. This experience gave her an inkling of what she was capable of. 'When they asked me questions, I was able to answer them, and that was the first time I knew I had this ability in me. Till then I was only confined to home and school,' she recollects.

Smrithy is grateful to Bubbles for helping her grow: 'They are the ones who nurtured me. I didn't know my strengths; I didn't have confidence. I was just a mother with problems.' The principal and the coordinator of Bubbles were presenting a paper each at a national conference in Jaipur. They asked her also to send the organizers an abstract of a paper about how she uses Avaz. When it was accepted, she was terrified. 'How could I go there and speak?' she wondered. 'Mine was maths background, and typically maths types are not strong in language. My English was poor. A friend said, "I will write out whatever you want to say." I presented the paper and my stage fright went away for good.'

After that she attended an international conference in Mumbai, accompanied by Rajesh and the kids. She recounts, 'My confidence level grew.' When G. Vijayaraghavan invited her to Thiruvananthapuram for the international autism conference he holds every year, she attended. 'I went alone for the first time!' she remembers. Smrithy also gave a motivational talk at NISH the day prior to the conference – speaking about which she says, 'So the next day I could speak fluently and not like someone reading from a paper'. Avaz workshops for parents have become a routine, and she has been travelling on her own – once even as far as Punjab. 'I am not doing this professionally. The only thing on my mind is that I must do something for these children. I have no other ambition beyond that,' she humbly says.

The stress, however, has prematurely affected her health. A degenerating disc gave her back problems and she has a game leg too. That is why she makes sure she has enough time for herself. Self-care and grooming are important to her, and so are weekend outings and road trips to different places, from which she returns refreshed and with renewed energy. She says that she no longer waits on her family hand and foot: 'I make the food; once it's in the kitchen, Aditya and Rajesh can take it by themselves when they want. I am strict that way, but I've set limits. Otherwise it would be a big struggle.'

Smrithy looks back with guileless awe at her own transformation: 'From being just a depressed mother... How I changed!' She is no longer that timid girl from Padinjare Vemballur. 'Autism is a lifelong journey,' she says. 'Our journey is as a family. It's not just me alone.'

———

Janaki Narayan was brought up in a liberal family in Coimbatore, but was married into a conservative one in Chennai. Her husband Ravi was an Indian Institute of Technology (IIT) graduate working in Delhi. He would come to Chennai, on and off, where she lived with her in-laws. She would also dash off in between to her parents in Coimbatore. Siddharth, born in 1983, was a breech baby. At three months, he was unresponsive and would just keep lying still. Doctors took it casually. 'Late bloomer,' they said when he couldn't complete his developmental milestones. It took over a decade for him to be diagnosed with ASD.

Janaki's in-laws found it extremely difficult to accept their grandson's disability. They took her and Sid to every temple they could find, seeking hope through pujas and all kinds of 'cures'. Janaki believes that her parents too must have suffered a blow, although they didn't express it openly. Meanwhile, Ravi got a job in Pune, and the couple moved there. Since he travelled a lot, she was Sid's full-time caregiver. After they moved to Bangalore, they had another baby, Shravan, in 1991. They were comfortably off, living in their own house and employing helpers.

Janaki first admitted Sid to a Montessori school, but he would simply sit quiet and not stir. Then she put him in the same school as Shravan, who quickly outstripped him. Teachers constantly compared the brothers who were eight years apart. Shravan got tired of conveying teachers' complaints about the 'badly behaved' Siddharth to their parents. Fortunately, the Brindavan School for children with learning disabilities had just opened its doors. They admitted Sid there in 1994. Like Smrithy had done, Janaki too started to get involved in the functioning of the school.

Things were going fairly smoothly when Ravi suddenly died of a brain haemorrhage. The devastating bolt from the blue left her a widow with two young children to look after. She refused to allow her in-laws to make Sid perform what was deemed to be the eldest son's duties such as ritually lighting his father's pyre. She knew that it would deeply traumatize him. Her parents did not want her to stay on in Chennai and brought her to Coimbatore. It was a significant change for the children – losing their father first and then changing (regular and special) schools. Although her family was a tremendous support, she now had to deal with society's behaviour towards the 'inauspicious widow'. She went through a long period of healing, trying to regain her bearings. Ravi's IIT old boys' network rallied around them and became their surrogate family. Her brother in the United States invited her over, urging her to take a break and leave the kids behind with their grandparents. It was a life-saver that propped her spirits up and revitalized her.

Then the well-meaning IIT group got into action looking for matrimonial alliances for her. A couple of men expressed interest in marriage, but they weren't ready to take on the responsibility of Sid. In each case the suitor would invariably say, 'Leave him with your parents.' She put her foot down. 'We're a package deal,' she told them.

Hari Narayan proved to be the ideal match. He was a widower with a daughter, and he was keen on forming a bond with the boys – and with Sid in particular. As it turned out, they formed one healthy united family. Janaki remembers a vacation they took together to Mauritius; it was a time for bonding – for the three children and the couple as well.

Janaki and the kids underwent another change of scene after the marriage – a return to Bengaluru, with Sid back in familiar Brindavan. Janaki did a course at Karnataka Parents Association for Mentally Retarded Citizens (the parents' association in Karnataka that runs orientation courses for teachers on handling kids with special needs), and joined Brindavan as a teacher. Now, she is a volunteer faculty as well as the co-coordinator of a programme for parents where she and her colleagues teach parents strategies to help their kids at home.

Janaki discovered that Sid's strength – besides his stupendous memory for incidents, though not for numbers – was in his hands. A friend of Janaki's kept him occupied with data entry work; a driver would pick him up and drop him back home. One day, a visiting senior employee of Sasken Technologies noticed him and suggested he do the same work for them for a salary. Sid found out their address; his only concern was how he was going to reach the office. When Sasken asked him if he would like to join, he gave them a perfectly logical answer: 'I'll ask my driver and get back to you.'

Janaki is at peace now. She says, 'Slowly, with the wisdom of growing years, coping mechanisms kick in and one learns to just enjoy the present, and not take life too seriously. I entered the special education world because of Sid. I became a better human being because of Sid.'

## Children of PwDs

What happens when the tables are turned? When both parents have disabilities and the child does not, the child might partly take on the adult role in the relationship. If the parents are leading independent lives, the child also learns independence early in life.

This was the case with 36-year-old Neha Arora, whose parents came from liberal-minded, though financially strained, families in Delhi. Theirs was an inter-caste marriage, arranged via a matrimonial ad by her mom's grandfather and dad's father. Neha's great-grandfather was a man of progressive views who, way back in 1945, had got his daughter-in-law remarried after his son's death. Neha's mother Achla had contracted polio when she was ten months old, and later became a wheelchair user, but her condition did not stand in the way of her marriage to Satish Chandra.

Satish had lost his vision when he was 22. When his younger brother offered to take care of him – that is, have his blind brother depend on him for all his needs – their father put his foot down. Nothing doing, he said. Satish would have to learn to fend for himself. He sent Satish to the National Association for the Blind (NAB) in Hauz Khas (Delhi), which trained him to lead an independent life.

Satish and Achla started their married life in a rented house where they shared the kitchen, bathroom and toilet with another family. They couldn't afford to have children. But after Satish got a government job in Agra, teaching children of prisoners, Neha's elder sister was born – now that they had some measure of financial stability. Achla did odd jobs – she stitched clothes, operated a telephone booth and so on. Ten years later when she too landed a government job in the Registrar of Property office, they had Neha.

'They made us independent very early,' Neha says. She remembers how her sister would lead their father by the hand when they went out. From the age of four, Neha would be sent by their mother to the local shop to buy groceries. When she was in the fifth standard, Achla gave her a shopping list and told her to take a rickshaw to their regular provision shop in the market 5 km away. She had told her: 'Buy everything on the list and, with the money left over, buy something for yourself.' Neha remembers buying herself a metal pencil box. The next year Achla gave her the school fees and said, 'Go deposit it in the bank attached to the school.' Later, when she joined a local engineering college, she realized that her classmates did not even know how to write a cheque! Neha's 'disability gain' was her self-sufficiency, which has taken her far in life.

Her parents were also the reason she started her own company, Planet Abled. Because of their disabilities the family had never ever gone on vacation. Sometime after Neha got her first well-paying job in Delhi, she thought of treating her parents to a holiday – only to discover what a frustrating ordeal travel was for PwDs. Obstacles cropped up one after another on their way. Neha had the courage to quit her corporate job and start Planet Abled, which provides accessible tourism for PwDs. Yet again, the disability of one (or in this case two) had opened up possibilities for many.

# 6

# GUIDELINES FOR PARENTS

PARENTS OF CHILDREN WITH DISABILITIES COMMONLY experience a potent mix of emotions: fierce love tainted by disappointment, a sense of failure for having produced an 'abnormal' child, protective instincts going on overdrive, stress and frustration from caregiving, worry about the potential and actual social rejection of the child and – by association – of themselves, and the spectre that looms over them all: 'what happens after I'm gone?'

No parent of a child with disabilities – none of those we've told you about – has ever found it smooth-sailing. Every single one of them has had to breast the tumultuous waves of denial to reach the tranquil shore of acceptance.

## Denial

For practically every parent, denial is the starting point. There is a saying in Malayalam that roughly translates as: In the eyes of the crow, only her baby is golden (fair). Her maternal instinct makes her not see the truth as it is. Poonam Natarajan, who has gone through her own share of inner turmoil, recalls a doctor-mother who simply couldn't accept that her child had a disability. Gitanjali

Sarangan of Snehadhara says, 'The child won't even be able to hold a pencil and the parent would say, "We want the child to do copywriting from newspaper, teach [her] a-b-c-d 1-2-3."' But she adds, 'That is slowly changing.' Poonam too optimistically echoes her: 'Things have changed a lot. Even illiterate parents see things on TV; there's an information boom. Parents are more aware and come to terms [with their child's disability] more easily.'

However, denial still prevails. As Janaki Narayan of the Brindavan School remarks, 'When we talk to the parents, some of them don't want to hear what we have to say. Then they go doctor-shopping – who will say what they want to hear, that there is nothing wrong with your kid. Then they go school-shopping – if one school says your kid has a problem, go to the next...until you find one that accepts you.' But Janaki empathizes with them too: 'I understand parents. It's because of the stigma that society places on a disabled child.'

One such couple came to Sense Kaleidoscopes, an art school for those with autism and Asperger's Syndrome run by Anima Nair and Akshayee Shetty in Bengaluru. The parents were in complete denial, not even wanting to hear or say the word 'autism'. Their son was 18 and had completed ninth standard in an international school. He didn't know the basics of numbers and couldn't even string a sentence together, but his mother wanted him to write the board exam through the National Institute of Open Schooling (NIOS).

Anima says that the more well-off parents of children with autism often put their child in expensive mainstream schools that are happy to keep receiving fees until the tenth standard. Once it's time for the kids to write the board exams, which they can often never hope to pass, the schools bid them goodbye. Mini Menon of Endeavor ELS, cites an instance of the parents of a 20-year-old with DS. The parents insisted on sending this 'child' to school and paying the fees in the vain hope that someday he would be able to write the NIOS exam.

Sometimes these unreal expectations are catalysed by popular cinema's glorified portrayals of disability. It's as though parents are constantly searching for some quality that will 'redeem' their child in the eyes of society. In Gitanjali's words, 'After [the popular Bollywood film] *Taare Zameen Par* every third boy is an Ishaan [the film's protagonist, a child with dyslexia].' Parents imagine that within every child with dyslexia lies a hidden talent for creating great art.

Buckling under social pressure, parents try every possible way to mask their child's disability. Mini describes how some parents sneak their special-needs child into a mainstream school by heavily medicating them to hide their 'behaviours'; but soon enough, when teachers find out about the child's disabilities, they get shunted to the special section. The schools that have woken up to this practice have stipulated that all kids will be observed for a trial period of a month before deciding where they might fit in.

## Diagnosis Isn't Everything

The right diagnosis can drain denial out of the clouded minds of caregivers, fix their ways and give them a sense of purpose. But why is it that so many doctors make dire predictions? Many PwDs and parents we spoke to were practically given ultimatums by medical professionals. Could it be that while intending to not give parents false hopes, medical professionals are swinging to the other extreme instead?

Priyanka Malhotra's doctor told her that her son Nipun's arthrogyposis would condemn him to the life of 'a wooden doll'. When co-founder of the incubator Artilab, Mohan Sundaram was just sixteen, the neighbourhood doctor in Chennai who diagnosed him with MD casually told him he had another five years to live. He cried himself to sleep that night. Jeevan B., a software engineer at Microsoft, was born with osteogenesis imperfecta (OI), a rare disease commonly known as brittle bone disease. 'Doctors predicted I wouldn't live more than a day, that I wouldn't see the sun rise,' he says. In the 1960s, the parents of musician Ghatam Suresh who had contracted a severe case of polio at the age of two-and-a-half were categorically told by a doctor, 'He won't be able to walk.'

Gagandeep Singh Chandok, who has Thalassaemia Major, says, 'The doctor told my parents that this child will not live more than 21 years of age. My parents were broken. Shattered.' Gagandeep, who is now the president of the Thalassaemia and Sickle Cell Society (TSCS) of Karnataka founded by his father Guninder Singh Chandok, says that even today many doctors voice the same prognosis: 'I have parents coming to me, [whose] doctors have told them, "Your child will not live beyond 16 or 21," and they're devastated. I tell them, "I'm 36, I know persons [with this diagnosis] who're 40, [or] 60." Then you calm them down.'

On the other hand, Geetha Sridhar of Sahas, with pupils mainly from the working class, has a different experience to narrate: 'Doctors in our local hospitals won't reveal the truth to underprivileged parents. They tell them, "After some time he will become all right," and parents have false hopes. We tell them: "No miracle will happen here."'

Making matters worse, we in India tend to treat doctors as demigods and have unquestioning faith in their pronouncements. Developmental paediatrician Vibha Krishnamurthy at the Ummeed Child Development Centre in Mumbai, addressing the India Autism at Work (AaW) Summit 2019, speaks about what patients in India often believe doctors are supposed to be like and do: Know everything (or at least pretend to!), be emotionally detached from the patient, have the power to decide their fate and be responsible for whatever happens to them.

It is useful to bear in mind that the model that doctors follow is what Vibha calls 'the medical triad': 'What is the problem? What are the symptoms? What are the signs of the problem?' Once they have the answers to these questions, they then diagnose and treat the 'problem'. '*But disability is not a disease or a problem,*' she says emphatically. 'We need to bring in the second expert. We need to invite the child into the room.' The doctor should train herself to ask different questions. In the 'new triad', which does not follow the medical model, the focus is on hopes, strengths and skills. She ought to ask parents on each visit: 'What do you hope to achieve today? Why is that important to you? And what are the strengths of the child?' The doctor then has permission to be curious, say: 'I don't know', and be vulnerable.

Speaking of diagnoses, Temple Grandin mentions a rather disturbing example in *The Autistic Brain* of how a simple typo could have brought about any number of wrong diagnoses.[19] Autism wasn't mentioned in the first two editions of DSM and was listed in DSM-III in 1980 as 'infantile autism' in a larger category called Pervasive Developmental Disorder (PDD). The 1987 edition of the DSM called DSM-III-R carried a new category: PDD-NOS (not otherwise specified). (Also, infantile autism was changed to autism disorder, which would become ASD only in DSM-V.) In 1994, DSM-IV described PDD-NOS as 'a severe and pervasive impairment in social interaction <u>or</u> in verbal or non-verbal communication skills'. Believe it or not, this was a typo! It should have been '*and*', not 'or'! That is, it involves impairment in both social interaction *and* communication skills. The error was later corrected, but meanwhile how many wrong diagnoses had been made is anybody's guess.

Diagnosis, however crucial, cannot be the last word in the caregiver's manual. And the medical model, as we have tried to

---

[19] Temple Grandin and Richard Panek, *The Autistic Brain: Thinking across the Spectrum* (New York: Houghton Mifflin Harcourt, 2013), p. 18.

show, certainly has its drawbacks. Focussing on hopes, strengths and skills seems to be the more sensible option.

But before that can happen, the parents need to accept the child's disability. Denial solves nothing.

## Comparisons

Another form of denial is the conviction that one's child with disability is 'better' than another with the same disability.

At the junior centre of Brindavan School, coordinator Rajani Padmanabhan had just finished speaking to a mother who wanted to admit her son. The mother had visited the centre previously but since he was not so much an LD child as one with behavioural issues, Rajani had recommended another school. The mother told her, 'Yes, I went there, but *wahan ke bachche ache nahi hai* madam, *mera bachcha kaisa waha padega?* (The children there are not good, madam, how can my child study there?)' Although she recognized that her son was different from the NT ones, she didn't want him to be among children whom she considered 'even more different' than him!

'Among our own parents we have a caste system,' Rajani says with a sigh. In fact, 'caste' is a recurring word among the special educators we meet. Merry Barua, founder of Action for Autism (AFA), tells us she had written about the 'disability caste system' 15 years ago in the AFA journal. ID is right at the bottom of the pyramid; and within ID, autism right at the bottom. Even in autism, 'high functioning' is a higher 'caste'! 'Parents discriminate – [they think] how can we put our child along with "those kind of children"? I say, if your child is put in a regular school won't the other children's parents be referring to your child as "those kind of children"?' she tells us.

Anima Nair observes that parents of children with ASD in particular often simply cannot form a support group because of this habit of comparing. Much sharing happens among parents of children with disabilities such as DS or CP because the symptoms are similar, but since each child with autism is different every parent is more likely to have a tendency to think that their child is better than the rest. Anima many times finds a total lack of empathy in these parents towards other children with autism.

Gitanjali Sarangan too has found parents adopting the 'my child is better than yours' attitude combined with 'she will get worse through contact with yours; she'll pick up bad habits'. A group of Snehadhara parents asked her if she would create a residential facility for just their 10 children with ASD. What about the others at the centre? 'Oh, they are not our type,' they replied. 'It's like casteism in autism,' Gitanjali tells us. She is often told by parents, 'Don't put this child with that child because she is so bad.'

When Manjula Kalyan of Swayamkrushi tried to start an inclusive primary school, she failed, because parents of average children did not want their kids to mingle with kids with disabilities; the average children would 'get influenced and learn their behaviour [that is, the behaviour of children with disabilities]', they said. Then she found that even among parents of children with ID, there was a divide: parents of educable children with ID did not want to admit their kids along with 'those kind' of kids (kids with severe ID).

## Overprotection

Parents don't realize the dangers of infantilizing the child with disabilities. In an effort to make her life easy, they may start doing everything for her instead of taking the trouble to teach her how to do it herself. Overprotection leads to dependency, which can cramp her future.

Shanti Raghavan, founder of the multi-award-winning Enable India, points out that parents do not give children with disabilities an opportunity to be responsible. 'If there are two sisters and one is even slightly disabled, who will the parent send out to the shop to buy something? The answer is obvious. So PwDs do not get a chance to make mistakes and learn from them and face the consequences of their actions.'

Shanti frequently witnesses the lack of exposure that comes from mollycoddling. 'As Indians, we're over-emotional, less practical.' When PwDs come in as potential employees to Enable India for employability and life skills training, group discussions are organized on how to solve the problem of social integration. Trainees themselves work out solutions to issues such as parents not allowing them to go out and be independent. 'Even after overcoming all barriers and getting a suitable job, the mother might say, "*Paapa* (poor thing), why go through all this trouble? Let her not take up the job." The NGO-way would be to counsel the parents. But here, they find the solution themselves. Each person has done different things to convince their parents,' she says.

Shanti understands the parents' concern, though: 'Every person has their own journey. Every PwD has their own journey of becoming independent. Every parent has their journey towards letting go.' She gives us the example of Hema, a blind 30-year-old mother of one, who came to the training session on the first day led by her mother. She had never gone outside her house without her mother holding her hand. Shanti recalls that she exaggerated wildly when telling the mother she could take 20 years to make Hema independent, '[For the] first five years, be next to her all the time but don't hold her hand. Next five years, walk behind her so that you can catch her if she stumbles etc., etc. Some rubbish I said. The next day Hema came in an auto and got out, without her mother. Something opened up in the minds of both mother and daughter, and that's all it took.'

Describing one of the training sessions for the blind and VI, Shanti says that on the first day they are given oral instructions to help them get to the food at lunchtime. They are told where the food is located and how it is arranged. This is usually the first time they find their way to and serve their meal independently, and not simply eat whatever someone puts for them on their plate!

'Indian families aren't too good at making their children, even NT children, function independently,' says Vibha Krishnamurthy at the aforementioned AaW Summit. 'Allow them to make choices and decisions early in life. Respect their right to say no. Obviously there are situations when children cannot be allowed to say no – for instance, if the whole family is going out, the child cannot choose to stay at home. But there is no harm in asking, if you're going out, "What shoes do you want to wear? What dress?" And if those choices are inappropriate, that's okay.'

This capacity for independent thought and action should be encouraged and nurtured particularly in children with disabilities. It will reap rich benefits in adulthood when they take the step towards independent living.

## Fear and Guilt

All parents start out with fears, so don't be ashamed to admit yours.

When a child with disabilities is a firstborn, parents tend to be fearful of having another. After Gagandeep Chandok was born in Bangalore in 1983, his parents Guninder Singh and Savinder Kaur were too preoccupied with him to even dream of having another child. 'They wanted to focus all their attention on their only child,' says Gagandeep. 'Besides, treatment was expensive. It was a tough life.' People kept trying to convince them, and it took eight years before they finally caved in. 'My mom did [undergo] pre-natal tests to make sure my brother was fine before he was born,' he says. Gagandeep's younger brother Amrit was born in 1991.

Coincidentally, in the very year that Savinder Kaur had her second son, Sid's mother Janaki Narayan (whom we have met previously in this book) living in the same city also had her second baby, and went through an identical dilemma. After Sid was born with CP in 1983, Janaki had misgivings about conceiving again. She too took eight years to do so, and only went ahead after genetic testing had allayed her qualms. She laughs now at the memory of her panicking when it was time to give birth to Shravan in 1991. Her doctor still teases her about it – she kept saying 'I want a normal child, I want a normal child' aloud in the OT!

Mothers like her are confident and secure enough today to not only admit their previous fears but also see the comical aspect. Priyanka Malhotra had just found out, after months of trekking all across Mumbai for a school that would admit Nipun, that St. Mary's was willing to open its doors to him. Nipun had answered all the 'practical stuff [and] sensible questions that Father Joe asked him'. Priyanka, who was full-term pregnant with her second son Manek at the time, was so elated by her success that she ran out of the building and fell down flat, hurting herself. 'I refused to have any X-rays or painkillers, because I couldn't risk another child with a problem. So although I was in agony, I had my first painkiller only after delivery.' Just before her delivery, she was terrified she wouldn't have a 'normal' child. 'My husband Pravin took me to Jaslok, but I said if I have another child with a problem I'll jump out of the window. So he took me to Breach Candy.' Which, being a single-storey building, posed no danger since she could no longer leap off a higher floor there!

How rare are the parents who despite having a child with genetic disorders avoid testing before having their second child. Suchitra Shenoy, author of *Mindful Parenting: The First 1000 Days* and one of the speakers at the India Inclusion Summit 2018, describes how moved she was when one such couple – Rajeev and Monisha – who had a son Mihan with DS refused to test for trisomy 21 also referred to as Down Syndrome (the chromosomal irregularity that causes the syndrome) when the lady got pregnant again.

Mothers in particular seem to go through an irrational feeling of guilt after they give birth to a child with disabilities. There's the nagging question: Is it my fault? Janaki admits, 'In all honesty, the gnawing feeling of "where did it all go wrong?" is perpetually there.' In her case, she had a difficult delivery; Sid was a breech baby. After discovering that there had been placental infection, she wondered if she was responsible somehow. She had been working for the Red Cross Society. 'Did I catch the infection there?' she would ask herself.

Mothers start digging into their past and scrabbling for any shred of reason to understand why their child might have been born this way. Such guilt-ridden thoughts, however improbable they may be, haunt many parents, and there's no way to get rid of them other than to get a grip on oneself and decisively shake them off. Instead of asking 'why', try and learn to say 'so what?'

## After Me, What?

The biggest question that looms over parents of children with intellectual, neurological or multiple disabilities especially is this: 'What happens after I am gone?'

Do you leave them in the care of siblings (if they have any) or 'reliable' relatives? Do you place them – god forbid – in an institution, despite all that it implies in a country like India? How will they manage their finances, handle legal matters, or plan their lives?

Developed countries made the move long ago from institutions to nursing homes, group homes and assisted living facilities. There are entire communities – millions of the PwD population (which includes the aged) – for whom support systems are in place. There are counsellors, health care workers, social workers, therapists and others to help them lead healthy, independent and active lives. In many European nations these facilities are state-funded. Of course, not everything is hunky dory; there are unchecked rotten eggs in the basket, and slashed healthcare budgets have been affecting the most vulnerable adversely.

Meanwhile, we in India are only just beginning to think of options to institutionalization. Article 19 of the UNCRPD seeks to promote and protect the rights of PwDs to live independently within the community. In the 1980s, the Indian government initiated Community-Based Rehabilitation (CBR) Programmes, which were meant to integrate PwDs into the community. CBR was naturally aimed at the rural poor, since the government in a vast land like ours is all about reach and spread. The focus of rehabilitation has been on integration with family and community, accessible environment, medical intervention and vocational training. By its multi-pronged approach, through its many wings and branches – the MSJE's district rehabilitation centres (DRCs) and grant-in-aid for promoting CBR, the RCI's training of CBR workers, the National Trust's fostering of programmes that promote PwDs' independent living in the community – supplemented by the many NGOs in this sector, the country's 'disability and inclusion' map shows scattered patches of green.

While the government millipede crawls on, the anxieties of urban parents grappling with the big question – 'Will my child be able to manage on his/her own?' – remain. The good news is that there are pathbreakers in the Indian disability sector who are actively planning to set up independent and interdependent living facilities for PwDs, where they can live, work and enjoy their leisure. Models have been evolved that can be replicated countrywide in both rural and urban contexts.[20]

While these promising ventures take shape, urban parents are groping for and finding their own solutions. Anima Nair, mother of Pranav who has ASD, says, 'I'll sell my gold; I'll sell the freaking

---

[20] Read more about them in Chapter 26, 'Helping Them Live Their Way'.

house if needed, and put the money in his bank account.' Her only concern is to see that he is not cheated. Janaki Narayan's POA (plan of action) is this: 'Plan ahead. Set up the trust deeds. Find out who will be in charge of the money. It is a commitment for life.' She has put what Sid earns into his account and set up a trust fund with her other children in charge. This is money they can take out only for his medical care. As a precaution (since nobody's future is carved in stone), she has also found a care home in Coimbatore that takes in the elderly and disabled, and has excellent facilities, doctors on call and caring attendants. She takes Sid there once in a while so that he becomes familiar with the place and will not feel like a fish out of water if and when he has to live there one day.

Poonam Natarajan has in mind a new kind of trust fund for adults with ID and DD. It will be one of the pillars of the new resource centre that Vidya Sagar is setting up to tackle the 'after me, what?' problem. Poonam calls it the Trust Enabled Decision-Making with Support System or TED-S (a mischievous play on TEDx). 'Many parents who have saved money for their child want to set up a trust for the future with it, but most of these are set up in a very stereotypical way – with three or four trustees who are either siblings or friends of the parents,' she says. 'We find this does not work well. We are trying out setting up a trust with a support circle or a first circle of friends, ideally those around the same age as the PwD, who will support him/her in all domains of life.'

Vidya Sagar has identified 11 domains: Activities of Daily Living (ADLs) and hygiene, personal mobility, transport, communication, health and nutrition, finances, decision-making, safety, problem solving, leisure, recreation and social engagement. 'We are hoping that each member of the support circle will look after one or two domains,' Poonam says. 'Also, a separate system is being worked out for each person to replace a supporter if needed.' They will also employ a chartered accountant to regularly audit these trusts to ensure money is spent properly, and an oversight committee that can solve problems, remove unsuitable trustees and appoint new ones.

## Self-Care

One can never underestimate the sheer labour that parents put in to take care of a child with disabilities. Prachi Deo had seen, throughout her growing years, how her parents had tended to her brother Pranjan, and their example is ingrained in her consciousness. She says, 'You can empathize but you can never be in the shoes of a parent with a special needs child. The amount of work they can get done! The kind[s] of things they take care of, and do patiently over and over again, are incredible.'

Amid the routine, the ups and downs of daily living, parents sometimes forget to take care of their own physical, mental and emotional health.

Gitanjali Sarangan underlines the importance of psychological interventions for parents. 'Parents ask me, "What can we practice at home with the child? What can we do for our child?" I tell them the best thing you can do for your child is to please take care of yourself.'

Strained finances, strained relationships... It is not unusual to find marriages teetering on the brink. Janaki Narayan observes that the couples usually have to decide who the primary breadwinner should be. One parent has to give up their full-time job to care for the child with disabilities, and it is most often the woman. Janaki feels that there is greater pressure on younger mothers these days to continue in their jobs; she keeps hearing them complain about having been forced to stop working. They have a stronger sense of self and identity than women of the older generation.

Snehadhara gives the parents a weekly break from their children. The 'kids' stay on at the centre from Friday afternoon till Saturday, and the Snehadhara team takes on the responsibility for them. Seeing to them is not just a matter of feeding them and putting them to sleep, which in themselves are enervating tasks; they have individual needs and behaviours, and could have medical complications. For example, two sisters with CP are prone to epileptic fits. They get them at specific times: one during the day, one at midnight. They have to be closely monitored while they sleep, because an unattended fit could be fatal.

'Our Friday overnighters are for that one day when you can be by yourself,' says Gitanjali. 'I feel it betters your relationship with the child. You don't have to feel guilty about celebrating your life.'

Parents sometimes take decades to realize the importance of self-care. They are so preoccupied with caring for their child that their own needs recede into the background. It is when the child has attained some measure of stability that one fine day they are pleasantly surprised to find: 'Hey, we still have some time left to enjoy life!'

'I had no social life; nothing,' Priyanka Malhotra recalls. It's a different story today, but Nipun hasn't forgotten how his mother's life used to revolve entirely around him. 'Sometimes he asks me, you spent your entire youth on me – not knowing whether you'll get results. But any mother would do it for her child.'

Sujatha Kanithi from Hyderabad is another mother who had no time to breathe while she journeyed with her daughter Shravya every step of the way. She could relax only after Shravya became the first blind student to do a postgraduate diploma from the Indian School of Business (ISB). Shravya tells us, 'I'm asking her to enjoy herself now, [and] do whatever she wants to do. Very recently, she started building a network of friends for herself – goes walking with them, goes for trips with them. It's very important. She's literally lived for me. Now it's time that she lives [for herself].'

Janaki has a little list of tips for parents. It is no earthshaking piece of wisdom taken from some wellness coach or self-help guru.

It is a homegrown list based entirely on experience – her own and of others whom she has encountered. She tells every parent:

- Celebrate small successes.
- Be aware of your child's strengths; build on them.
- They are children first and 'special needs' next.
- Don't forget to laugh.
- Follow your passions too.
- You don't have to be a helicopter mom or dad.
- And don't blame yourself.
- Use family as your support system; don't distance them.
- Spread awareness.
- Tell the community to help you out.

Janaki concludes: 'It's in giving my time and helping other parents like me that I finally made peace with myself. I see my own self of long ago in the frightened and desperate faces of young parents, and assure them that this too shall pass.'

Parents of children with disabilities often seek solutions from Priyanka Malhotra. 'When people meet me they think I have a magical remedy for them,' she says. 'They should just believe in their children. Understand them. Know them.'

# 7

# SIBLING RELATIONSHIPS

PARENTS WITH TWO KIDS OF DIFFERING ABILITIES, ONE NT and the other with ID or DD, might find themselves in sticky situations. Those who bestow all their attention on their child with a disability might unwittingly pressure the sibling to 'make up for' the 'lack' and become a high achiever. NT siblings might feel jealous or neglected. They might feel burdened by having to play the role of protector or embarrassed by public reactions to what is seen as 'abnormal' behaviour.

On the other hand, siblings who are aware and involved in dealing with the disability often turn out to be compassionate, understanding and generous human beings.

Anita Sharma who runs On My Own – a driving school in Jaipur for those with mobility impairments – says she faced no problems in school because of her physical disability (she contracted polio as an infant), but as she grew older her siblings did have to fight on her behalf when schoolmates referred to her by derogatory names. She remembers her brother getting into a fight with his classmate who had said *'Teri behen langdi hai'* ('Your sister is a cripple').

When people started seeking to establish a matrimonial alliance with Janaki Narayan's younger son Shravan, the moment they heard of his brother Siddharth having autism, they would hesitate. Shravan repeated the same words that Janaki herself had used in the past, when well-meaning friends were trying to fix her up with widowers after her first husband died: 'We're a package deal.' He said, 'If you don't want my brother, I'm off limits too.' Janaki says musingly: 'It never ends, does it?'

Prachi Deo has unequivocally taken on the responsibility of caring for her *dada* (older brother) Pranjan who has DS. It was a natural follow-through of their close bond since childhood. 'It never really hit me that he and I are different, although I realized that we were going to different schools and he didn't come to the playground with me. I used to play with him at home and always insisted that he have the same experiences I do. He has a few sensory issues and some difficulty handling new experiences,' she says. 'I insisted that *dada* also come and see the Taj Mahal, but the marble was hot, and he couldn't communicate that he couldn't walk there, and dad had to piggyback him to the tour bus. I insisted that he come to the beaches but he didn't like the experience of his feet sinking in the sand. So after I got married, my husband had to piggyback him when we went to beaches!'

Personal decisions are always weighed against her need to be around her family, she says. 'The decisions of travelling or moving to another city were very difficult for me. Even before marriage, I said, "I have to have this talk with the person I marry that I come as a package deal." Luckily I fell in love and married a person whom I knew to be a good enough human being that I didn't have to explicitly have that talk. Because I had the confidence that he would be with me through thick and thin. So being a sibling of a person with a disability helped me to find a wonderful life partner.' Talk about disability gain!

When her husband wanted to go to the United States for his PhD, Prachi was torn. She finally accompanied him on his four-year term but when their stay was extended by another four years she found a job with an Indian company that allowed her to be in

India for four to five months a year. Her natural anxiety for her parents back home increased a hundredfold when their health deteriorated.

Prachi can identify with the concerns of youngsters who attended her workshop in Nagpur for siblings of PwDs. They were teenagers or in their early twenties, and they had doubts like: Should I take up a job in Bengaluru, because if I do my mother will have to take care of my brother who has CP and she won't be able to lift him; I have to go away to study and I don't know if I should be doing it; or I don't want to get married for fear of what kind of husband I will have. 'I know of a sibling who didn't find a good husband and who had her marriage breaking up,' she remarks.

Prachi has to schedule our interview too such that it does not clash with her brother's routine. Every evening, at a specified time, she goes for a walk with her *dada*. He'd fret if she was late, but when she turned up he'd call her the best sister in the whole world! Perhaps his assessment isn't too far from the truth.

———

Often, the NT sibling takes over as the legal guardian once both parents die. Although there is information about guardianship on Nayi Disha, the website that Prachi started which provides information on ID and DD, the irony is that she is struggling to get guardianship herself.

Under the National Trust Act, you can apply for the guardianship of children with autism, cerebral palsy, mental retardation and multiple disabilities after they turn 18. The Trust has appointed a Local Level Committee (LLC) in each district, which is empowered to approve or remove legal guardians. The LLC, headed by the district collector, includes an NGO representative and a PwD. Priority of guardianship is given to either or both parents. After the parents die a sibling cannot automatically take over; they have to re-apply to the LLC.

Prachi, personally, is frustrated by red tape. 'When the biological father himself says I want my daughter to take care [of her sibling], why should we need permission from the LLC for that?' she asks. 'Why would you put a district collector, who is responsible for the revenues of the entire city or zone, to take care of this when they have other priorities?' When she approached the district collector, he shooed her away saying, 'This is not my business.' He sent her to the revenue officer who said that unless the district welfare officer says so, I can't okay it. The district welfare officer had no idea about it and said, 'We've given guardianship already, so how can we give it again?'

Former chairperson of the National Trust Poonam Natarajan agrees that there are 'many issues in the functioning of the LLC'. She points out that the very question of guardianship and the PwD's 'legal capacity' has been debated in the UNCRPD, throwing up diverse views on the matter.

———

Mahima Nair has just finished her fourth glass of iced tea the evening I (C.K. Meena) meet her in Bengaluru. She's 15, on spring break from her international school where she is doing her IGCSE.

'Clean your room!' comes the eternal order that mothers have issued down the ages almost since the beginning of time. Mahima's mother Anima Nair is anxious that I find 'at least a place to sit' in her daughter's room when I go over to talk to her.

We end up sitting on her large bed and chatting about everything from her tomcat Caramel to Trevor Noah. 'He's awesome,' she proclaims, expressing her fondness for the comedian and TV host, before she moves to the subject of the books she reads (*To Kill a Mockingbird*, *Catcher in the Rye*, *The Kiterunner* and *1984*). 'I tried a Charles Dickens book once but it was really hard to understand', she says, and tells me that her favourite authors are Stephen King,

Neil Gaiman and Jonathan Stroud. She loves fantasy. At school, besides maths and English, she chose French, physics, chemistry, global perspectives, and information and communication technology. And oh yes, she wants to be a pilot – a 'weird obsession' she's had since the age of six.

Beside her bed, I notice a miniature mattress and a bolster. It is Caramel's bed for the summer; in the winter he likes to curl up in the *razai* lying all crumpled next to it right now. A guitar and a ukulele in their black cloth covers are propped up against a wall. Besides these instruments that she plays, she takes piano and vocals lessons from a Trinity College graduate who comes next door to teach her neighbour. Some of the posters she has made are stuck on the cupboard. 'I stay here [in this room] 90 per cent of the day,' she explains. She shared a room with her brother Pranav, who is 18 now, only when she was little, she says. 'We had twin beds, and then I wanted my own space, very early.' Now it's her room, and hers alone.

Pranav is on the autism spectrum. 'Honestly, from a really young age I knew what autism was; I instinctively knew that he was different,' she recalls. This awareness was perhaps in no small part instilled by Anima. The first school they both attended was inclusive and had children with disabilities along with the average ones.

How was it for the two of them growing up in this gated community? Mahima says the neighbouring kids all know of his condition and they would play football and cricket together. The siblings used to play together online when they were younger. She says, 'We used to play a lot of games on the computer, compete against each other; we'd find games on so many websites and play. Now we usually just do our own thing. I do my own stuff, he does his own; we're cool with it.' Pranav's 'stuff' is his art. He sold two of his paintings, she tells me with a touch of pride. (Anima had earlier informed me about it when I met him and the other artistic talents at Sense Kaleidoscopes, where he studies.)

'I moved schools a lot,' says Mahima. Didn't she fit in? 'They were just bad choices, I guess!' she retorts. She shifted to the international school in Grade Nine and likes it a lot. It is inclusive and disability-friendly, has a huge campus, 18 different sports and 'very good' teachers.

Do her school friends come over? 'Frequently,' she says. 'Mostly for projects that we say we do but never do. We usually end up watching Netflix.' And how do they react to Pranav? They're 'open-minded', and besides, they know a good deal about autism – mainly because the school is inclusive, 'and they get a more detailed insight from me'. Even if they hadn't known much, she says, they're 'genuinely kind people' who would anyway have treated him well.

The outside world is not so kind. Growing up, she has been acutely aware of that. There have been the usual prejudiced reactions from the ill-informed. 'I've met so many of these people when I was small,' she remembers aloud. Besides grown-ups, there were some kids in her class who thought autism was 'a bad thing' and 'quote unquote, weird', she says. 'I used to be a very short-tempered kid; I'd get very mad and fight with the schoolkids.'

But now that she is older, she handles prejudices in a mature manner. When older people find Pranav's behaviour 'an embarrassment because he doesn't behave the way you're supposed to', she knows that their attitudes spring from 'cultural values, [and] traditional beliefs'. 'You can't really convince someone that deeply traditional. I know whatever I say won't change things. I don't really care about it now,' she says and then adds wisely, 'I used to protect him, but you can't do that too much; he's also got to learn. When he's alone, he's got to know how to deal with that.'

The door opens and Pranav comes in to ask his sister, 'We are going to see the land thing at 5.30, would you like to come?' She says, 'I'm sorry, I've got some work to do, but you go, enjoy yourself.' He reaches out to shake my hand and say hi. I tell him I've met him at Sense Kaleidoscopes with his mother. 'Yes,' he says.

'We're leaving at 5.30 in the evening.' 'That's after 31 minutes,' I say, checking my watch. 'Yes, it is,' he says and leaves.

Their parents are checking out some land, Mahima explains, 'That kind of thing really bores me. Drives don't interest me either.' Pranav likes to go on drives, though. 'He's one of the happiest people I know. He's always full of joy. I say, hey, come on, learn from him. I should learn from him too.'[21]

———

Smrithy Rajesh is showing me (C.K. Meena) one of her many videos on her YouTube channel. This one is of 13-year-old Aditya talking about his 11-year-old brother Addu who has ADHD and ASD. He is reciting what sounds like a scripted piece he has memorized on Addu's achievements and how he used to be jealous of him, but now plays with him and shares his bed. Shots of him playing basketball with Addu, linking hands and dancing with him and accompanying him on the electronic drum pad to play his favourite nursery rhyme, end with him saying, 'He's the best brother I could ever hope to have, and I love him very much.'

'And you fight with him too, now; confess!' I tease Adi, who has that endearing awkwardness that NT kids his age usually display.

He shakes his head. After a considered pause he replies, 'Irritating is not fighting.'

'When he gets bored he hits me,' he says, nodding matter-of-factly. It moves me, somehow – the image of this mild-tempered teenager resigning himself to his brother's knocks. In the best of situations, siblings of kids with autism are known to be mature

---

[21] Anima Nair writes in her blog about the unfairness of having too many expectations from siblings of PwDs. She tells us that although her daughter Mahima loves her brother Pranav who has autism and says she will look after him, she should not be expected to continue looking out for her brother all her life.

beyond their years. But Smrithy is well-aware of the dangers of having too many expectations of them; it's a danger she has warned parents of in the paper on the role of siblings that she wrote for her diploma.

Smrithy brings me a plate of homemade *achappam*, the brittle, delicately sweetened Kerala speciality fried in coconut oil. Her mother-in-law specially made and sent it over from Kerala for Addu's eleventh birthday (in 2019). I offer it to Adi, who grimaces in response.

'What? You don't like it?' I enquire. Smrithy says he dislikes all traditional food.

'You mean you like...KFC?' I ask, again trying to draw him into the conversation.

'Yes!' he utters triumphantly.

'Aaargh!' I clutch my throat in exaggerated disgust.

Smrithy describes how, when they go to her native village in Kerala on vacation, Adi complains that his grandmother doesn't know how to cook! She prepares only traditional food, which Adi the archetypal metro kid turns up his nose at.

'What is Addu's favourite? Does he have any?'

'With him you can never tell,' says Smrithy. 'One day he'll say he likes a dish, and if you serve it to him the next day he won't want it.'

Adi reads voraciously and widely. He's devouring Harry Potter at the moment and prefers the books to the films. Smrithy says that while Addu is constantly physically active, Adi hates moving his butt and has his nose buried in a book all the time, frequently deaf to his mother's call to come and eat. They get the daily local English newspaper on and off, but they buy it regularly during Adi's vacation because he likes reading it. She wonders aloud where he got the habit from, since neither she nor her partner Rajesh are readers.

I think I know the answer. It's the silent TV. Addu can't stand the noise of the television, and it's switched on softly only after he goes to bed late at night.

'You must be the only kid in your school who doesn't watch TV,' I tell Adi.

Another triumphant 'Yes!'

'That's why you're a reader.'

Later, he picks up Temple Grandin's book on autism from the shelf and shows it to me. 'He read it even before I did,' says Smrithy. From his collection it is evident that his reading spans across not only children's books but anything he can lay his hands on.

Before I leave, Rajesh calls Smrithy from the camp where he and Addu have gone for the weekend. Smrithy shows me WhatsApp images he has just shared of the twosome trekking and boating and so on. When they return, no doubt, the 'best brother' will be back to irritating, and playing with – and loving – his patient older sibling.

# 8

# EARLY INTERVENTION, IF NOT PREVENTION

THE SOONER A CHILD'S DISABILITY IS IDENTIFIED, THE sooner one can intervene with appropriate therapies to help them meet their developmental milestones and get smoothly integrated into society. But the aim of the government, medical fraternity and indeed of society at large, is to prevent children from acquiring disabilities in the first place. The widely accepted sequence is: (1) prevention, and if necessary, (2) timely diagnosis and (3) early intervention.

With these aims in mind, the March of Dimes Foundation, established by United States President Franklin D. Roosevelt in 1938 to combat polio, was the first to provide global estimates of birth defects in a report in 2006.[22] It estimates that while 6 per cent of the total children born worldwide every year have serious birth defects, up to 70 per cent can either be prevented or mitigated. The report counters the misperception that preventing birth defects would require costly, high-tech interventions that the health budgets of low- and middle-income countries cannot accommodate. The

---

[22] 'March of Dimes Foundation, Global Report on Birth Defects' (New York: March of Dimes Foundation, 2006).

'feasible and affordable'[23] interventions it recommends include 'family planning, optimizing women's diets, managing maternal health problems and avoiding maternal infections',[24] which would also reduce child and maternal mortality, and disability.

In India, policymakers and experts have begun to accept that not dealing with birth defects creates a far greater financial burden as these babies need long-term care and management. In 2005, the government of India launched the Janani Suraksha Yojana, a safe motherhood intervention under the National Rural Health Mission (NRHM) with the objective of reducing maternal and infant mortality. In 2013, it launched the Rashtriya Bal Swasthya Karyakram (RBSK), a child health screening and early intervention programme that aims to screen over 270 million children for the 4 Ds: Defects at birth, Diseases, Deficiencies and Development delays including disabilities. The key feature is the continuum of care extending over different phases of the first 18 years of a PwD's life.

The subject matter of Pavitra Chalam's award-winning documentary film *Rooting for Roona* (currently available on Netflix) is birth defects, which are seen in six out of 100 babies born annually in India and adding up to 1.7 million babies born with birth defects in the world every year. As part of a grassroots initiative associated with *Rooting for Roona*, Pavitra's company Curley Street has developed an impact campaign focussed on preventive maternal health. In partnership with local healthcare organizations, it has developed video content geared to the needs of rural India covering topics such as anaemia, high-risk pregnancies and nutrition during pregnancy. This can serve as resource tools for frontline health workers such as ANMs (Auxiliary Nurses and

[23] Ibid., p. 5.
[24] Ibid.

Midwives), and ASHA (Accredited Social Health Activist)[25] and Anganwadi (rural crèche) workers.

## Catching Them Early

India is nowhere near putting systems in place to provide early intervention services for children with disabilities the way Western nations have done. Commenting on the plight of urban parents, Poonam Natarajan says that although 'clinics [that can aid early intervention] have mushroomed, they charge by the hour, and parents run from one clinic to the other because each handles a different area: one for speech therapy, one for vision, one for occupational therapy, one for physiotherapy.' This piecemeal approach fails to identify the child's overall needs. At Vidya Sagar, a multidisciplinary team decides what is best for each child and sets aside four to five weeks a year to draw up Individualized Education Plans (IEPs) for them. 'The child comes to us at eight or ten months old,' says Poonam. She adds with a smile, 'We have on our staff some of our alumni who came to us for Early Intervention even before they were one year old! They grew up in the centre and now are disability advocates in the Disability Legislation Unit.'

The country also faces an acute shortage of qualified professionals, such as speech therapists and occupational therapists. So if we're talking of intervention at a national scale, there would first need to be coordination between all the government hospitals and Anganwadis, ASHA and community health workers, for timely diagnosis, and enough centres fully equipped to deliver intervention services. And for every state, district, town and village to achieve this – to mesh the thousands of cogs in the government wheel – would take a long time indeed.

---

[25] Local women trained to act as health educators and promoters in their villages under the NRHM.

Predictably, Kerala has shot ahead of the other states. Its State Initiative on Disabilities (SID) is part of its historically robust health delivery system that is as good as or better than that of many 'developed' nations. Dr Mohammed Asheel, on deputation for five years as executive director of the Kerala Social Security Mission (KSSM), points out that the Infant Mortality Rate (IMR) of Kerala is comparable to those of Scandinavian countries.

As Dr Asheel turns his laptop screen towards us, we can see tables and numbers. With a single click he can check the number of babies born on any given day in any of the 66 'delivery points' (centres where babies are delivered) in the state. What's more, the data indicates how many of those babies are 'high risk'. Every point – from large district hospitals to District Health Centres (DHCs) and a few Community Health Centres (CHC) – tags babies at risk of acquiring a disability and relays real time data to KSSM. Each DHC has a Junior Public Health Nurse (JPHN) provided with a tablet to enter data on every newborn screened there.

All delivery points are fully equipped to make early intervention and, sometimes, prevention possible. Antenatal screening can detect some disabilities in the initial stages, Dr Asheel explains. Certain disabilities, including congenital heart defects, are identified through the Nuchal Translucency (NT) scan in the twelfth week of the foetus. In the second trimester, the Triple Test detects DS and other genetic anomalies. The hearing of a one-day-old infant is checked with an Otoacoustic Emission (OAE) screener.

Prevention precedes intervention, as we have mentioned before. In 2017, SID adopted Anuyatra, a life-cycle approach geared towards tackling disability through measures ranging from prevention to assisted living. Anuyatra works through IEC, another one of those ubiquitous abbreviations – Information, Education, Communication. But it is not just a meaningless mantra in this instance. Kerala's legendary 100 per cent literacy and its high education levels ensure that IEC works pretty well on the ground. Citizens are told about the risks of consanguineous marriages, early marriages, late pregnancies and iron deficiency – all of which could lead to congenital or acquired disabilities.

Twenty-five Mobile Intervention Units (MIUs) are conducting outreach programmes and providing therapy for children in need of them. There is one MIU for every six community development blocks, and it visits each of the six blocks once a week. Each MIU is supposed to be equipped with a developmental therapist, speech therapist, physiotherapist and special educator, but there is a shortage of professionals. They say that they are attempting to rectify this at the earliest.

With the gung-ho attitude of someone eager to get things done on a war footing, Dr Asheel describes how Anuyatra's work will help, for instance, include deaf and HI children in mainstream schools: OAE screening on day one, BERA test in the third month to confirm hearing loss, hearing aid fitted in the sixth month and cochlear implant in the eighteenth. At two years the child goes to a Special Anganwadi (state-run rural child care centres for kids with disabilities), and by the time she goes to a mainstream school, she should be able to hear.

Further, SID is in the process of establishing District Early Intervention Centres (DEICs), training Anganwadi workers to detect disabilities and strengthening the existing special schools for children with ID. (Special Anganwadis are just being set up, but with a proactive administration one should see results sooner than later.) It has already kick-started Project Autism at various government medical colleges and institutions that offer early intervention and therapy services.

Early intervention is also one of the main objectives of NISH in Kerala's capital Thiruvananthapuram. 'We give speech and language [therapy] as early as possible,' says Professor K.G. Satheesh Kumar, the executive director, explaining that the brain's plasticity (ability to change and adapt) attains its maximum potential at the age of three, after which the deaf child can't fully develop speech.

NISH adopts a Total Communication approach, using a variety of means of communication: Sign, auditory, oral, or using visual aids, depending on the individual child's needs. Total Communication can involve gestures, facial expressions, body language, lip reading, touch, taste, or the use of pictures, symbols or objects. The child and parents must be able to communicate in Sign, which is why teaching it makes simultaneous use of Sign, and speech. Both children and parents are taught for one hour in Sign and then the same lessons are repeated in English for the next hour.

Explaining that the goal of early intervention is to achieve integration 'at the earliest', Dr Suja Mathew says that the youngest child who comes to NISH was brought in when she was only 52 days old. Since hearing aids are fitted at six months (and implants at 18 months), they make maximum use of the child's new ability to hear by subjecting her to a wide variety of sounds – low, high and of varying frequencies – and constantly altering the sound level of the hearing aid. 'It's like mike-testing!' says Dr Suja. 'We have to check if the device matches the child.'

The child first learns to receive content and then receives content to learn. Before the child is admitted to preschool, the Parent Infant Programme involves training sessions with the child and the parent to equip the former with receptive and expressive language. The aim is to develop the child's auditory perception without her depending on lip-reading or visual cues. In an integrated classroom, the deaf and HI will have better and more role models, which will automatically raise their academic level.

## Implanting Hope

The hearing aid is the most common form of support provided to HI and deaf children as part of GOI's early intervention services.

Cochlear implants, however, are expensive. The electronic device alone costs a minimum of ₹6 lakh and, depending on the type, the price can go up to ₹15 lakh; add to this the cost of the surgery and post-operative therapy, and it's out of reach for the average Indian. It was only in 2015 that the MSJE included cochlear implants in the list of Assistive Devices (ADs) provided to PwDs under the central government's Assistance to Disabled Persons for Purchase/Fitting of Aids and Appliances (ADIP) scheme – at full or half concession depending on the person's income.

Long before this, however, a private hospital in Surat, Gujarat, had started providing free cochlear implants without any fanfare to economically weaker sections of society. At the turn of the twenty-first century, businessman Parag Shah got his three-year-old son Sumit fitted with a cochlear implant in Belgium. It was a life-changing surgery for the boy, who was subsequently absorbed into mainstream society. Parag wanted to bring this novel technology not only to India but to his hometown. He mooted the idea to his ENT (Ear, Nose and Throat specialist) surgeon friend Dr Vinod H. Shah who had been running Shruti ENT Hospital since 1965.

In 2008, the hospital conducted its first cochlear implant surgery, funded by Parag, on the two-and-a-half-year-old daughter of a loom worker. The two friends decided to form the Chinmaya Trust to help many more poor deaf children gain the same advantage that Sumit had. Dr Vinod was joined by his son Dr Saumitra Shah, who had trained under the reputed ENT surgeon Dr Mohan Kameswaran of Chennai, and offered to perform the surgeries for free, while Parag would cover the costs of the implant and the subsequent maintenance as well as the year-long therapy.

If you are imagining that there was a beeline of poor patients in need of free implants instantly at the hospital, you'd be wrong. They had to hold awareness camps to familiarize the public with this new technology. 'Acceptance was the first problem,' says Dr Saumitra, 'and the second was the stigma.' The implant has an external unit, which includes a sound processor, microphone and transmitter that fit behind the ears and around the head. A device that visibly displays a person's disability attracts social stigma, and more so when it bears an unfamiliar shape.

In 2015 when the state government started conducting cochlear implant surgeries in designated government hospitals, it was persuaded to extend its programme to Shruti, which is now the only private hospital that does cochlear implants in the whole state. The government procures the implants and the rest is taken care of by the Chinmaya Trust, with Parag bearing the bulk of the financial burden and of course Dr Saumitra foregoing his standard surgery fee.

Till date, the trust has benefitted over 900 children and adults who were deaf or severely HI. Around 90 per cent of the children have been mainstreamed, says Dr Saumitra. He reaps his greatest reward in the follow-up five years after the surgery when he witnesses the progress that each patient has made.

## The Challenges of Measuring Disability

Getting a disability certificate that names the type and degree of disability – and the accompanying Unique Disability ID (UDID) card, which is being issued at a snail's pace – entitles an Indian citizen to all sorts of concessions and benefits.

The RPwD Act defines a 'person with benchmark disability' as someone with not less than 40 per cent of a specified disability, where it can be measured, and includes disabilities that cannot be defined in measurable terms. The assessment criteria for all measurable disabilities are specified in numerical detail. The Act even sets the bar for dwarfism: You have to be equal to or less than 4 feet 10 inches or 147 cm in height to qualify!

A mental disability is measured in a specified range of percentages that indicates whether it is mild, moderate, severe or profound. The WHO assessment tool has been modified for the Indian context as the Indian Disability Evaluation and Assessment Scale (IDEAS). It covers many disorders but it isn't comprehensive. For example, for ASD there's the Indian Scale for the Assessment of Autism (ISAA).

Merry Barua of Action for Autism, has been fighting for years to correct the common perception of autism as an intellectual disability. 'The discourse in India has always been that autism is a fancy form of intellectual impairment,' she says. The RPwD Act too mentions autism – and dyslexia too, incidentally – as an ID, but Merry points out that a lot of people with both these conditions have no ID whatsoever, and are therefore not getting disability certificates.

The Autism Certification Medical Board consists of a clinical psychologist or rehabilitation psychologist, a psychiatrist and a paediatrician or general practitioner. Merry believes that although the board members may have diagnosed people with autism, 'they have not worked with them and so they do not understand the multiple and complex ways in which autism manifests'. ISAA often doesn't catch those who are on the severe end of the spectrum, she says. For instance, when the person who is testing asks parents whether the child has 'problems with communication' they say 'no', just because he talks a lot. But being vocal is not the same as communicating.

Clinical assessments could be useful for teachers, but wouldn't they be able to identify a child with a learning disability even otherwise? As Rajani Padmanabhan of Brindavan School says, 'Educators are qualified enough to find out the gaps in learning. A good classroom teacher will know that this child is not able to read cat-bat-mat, [and] not able to understand when we make a sentence.' However she admits that they usually need both cognitive and functional evaluations to give them an overall picture of the child's educational level. 'Although we do rely on the psychologist to give us an assessment of what is the difficulty, we rely on ourselves for the educational evaluation, which is something that the psychologist can't give us. If the child doesn't have too many difficulties we don't even want a label. Of course the label is only for internal knowledge, not to be mentioned outside.'

## Mental Illness and Health

'Measuring' mental illness comes with its own set of challenges.

The fluctuating nature of psychiatric illnesses makes certification a fraught exercise. A permanent disability certificate is rarely issued in these cases, because the certifying authorities have to be convinced that there are absolutely no chances of further improvement. A temporary certificate valid for five years is the norm. Manoj Chandran of the White Swan Foundation for Mental Health describes how it has become a catch-22 situation: If you're on medication and your illness subsides, you may not be eligible for a certificate when you're assessed. But to continue taking the medication, you need a certificate! Therefore you'd probably have to stop the medication and present yourself to be assessed during the active phase of the illness on a day when you're least lucid.

Diagnosis followed by intervention is the right way to go – but why not prevention? We as a nation haven't paid sufficient attention to self-care. 'Mental health is something that belongs to everybody,' says Neha Kirpal, founder-director of the annual India Art Fair and one of the World Economic Forum's Young Global Leaders. 'Just as we look after our physical health every day, we need to be able to nurture our mind.' Mental health is not a silo, she explains. You have to look at it in a holistic way, because if you're a cancer patient, for instance, or have a respiratory problem, your mental health suffers.

Grim statistics roll off her tongue: Globally there's a suicide every 40 seconds; in India, every 17 seconds; students kill themselves every hour; and there's an attempted suicide every three seconds. Prevention and early intervention are Neha's major concerns. 'Fifty per cent of all psychiatric problems can be diagnosed before the age of 15,' she states. 'And 60–70 per cent of those in jails have a mental health problem; if you deal with that, there'll be less crime. If you work towards a society where you have a stronger sense of self, and you're feeling more empowered and better about yourself, you'll do less harm.'

When mental health care – fragmented and limited though it be – is concentrated in urban centres, can digital technology help scale intervention services to cover rural India? It is a radical idea. We already know that India boasts of a staggering 1.2 billion mobile phone subscriptions, and if you discount phones with multiple SIM cards it works out to over 700 million unique users. More pertinently, over 500 million of them are smartphone users, almost equally split between rural and urban areas.

The question is: would a farmer or a migrant labourer who watches YouTube and WhatsApp videos in their spare time also use the cellphone to access (let alone pay for) mental health care?

Neha is placing her bets on digital-led omni channel platforms founded on a 24/7 accessible, decentralized and person-centric approach, rather than from a top-down clinical or pharma perspective alone. In fact, she is the co-founder of InnerHour (along with Dr Amit Malik), a personalized digital mental health platform that supports over a million users from over 150 cities around the globe. It's like a Fitbit for the mind, tracking your moods and well-being, offering self-help programmes and counselling services in eight languages with a team of 120 therapists. It offers a step by step guide, providing insights, setting goals and recommending activities customized to your needs, such as easy exercises to keep you aware and motivated. Going forward, Dr Amit and Neha are focussing on full service curative care management for the entire range of mental health conditions, soon opening primary care centres and acute care facilities, all supported by the same digital platform for seamless continuous access 24/7.

To identify potential mental health problems in the country, there should be a specialized workforce, says Neha, citing an example of the founder of the not-for-profit Sangath in Goa, Vikram Patel, who has devised a training module for barefoot counsellors. 'How do we train laypersons [and] frontline workers like gynaecologists, paediatricians, general physicians, the police force and teachers, to intervene?' she ponders. Her mental health platform plans to do extensive community building around mental health conditions online, and with support groups and training programmes for universities, corporates and healthcare workers.

The White Swan Foundation has been training teachers to identify mental health problems among students. It has trained 400 teachers so far through a six-hour workshop, focussing on adolescent behaviour in the classroom. It usually takes about two of those six hours to make government school teachers realize that this isn't one of those standard teacher-training sessions to improve their teaching skills. They are encouraged to first speak about the difficulties they face and understand their own mental health, because their well-being affects how they handle their pupils. Finally they are told about the adolescent phase – the biological changes that happen and how it affects the child's behaviour. Armed with this knowledge they can identify signs of distress in the classroom instead of just putting it down to disobedience or indiscipline. These teachers will be urged to train others – a train-the-trainer method. Also, White Swan is trying to get the government to include a session on mental health in their regular teacher-training sessions.

## Prevention, a Prickly Question

Now you might wonder what could possibly be debatable about a perfectly reasonable step like preventing a disability.

As we stated right at the beginning, the aim of government, the medical fraternity and indeed society at large is to prevent a child from acquiring a disability. Therefore few would disagree with Christy Abraham, former chief executive officer of the Association of Persons with Disability (APD), when she says, 'There is a need for more prevention. Not just paediatricians but also gynaecologists should spread awareness on preventing disability in the womb.'

So can there be any reasonable argument against prevention?

'Nip it in the bud', is what we usually say. Let there be no more people being born with or acquiring disabilities in the world from now. Through science and technology we can create the 'perfect' human race. Can you see where this is going?

If we tell you that by saying disability should be prevented we devalue PwDs who live among us, you may protest vociferously: 'Come on, this is carrying it a bit too far'. Well, if you think we sound extreme, you should hear some of the militant voices from the international Deaf community.

Many radical Deaf activists in the West have made the controversial claim that cochlear implants are a tool for cultural genocide. They believe that when parents and doctors convert a deaf child into a hearing one, they are obliterating Sign, forcibly introducing speech and wiping out an entire community.

We're not taking sides, but if you extend their argument to all other disabilities, you cannot deny that it poses ethical questions to which there are no easy answers.

If future scientists are able to discover every 'faulty' gene that causes a physical or intellectual impairment, doctors can pluck it out of the foetus like a weed from a garden. Similarly, advanced technology will be able to easily 'fix' disabilities acquired through accidents or old age – cyborgs already live among us with bionic limbs and exoskeletons, and there are deep brain implants to treat movement disorders and whatnot. Eliminating disability altogether would certainly cost the government less. It could save a gazillion rupees on subsidies, therapies, medical support, special education, creating fully accessible environments... No need to talk about inclusion. And you can kiss compassion goodbye.

You didn't blink an eye when you read about Dr Asheel mentioning the NT scan and Triple Test to detect 'anomalies', did you? You took it for granted that if parents found out they were going to have a Down baby they would naturally decide to get the foetus aborted. After all, India's Medical Termination of Pregnancy Act allows abortion beyond the 12-week stipulated period for up to 20 weeks if there is a risk of 'physical or mental abnormalities' that would render the child 'seriously handicapped'.

But what would you say to a Pranjan or a Sid or a Nipun if they asked you, 'Should we never have been born?'

Nobody can point a finger at parents for exercising their legal right to avoid the financial and emotional burden of raising a child with a disability in our country. On the other hand, if our country and society were inclusive and they wholeheartedly supported every child with disabilities to grow up to lead a healthy and fulfilling life, those parents might think twice before taking a decision.

Can every parent of a child with a disability say – hand on heart – that they have never wished they'd had a 'normal' child instead? On the other hand, can't every parent also say that they would never exchange their precious, unique child with disabilities for any other in the world?

The anguish of bringing up a child with disabilities cannot be wished away, but neither can the rewards of doing so be discounted. 'Prevention' isn't so simple, after all.

# 9

# INCHING TOWARDS INCLUSIVE EDUCATION

IN INDIA, CHILDREN WITH DISABILITIES (OR CWSN IN government-speak) have the right to free education from the ages of 6 to 18. That's four years of free and compulsory education, more than non-disabled children are entitled to.

CWSN are legally entitled to choose the neighbourhood or special school they would like to attend. The RPwD Act directs state governments to 'endeavour' that *all* educational institutions admit them and provide support, access to all facilities on campus, and reasonable accommodation for their inclusion. Government and aided institutions of higher education must reserve not less than five per cent of its seats for PwDs.

Fine words, but don't they ring a bit hollow? We know there is no glorious array of special schools for children with disabilities to choose from when there aren't enough viable regular schools in the country. When regular schoolteachers themselves are in such short supply – over a million job vacancies, according to the Ministry of Human Resources Development[26] – you'll have to search for Special Ed. teachers under a microscope.

---

[26] Anisha Singh, 'Teacher's Crisis In India: Country Falls Short Of 1 Million School Teachers', *NDTV*, 4 December 2017.

Reserving seats in higher education would make sense only if children with disabilities could enter school in the first place and actually make it to college. Even the dubious statistics of the Census show that in 2011 almost 40 per cent of India's children with disabilities (which includes 50 per cent of those with ID) have either never attended school or dropped out, while graduates with disabilities constitute a single-digit percentage.

Formal education for PwDs has, however, existed in India since the nineteenth century when the British set up schools for the deaf, the blind and the 'mentally retarded' (an old term for those with ID, it is unfortunately still in vogue in government circles). The Indian government launched a scheme in 1974 to integrate 'handicapped children' in mainstream schools and encouraged special education in the 1980s, as a result of which NGOs set up several schools for deaf, blind and 'MR' students. The government launched Project Integrated Education in 1987 to encourage enrolment of CWSN in mainstream schools. Over the decades, the government has moved from calling for integration to speaking of inclusion.

But on the ground, what is the quality of education that children with disabilities in government schools (in the few places where they exist) are receiving? Most teachers seem to just tolerate their presence in the classroom and ignore them most of the time, because they are not equipped to handle them.

Take the example of Ganesh Mani, the bubbly proprietor of Jehovah Jirah Industries which employs only PwDs. Ganesh, who comes from a low-income family in Bengaluru and is the youngest of eight siblings, contracted polio at the age of five. He says that his early childhood was spent just sitting in the house, eating and sleeping. His mother would carry him to the nearby government school where the teachers ignored him. As a result, 'I knew nothing, did nothing, I was *ek dum* (absolute) zero,' he says.

He was 12 and still in the fourth standard when his mother shifted him to yet another government school. There he was demoted to the first standard, because that was the level of education he had received! At 14, his mother changed his school again – this time, he was admitted to the seventh standard in a private school. The teachers there showed a little more interest in teaching him, but it was too late for him to catch up. He kept getting (as he describes it in Kannada) 'big, big eggs' in all subjects. He wrote his tenth standard final exam when he was 18 years old. 'Big pumpkin I got,' he says cheerfully.

If this was the experience of a boy with a physical disability in a government school in a state capital and metro, you can imagine the plight of the thousands of children with various types of disabilities enrolled in schools in rural and far-flung regions.

## Training in Special Ed.

It is unfair to compare the Indian situation to a high-income nation such as the United States, which has hundreds of special schools, but the differences are too obvious to ignore. In regular schools there, no child can be rejected because of a disability, and even those with severe disabilities are included. A typical school has a resource pool of full-time professionals: special educators, speech and language pathologists, board-certified behaviour analysts and school psychologists. The inclusive classroom has a special educator who engages with each child with a disability, for whom an individualized plan has been drawn up. *The cost of educating each child with a disability which the government bears is almost three times the cost borne by the parents of a child in the general education system.*

A Special Ed. teacher for each child with a disability is possible only in wealthy countries. Meena Cariappa, founder of Sahas Opportunity School in Madikeri, points this out and asks, 'How can we in our country afford that? We're talking of the multitude, not the elite.'

Since the few qualified special educators we have are mainly clustered in special schools, it makes sense to remedy the shortfall by training regular teachers to handle children with disabilities.

Janaki Narayan suggests that the regular B.Ed. (Bachelors in Education) course include Special Ed. and that schools include the subject as part of their orientation for new teachers. Siddharth Jayakumar, senior banker and India's first Certified Documentary Credit Specialist (CDCS) who has CP, echoes her view: 'Every teacher should be able to handle a child with a disability, and this should be included in the B.Ed. curriculum.' Gitanjali Sarangan has a more drastic opinion: 'You can do inclusion only if you ban special educators. Everybody [in the teaching profession] should be able to work with all learners.'

The government is on the same page. In its inclusive education guidelines for CWSN it states: 'Lack of specialized personnel can only be met if general education courses are reformed, and it is ensured that all teachers are able to address diversity in the classrooms... Training general teachers [in] adaptations to teach CWSN should be the main focus area because of the shortage of sufficient special educators in the states.'

The nation's capital appears to be a step ahead when it comes to inclusive education and disability training for general teachers. It is making 'giant leaps' says Uma Tuli of Amar Jyoti Charitable Trust. Merry Barua of AFA, claims, 'In schooling you'll be amazed at what's happening in Delhi. We've had inclusive education for at least 10 years, although I still say it's not enough.' It's been 20 years since AFA started getting kids ready to join mainstream schools, and those with mild to moderate ASD have been gaining admission in these schools, she says. Simultaneously, over the years, AFA has been systematically holding training sessions and workshops for teachers of schools in and around Delhi. 'If your regular teachers learn how to support people with autism, they can support people with other learning challenges as well,' Merry concludes.

The venerable SSI was set up by Dr Mithu Alur in Mumbai in 1972, and it soon sprouted wings. Dr Sudha Kaul set up Spastics Society of Eastern India in Kolkata in 1978, and Dr Mita Nandi began SSI North in Delhi in 1978.

Alternative Strategies/Services for the Handicapped (ASTHA), a community-based organization founded by Radhika Alkazi, specifically targets children with disabilities from low-income families. It has been working in Delhi's slums since 1993 and started with two aims: working with kids with multiple and severe disabilities, and providing information to PwDs and their families. ASTHA has enabled more than 250 children with disabilities to access mainstream schools in their quest for an inclusive education.

And then of course there is Amar Jyoti by the visionary Uma Tuli. 'People thought I was a mad woman trying to do something which was not going to happen!' Uma says gleefully, recalling the inception of Amar Jyoti in 1981 when she took in an equal number of children with and without disabilities. The school has maintained this ratio roughly ever since. It's a self-contained campus offering education, skill training geared to employment and medical intervention including therapy. Experience has taught Uma to take a holistic approach and offer the type of education best suited to each child's needs – there's integration and inclusion, classroom and home-based education, standard curriculum and NIOS. Equal opportunity and full participation are the watchwords of the school.

The MSJE has formed a task force with Uma as its chairperson to design a model inclusive school that can be replicated in other parts of the country. The Ministry is willing to start one each in the nine national institutes that are likely to already have all the resources needed for the schools.

Besides the Special Ed. diploma courses run on the Amar Jyoti campus, the Directorate of Schools also sends them groups of teachers for training in Special Ed. Uma strongly recommends multi-category disability training, because specializing in just one disability will narrow the scope of the teacher. Since you can't expect teachers to specialize in each of the 21 disabilities listed in the RPwD Act, there can be chapters on each disability in the training course, she says. 'Besides these, multi-category special educators also train regular teachers to be sensitive to disability.'

## Long Way To Go

What's happening in Delhi isn't true for the rest of India. How far have schools across the country implemented inclusion following the mandate of the Right of Children to Free and Compulsory Education (RTE) Act introduced in 2009, which was reinforced by the RPwD Act in 2016? The government has been pushing inclusion with renewed vigour, but are its schools disabled-ready?

There is no point jumping the gun when there are no disability-trained teachers, leave alone special educators. At an international conference held at Amar Jyoti in 2019, one of the points raised was a familiar one – the bugbear of our administration in fact: 'insufficient data'. Unless one knows how many kids with disabilities and what type of disabilities are there in each school, how would one know what kinds of teachers to provide?

Manjula Kalyan of Swayamkrushi wonders how government schools that often cater to underprivileged children were going to become inclusive if they lacked basic resources. Elaborating on this, she says, 'From 9 a.m. to 4 p.m. the children with disabilities are in a class of 40 children in the regular school where there is no occupational therapy, speech therapy or physiotherapy. After 4 p.m., will their parents be able to afford to take them to expensive therapists?'

'There's a big question mark over inclusive education,' says Geetha Sridhar, principal of Sahas, voicing her fears over the Karnataka Government's announcement of ₹15,000 for parents who admit their children with disabilities to government schools. Although private opportunity schools like Sahas do not charge for tuition, the money might lure parents away towards government schools where facilities are not likely to be adequate, Geetha worries. 'What kind of education will they get there? The teacher has no time to pay special attention. Why should she take the effort when she has a class of 40 students to handle?'

Sahas has managed to change the mindset of the local community over the quarter century of its existence. Awareness has gradually improved and parents – including masons, carpenters, domestic workers, farm labourers and others from economically weaker sections – have started bringing their children with disabilities to Sahas much sooner than they used to; in the past they were 8 to 10 years or even older when they were admitted. There are well-meaning teachers and schools, too, who identify children with learning disabilities in their class or school and refer them to Sahas.

Poonam Natarajan of Vidya Sagar, is especially concerned about the misuse of Home-Based Education (HBE), a scheme created through a 2012 amendment to the RTE Act. Children with severe disabilities were given the 'right' to opt for HBE, but what actually happened was that many principals of government schools used the amendment as an excuse to order parents to keep kids with severe disabilities at home. These children are enrolled in schools but in reality are left to languish in their homes, their disability worsening while they get neither treatment nor education, says Poonam referring to the situation in Tamil Nadu.

In 2000, the Tamil Nadu government divided all its blocks among 43 NGOs to promote inclusive education. Vidya Sagar got assigned six blocks, each with 80 to 100 schools, and they had 18 special educators. They conducted assessments and drew up a programme for teachers on how to include children with disabilities, make worksheets and create a lesson plan. In 2010, the government decided they didn't want NGOs and said that they would do it themselves. 'And they're doing nothing,' says Poonam, adding that Vidya Sagar has now got permission to work in around 200 schools in 62 rural panchayats.

To follow the government mandate, many private mainstream schools, especially in urban areas, call themselves inclusive by merely setting aside 'resource rooms' for children with disabilities. These kids are then under the same roof as NT kids but in a separate room. How does this practice qualify as inclusion? 'They are working like two autonomous units,' an outraged Gitanjali Sarangan says. 'You hear teachers say, "He is a resource-room child"! This is like branding and labelling in the worst way. Take away resource rooms. Every teacher should be able to work with every child.'

Poonam Natarajan says: 'The teacher in the classroom handling kids with disabilities, with special educators supporting them – that is inclusive education. Otherwise, they become "your children" and "my children". When the teacher talks to children with disabilities, she refers to the special educators as *your* teachers.'

Special schools serve an important purpose, although having genuinely inclusive mainstream schools is the ultimate goal. Wherever possible, parents of children with disabilities strive for their admission in regular schools, however ill-equipped, in the belief that their children will have a competitive advantage. For example, Shravya Kanithi, the first blind student of the Indian School of Business in Hyderabad, is thankful for having studied in a mainstream school. 'Students in special schools are in a sort of bubble,' she says. 'Eventually, when they step out they have no idea how to deal with the world; it's a shock to them. It would have been detrimental to me if I'd been stuck in that environment.' Her mother Sujatha insisted that Shravya study in regular schools right through, although the struggle to cope was considerable. In fact the family shifted from Visakhapatnam to the state capital when she was six, purely on her account – there were schools in Hyderabad which integrated children with disabilities. That being said, Sujatha remarked that teachers were ignorant of methods for teaching those with disabilities, and she had to 'teach them to teach from the perspective of the visually impaired student'.

## Deaf at Greater Disadvantage

It is probably because India has only 304 Sign Language interpreters certified by the Indian Sign Language Research and Training Centre (ISLRTC), and oralism is heavily promoted, that the Deaf community has low educational levels. 'Children with hearing loss have a higher rate of not being enrolled in school, of lagging behind in academics and of dropping out of school within a few years,' Kalyani Mandke and Prerna Chandekar write in their research paper on 'Deaf Education in India'. Deaf schools don't have Deaf teachers![27]

Professor Satheesh Kumar of NISH, takes us through the route that deaf students generally travel. In the Deaf schools, hearing teachers who don't know Sign use gestural communication to teach. 'Over-compassionate teachers' nudge their students from one standard to the next and, since they are barely able to score even the minimum of 25 per cent required to pass, teachers often help them write their exams. When it comes to the state board exams too, teachers are known to 'help' students pass. The result is that when they finish their twelfth standard and come to NISH, they can't even read and write.

As for deaf children in mainstream schools, they struggle to lip-read what the teacher is saying. 'Resource teachers' are supposed to bridge their learning gap but, in practice, there is just one resource

---

[27] Kalyani Mandke and Prerna Chandekar, 'Deaf Education in India', *Deaf Education Beyond the Western World*, ed. Harry Knoors, Maria Brons, Marc Marschark, (Oxford: Oxford University Press, 2019), pp. 261-284.

teacher for the whole school, and it is common to see even several schools share one resource teacher, says Professor Kumar. The class teacher has low expectations from the deaf child, which in turn makes the child perform below par.

P. Rajasekharan and Shashaank Awasthi, founders of the Chennai-based company V-shesh which works with the Deaf, identified this obstacle a few years ago and have been addressing it in a unique way. Although Shashaank says that they fundamentally 'are a jobs company', they have been working in deaf schools in order to strike at the root of the issue. They realized that the deaf persons they placed, even those working in progressive organizations, were facing challenges that stunted their career growth. And their setbacks could be traced to a fundamental deficiency in their English language skills.

Raja (short for Rajasekharan) says, 'If the mainstream world communicates in English and you use Sign, there is a gap which is never going to be filled unless you empower the individual right from the beginning.' Since English is the ticket to employment, in the last four years they have been providing a bridge English curriculum in deaf schools. This English language learning programme, which is delivered over two to three years in Sign using well-researched and tested techniques, gets integrated into the regular school curriculum. Shashaank says, 'With English, the rest of the subjects will improve as well.' Their long term aspiration is to have deaf trainers.

What NISH does, on the other hand, is to put ill-educated undergraduate students through a one-year preparatory course in ISL, English and basic arithmetic. 'Of 100 students, maybe 20 will get through if we're lucky,' says Professor Satheesh Kumar. These students then go on to do their regular bachelor's degree (commerce, fine arts and computer science are the choices here). As for the others, NISH scrapes up what Professor Kumar calls a 'salvageable group' of students who go through a Higher Education Foundation

Programme. Those who still can't make it are channelled into skills development: an Advanced Skill Acquisition Programme in the areas of gem and jewellery making, fashion technology and animation. This is done in collaboration with various industries so that placement is guaranteed.

When candidates come into NISH, there are both speaking deaf and Signing deaf in their classroom. 'The government's priority is to mainstream. We aim to make the speaking deaf clearer in their speech,' says Professor Kumar. But there is a strong pull from the Signers towards the speakers to join their group, and this is a huge temptation for the speakers whose speech anyway suffers from a clarity problem. 'By the time they get to the postgraduate level, there will be no special courses. Inclusion is the goal,' he explains. In an inclusive postgraduate course, the peer group of hearing students helps raise the academic level of the deaf.

What many people don't realize, however, is that including kids with disabilities in a regular classroom creates advantages for neurotypical kids as well. A study done in Vanderbilt University by Erik Carter and his colleagues revealed that NT pupils in the United States showed a 15-point increase in grades in an inclusive classroom; they did better because when they helped coach their classmates with disabilities, they became more engaged with the curriculum. And children with disabilities in an inclusive classroom had higher academic achievement, better social and communication skills and fewer behaviour problems.

Inclusion benefits all.

# 10

# SCHOOLS OF MANY COLOURS

SHOULD SCHOOLS FOR CHILDREN WITH DISABILITIES BE special or inclusive? It needn't be a question of either/or. While there are a few model inclusive schools in India, special schools play an important role in underserved communities and among children with disabilities who require extra support and focussed attention.

One size doesn't fit all. Good schools shape themselves according to the needs of the population they serve. And the child is never seen in isolation: the school always works with the parents – and where possible with the local community – to bring about attitudinal change. The common approach of most of these schools is rehabilitative: assess and intervene as early as possible, provide appropriate therapies, familiarize children with ADLs and design IEPs with an eye towards employment.

One size cannot fit all. It goes without saying that in a vast country with wild disparities of income and glaring imbalances in resource distribution, schools have to function with limited means and bow to the vagaries of their environment. G. Vijayaraghavan states what is blindingly obvious to everyone in the disability sector: 'We don't have enough occupational therapists, speech therapists, [or] Special Ed. teachers. We don't have enough rehabilitation professionals.' We could recite a litany of other things that we don't have enough of, but instead we shall acknowledge the many schools that work among the urban poor or in rural and remote areas, valiantly making do with whatever is available to serve children with disabilities as best they can.

Here are a few examples: an inclusive school, two special schools, a learning centre and a care centre – each with different aims and working in differing socio-economic and geographical contexts.

———

Accessibility, inclusive education, employment: the Amar Jyoti school has focussed firmly on these three areas. Children are screened – their aptitude to subjects tested and their disabilities assessed – so that they can be streamed accordingly. 'Our methodology is to teach children the way they would understand, not teach them the way we want to. This is called reasonable accommodation,' Padma Shri awardee Uma Tuli explains.

Every square foot of the campus in Kakardooma (Delhi), is accessible. (The Gwalior branch was set up in 1989.) In the basement of the main building, the social work department keeps records of every one of the school's 500+ current students, all of whom have been assessed before admission. The department is in close contact with the parents of the students with disabilities, helping them navigate the rules and red tape around getting disability certificates, disability pensions and other benefits.

Medical care and rehabilitation is not just for the students but for the community at large. Besides the general out-patient department (OPD), pathology lab, X-ray room and so on, there's corrective surgery, occupational therapy, physiotherapy, audiology and speech therapy, and an orthotics and prosthetics workshop where simple ADs such as callipers and the Jaipur

Foot are manufactured and distributed under the government's ADIP scheme. At the child guidance clinic, parents are counselled and children assessed as part of the school's early intervention programme.

The school wing has colourful tactile diagrams – learning prompts – on the walls along the ramp that leads to different floors. Besides teaching Braille and Sign, the school holds preparatory classes for those who will go on to join an inclusive classroom; in one of them, we come across a deaf, ponytailed young instructor teaching lip-reading to a group of HI kids. There's a special training centre for deaf-blind children and those with multi-sensory impairment.

Children are trained in skills towards possible future employment depending on their aptitude and ability, and this helps them become self-reliant later, says Uma: 'Students have become fruitful earning members who support the whole family.' In the artificial jewellery making unit, we meet children with DS and autism; the latter tend to have an eye for colour and design. They are stringing beads, while a couple of adults give the final touches to fashion complete pieces of jewellery. We are greeted abruptly and loudly by a boy with ASD and another immediately reaches forward to feel the texture of the material of the trousers we are wearing. The pottery unit helps children who have impaired gross and fine motor skills by asking them to shape the clay by hand.

Skill development training, which is free of charge for all students, is offered at a nominal cost to members of the public who are below the poverty line or from EWS (Economically Weaker Sections, in government parlance). Five women from the neighbouring slums are at work in the tailoring unit, and we can see jute bags and folders displayed.

Amar Jyoti has also held mobile camps – each camp lasting five days – for PwDs to register for ADs, get them fitted and get disability certificates issued on the spot. '29 lakh certificates in one year was a record,' Uma Tuli informs me.

'All-round personality development is important for the differently abled,' she says. 'If a child does well in sports or in cultural activities, automatically their self-esteem increases and they start doing well in academics.' Amar Jyoti initiated wheelchair basketball and Ablympics in India – Uma herself was an all-rounder in sports, having played javelin throw, sprint running, volleyball, badminton and table tennis. Children with disabilities participated in the Republic Day Parade for the first time in 1995 – another Amar Jyoti initiative.

———

In the 1990s in Madikeri (Karnataka), just as in other parts of rural India, it was common for parents from underprivileged backgrounds to confine their children with intellectual disabilities to their homes, away from the public eye. It was in such circumstances that the Kodagu Vidyalaya (which in 2004 collaborated with Bharatiya Vidya Bhavan and prefixed BVB to its name) started a rehabilitation centre for children with disabilities in November 1996.

Meena Cariappa, the sprightly octogenarian who founded Sahas, recalls how they started with eight children in a corner of the Kodagu Vidyalaya's hostel dining room: 'We were given four hours a day and a cupboard. Like the story of the camel and the tent, we then got one room, two rooms and finally this building!' Sahas the Opportunity School now has its own airy, spacious building on the school's premises. Over 60 children with different physical and intellectual disabilities – kids with deafness or speech and hearing impairment, CP, autism and ID – receive individual attention, a formal or functional education depending on their abilities, and vocational training.

Activities in sports and the arts are a vital part of the school programme. The school is proud of the fact that many students have won medals at the state, national and even international Special Olympics. Many deaf and HI children from Sahas went on to do courses at Mysuru's JSS Polytechnic in computers, electronics or jewellery design, says Principal Geetha Sridhar. Geetha, who has been with the school right from its inception, is a home science graduate who was into pre-school education and later did a Special Ed. course at National Institute of Mentally Handicapped (NIMH), Hyderabad.

Meena Cariappa was in Delhi, teaching preschoolers from 1965 to around 1973. Later she and two of her friends started a nursery school at her home. One day the mother of a three-and-a-half-year-old boy with mild CP approached them and asked if he could be admitted. They agreed, and Meena found dealing with him 'very interesting'. After a failed marriage, when she had to close the home school and move out, she decided to concentrate on children with disabilities.

After doing a one-year diploma course in Special Ed., her knowledge of disability mainly grew on the job that she got in a school for children with disabilities run by a woman who herself had a child with DS. Meena worked there for close to two years, and for another two she individually handled children with disabilities for four hours a day in a room she rented. In 1989, after she and 'Nanda' (Air Marshal K.C. Cariappa) got married, her life revolved around the air force stations where he was posted. When they were at the Chandi Mandir Cantonment in Panchkula, the wife of the army commander there wanted to set up something for kids with disabilities. Meena took up the assignment and set up the school from scratch, with the commander's wife giving her support and infrastructure.

After Nanda retired and they came to Coorg (now known as Kodagu), word spread that Meena had a Special Ed. background, and the Kodagu Vidyalaya management asked her if she would set up the school for children with disabilities for them. Although they intended to handle only specific disabilities such as DS and CP, 'when people started coming [in] with children with other disabilities, we couldn't tell them "not here, go there" because there was no "there" to go to,' Meena says. For the first few years they received generous donations from the Kodava community. Now they get by with a combination of donations and government grants.

Most of the teaching materials are painstakingly handmade by the teachers themselves. Geetha shows us the picture-heavy and simple workbooks they use. For instance, they have created images and graphics through which kids with ID learn concepts such as big and small, hot and cold, far and near, and over and under. To help in ADLs, for those with CP in particular, there are lessons in eye-hand coordination and fine motor skills. Geetha demonstrates the 'tailor frames': buttons, hooks, zips and shoelaces attached to separate frames, on which kids can learn how to do and undo each item.

Sahas runs a 'mock shop' to teach the children the basics of buying and selling produce in the market. They learn how to make payments for items and also how to collect money for items sold, and give back the right change and make out a bill. They learn the basics of weights and measurement: how to fill liquid into litre bottles, weigh out items in grams and kilos, use a measuring tape and so on.

Mothers stay on at the school all day, since they come from places too far away for them to go home and return to pick up their children. 'We want them to earn while they're here,' Meena says. Therefore Sahas opened a tailoring unit where mothers earn an income by training children in tailoring.

A couple of years ago, the school's board of trustees decided to replace itself with a younger set of people. Five of the older board had died and the other three, including Meena, decided to resign.

'I'm actually a *faltu* (useless person) over here, busy poking my nose [in others' business],' she jokes. 'Now all eight trustees are younger, with clearer heads than I have.' She's sticking around for a two-year transition period. 'I'm at peace because I know it'll continue. It's nice when you start something to know it's going to continue in good hands,' she ends.

———

The prominent board outside the tile-roofed old bungalow announces 'The Autism School'. It is part of the Centre for Autism and other Disabilities Rehabilitation Research and Education (CADRRE) in Kerala's capital Thiruvananthapuram and has been set up by GVR. After he stepped down as the honorary director of NISH, he registered CADRRE in 2016 and opened The Autism School in September 2017, running it entirely on private funds. He got the once-dilapidated bungalow renovated to create a 4,000 sq ft space amid lush greenery.

The pupils here are mainly non-verbal. The staff-to-pupil ratio is 1:1.5 for toddlers and juniors, 1:2 for pre-teens and 1:3 for teens, and every child has an IEP. The 25 staff members (with the seven support staff) work together, following a holistic approach; the staff comprises speech language pathologists, occupational therapists, educators who include art teachers, child psychologists, a music therapist and an Ayurveda physician. There are no teachers with Special Ed. degrees, only regular teachers who learn and unlearn on the job, 'because there is a lot of unlearning to be done,' GVR says. Picture Exchange Communication System is the method followed, although they are 'open to any methodology that helps the child'.

Kids with ASD often have impaired motor skills, which affects their ability to grasp objects. To help improve these skills, the playroom has pegboard toys – for example, a board with slots of different shapes (such as letters of the alphabet, numbers or geometrical figures) into which wooden blocks of matching shapes must be fitted – and stacking rings, which are coloured plastic rings to be stacked on a peg in order of size to form a conical shape.

The sensory room has padded walls and is soundproof. Teachers call it 'the calming room', and it's usually used for beginners, to allow them to settle down, or else those who become overly agitated in the course of the day. Ayurvedic *shirodhara* sessions are made available too, for their calming effect.

The children spend a maximum of two hours indoors 'learning', after which it's time for (Carnatic) music therapy or dance therapy or going outside to the well-designed play area. Children with ASD commonly have sensory issues, which are addressed outdoors through hydrotherapy and tactile stimulation. They walk through shallow water or the wading pool, or sit in the aqua bath – all of which have bases that stimulate the soles of their feet. The floor surfaces have different textures – flat, undulating, rough, smooth, hard and soft – achieved by using different materials such as gravel, pebbles, sand and bamboo. There are also 'play stations' here, but not the computer kind! The 'brain gym' gets the child to pick up plastic letters and shapes from one station and walk to the next station to place them on the appropriate pegs on the board. The underside of the steps to the slide has a large plastic ball, which they can hit and punch.

The staff members begin their day with an early morning meeting to recall positive 'wow moments' of the previous day – an occasion to lighten the stressful atmosphere they generally work in. The day we visit, the 'wow moments' are kids sharing guava slices among themselves (thumbs-up for social interaction) and a child dancing to music for the first time (improvement in locomotor skills). There have been delightfully surprising 'wows' in the past, we are told. A teacher noticed that a little boy was unable to stack rings by placing the biggest one at the base and so on in descending order of size. After closely observing him she realized that he had his own method: he was stacking them in the VIBGYOR order of colours: violet, indigo, blue and so on in the order of the rainbow.

Another time, a boy who was being taught the numbers kept mumbling what sounded like gibberish. After a while the teacher realized he was saying the numbers in French! When she started teaching him the colours, he once again uttered alien words. 'Ah, he's saying them in French,' she thought this time. But he wasn't. It became a challenge for all the staff to figure out what language he was speaking in. At 11 p.m. everyone received the teacher's 'Eureka' message: it was Czech! As GVR explains, these kids spend a lot of time browsing online and pick up all kinds of information, and narrow, obsessive interests are one of their common features.

To encourage interaction with the outside world, the kids are taken on theme-based monthly outings to places such as the planetarium, fire station, police station and zoo. For instance, the theme of Transport entailed a ride on a double-decker bus; Food, a visit to the agricultural university.

After undergoing an intensive initial orientation, parents (along with grandparents if present) attend a workshop held over three weekends. CADRRE strives to keep parents and the wider family involved and motivated, and work hand in hand with the team to bring out the best in the child.

―――

While taking a few wrong turns when we walked through the narrow *galli*s (bylanes) of Jamia Nagar (Delhi), we could anticipate the sort of community learning centre ASTHA had set up here in July 2019. Located in a small rented space 'opposite MLA's office' – the only landmark to guide us when asking people for directions – it is indistinguishable from the other dwellings in this working class locality that has a largely Muslim population.

In both appearance and function, it seamlessly blends in with the local community.

ASTHA, founded by Radhika Alkazi, started 30 years ago with one child in a garage but quickly expanded its scope from being a centre for children with disabilities, which took on children with severe and multiple disabilities, to also becoming a resource centre for parents and a community-based organization working in some of Delhi's *basti*s (slums). In 2000, ASTHA started the metro's first disability helpline, from which emerged the National Disability Helpline inaugurated in 2005 by former President of India Dr A.P.J. Abdul Kalam.

After surveying the locality, ASTHA identified 30 children between the ages of 6 and 14 with CP, DS, and intellectual, visual and hearing disabilities. Those with severe disabilities needed home-based services. The staff at the learning centre consists of the project manager, the special educators, the social worker and community workers sourced from the neighbourhood.

The centre makes it a point to involve parents and the wider community in its activities. Since their aim is inclusion, they hold monthly meetings with parents of kids with and without disabilities to give them information and awareness on aspects of disability. After a team of specialists, including therapists, do an overall assessment of each child, they prepare the IEP and draw up a three-month plan along with the parents to set goals for the child. They also assist parents in getting disability certificates made and pensions secured.

Based on their age and ability, kids are grouped into pre-academic, academic and pre-vocational. Everyone is taught ADLs and social skills (including good touch and bad touch), besides health and hygiene. There are specially designed chairs for children with orthopaedic and locomotor problems, and wheelchairs for them to travel to and from home. Parents are trained in using the home environment for the child's learning. For instance, a parent can refresh a child's knowledge of numbers by using household objects, telling her 'bring me two onions and three potatoes'. Parents of (often bedridden) children who get home-based services are trained in how to care for them – the correct ways to lift them, to make them sit, to feed them and so on.

The principles behind the learning centre are in line with one of ASTHA's primary aims: Community-Based Rehabilitation.

———

At the Direct Care Centre of Snehadhara in Bengaluru, they do things a little differently. No IEP, no daily reports to parents, and the method they follow is not material-heavy. They work with the body and with the mind.

'We use a bouquet of art forms – music, dance, drumming, story-telling – in a therapeutic setting. It's a multi-modal way of working with learners,' says Gitanjali Sarangan, a practitioner of ABT. Snehadhara also runs a residential ABT certification course for representatives of organizations that work with special populations such as PwDs, addicts, children at risk and survivors of abuse.

Gitanjali did her master's in biochemistry but had wanted to work with speech and language pathology for a long time. In a special school she met Sneha, who was two-and-a-half years old with DS, poor eyesight and heart problems. What struck Gitanjali about the toddler was the magical effect she had on the other children. When the special school turned into a mainstream school, Sneha had no place there, or in any other so-called inclusive school, so Gitanjali decided to create a space for her, Snehadhara. Doctors had claimed that Sneha would be 'like a vegetable' and would never speak. 'Today Sneha speaks five Indian languages, dances, sings,' Gitanjali says. 'I wouldn't attribute it to ABT but to the fact that she was able to learn in her own way.'

When we met Gitanjali at Snehadhara, there were 24 adults working with 35 'children' with ID, CP, DS, ADHD and ASD; the youngest is three and the oldest, 40. 'One-on-one is not the way of learning,' Gitanjali says. 'We believe in group therapy.' The groups form naturally and are never disability-specific. 'The kids find their own buddies. They complement and complete each other beautifully. Some of them respond to each other much better than our facilitators giving instructions,' she adds.

Gitanjali doesn't tread the beaten path or blindly go by the book – the DSM or any other. Experience has shown her that when push comes to shove, kids with autism are capable of changing their inflexible routines and of interacting with strangers. 'Kids adapt. They break out of patterns,' she says. 'Violence and self-injury happens, but the kids are ready to overcome that.' During the weekly sleepover, for example, when a child realizes that there's a queue of 10 people outside the two bathrooms, he/she 'doesn't go through his rigid routine with the toothbrush'. In summer school, when they are taken to meet various people, Gitanjali deliberately doesn't 'prepare' them for the outings. 'We take them to as many places and meet as many people as possible. We've stayed away from places exclusively for kids with disabilities,' she explains.

Since kids with ASD are usually in isolation and know only the 'self', creating 'another' by building social roles is most important, Gitanjali says. Once a week they take the children to a mainstream school and conduct a joint session with NT children. Every Thursday, parents take turns to host a meal at home for a group of six kids, including their own. Once every two months, Snehadhara invites artists to perform for the children; through stage and audience, the boundary between 'me' and the 'other' is created.

Gitanjali is planning more interactions with senior citizens. She recalls a group from a home for the aged that had come to Snehadhara. The youngest was 92 and the oldest 97, and some had dementia. 'Children were automatically taking care of them,' she says. The way some of the seniors repeated a story over and over was like 'echolalia on another level'.[28]

———

Snehadhara and the other schools we've described represent varying approaches to education for our country's PwDs, who come from diverse geographical and social backgrounds. They might be inclusive schools or special schools, they might follow the mainstream syllabus or have IEPs, they might focus not so much on formal education as on rehabilitation and care, but they have a common objective: to fulfil the specific needs of the milieu in which they are located and to place the child at the centre. And even as they put the child's interests first, they ensure that they draw in the family and the community to complete the circle of care.

---

[28] Echolalia means repeating others' words or sentences, a common characteristic among those with ASD.

# 11

## INCLUSION VIA THE BODY

IF DISABILITY IS WHAT SETS PEOPLE APART, PLAY CAN
bring them together. Schools can foster inclusion both inside and
outside the classroom. Inclusion through sport is a great way to
inculcate empathy.

The school playground is often the first major experience
of exclusion in the life of a PwD. Rahul Bajaj, Oxford graduate
and visually impaired lawyer who is a judicial law clerk at the
Supreme Court, remembers being seated always in the front
row in school – totally isolated, with no friends and never going
out into the playground. Percussionist Ghatam Suresh who is a
polio survivor says that the physical training teacher in school
would discourage him from going to the playground, because he
automatically assumed that the boy was incapable of any physical
activity. Whereas Suresh, like any other child, was eager to take
part in sports and 'could do pull-ups and push-ups'. It was only
his brother (who also had polio but was less severely affected) and
his friends who would include him in their games, he recollects,
'When playing cricket I would stand and bowl. When batting I had
a runner.'

That the government should 'take measures to ensure effective
participation [of PwDs] in sporting activities' has been included in

the RPwD Act.[29] The government of India encourages para sports; there are now wheelchair sports of practically every kind in India – cricket, basketball, badminton, tennis, you name it.

But we're still in the realm of PwDs playing games and sports in isolation. Is inclusion possible in sport – PwDs and the so-called 'able-bodied' playing together?

## It's Not Mere 'Child's Play'

When young NT minds are exposed to the idea of inclusion, there is a good chance that they will practice it in adulthood. Umoya Sports, founded by Aditya K.V., enables inclusive education through sports. In eight schools and organizations (so far), most of them based in Delhi, Umoya has been conducting a programme in which kids with ID and DD engage in sport with NT kids.

Aditya was studying in an engineering college when he was bedridden due to sports injuries for six whole months. The level of inability and dependence he experienced left a lasting impression on him. After a stint in a software company, he applied for a two-year fellowship from Teach for India. As part of the leadership programme he was expected to be a full-time teacher in a government school in Mumbai. During his time there, Aditya noticed how, among the many underprivileged kids in school, those with ID were utterly neglected by the teachers. He conceived the idea of sports as an educational tool and started a successful sports programme for the ID kids using football; in fact, one of them eventually became part of the school football team. Later, Aditya joined an international school in Bengaluru, and when he saw the resource-rich school refusing admission to children with disabilities simply because they didn't have the wherewithal to

---

[29] RPwD Act, Chapter V, Section 30(1).

cope with them, he decided to do something about it. And that is how the idea of Umoya Sports sparked off in his mind.

We join the Umoya team to observe the sports programme they have created for Delhi's Jamia Nagar community learning centre. They are about to conduct a session of Purposeful Play at the local community hall. A group of children with disabilities and NT kids of different ages, along with some of their mothers, are waiting for us. 'This is not a therapy programme, although it is therapeutic,' Aditya explains. 'It is a sports education programme adapted to CWSN.' He explains that through a sports buddy system that pairs an NT kid with a child with disability, bonding and awareness are automatically created. 'The idea is to bring these kids together on the same platform, make it fun and goal-oriented,' he adds.

The concept of 'Adaptive Physical Education' – adapting physical education to suit children with disability – is common abroad but absent in India, says Aditya. The Umoya programme, called Joy of Play, spans 36 weeks and is spread over three terms. Every session starts with a warm-up and addresses three elements of body management: agility and flexibility, endurance and coordination. Principle of Play uses athletics, football and basketball to address both physical and social skills. Aditya formulated Joy of Play after gathering inputs from all quarters: NGOs, parents of special kids and even coaches that the Delhi Dynamos – the Indian Super League football team – sent across to mentor and assist him. Matching elements of each game to the skills that needed to be enhanced, and keeping in mind the different challenges involved in each disability, he was able to design games that were tailor-made for kids with particular disabilities. Umoya also creates workshops and modules for sports teachers to work with children with disability.

The children with disabilities at the community hall are a mix of kids with HI, CP and autism; most of them have problems with motor skills, balance and hand-eye coordination. Plastic chairs are quickly plonked at the back of the hall and the equipment – a ball, and plastic markers and cones in the colours orange, red, yellow, blue and white – is set up. The kids line up in a row, ready to run at the sound of a clap or whistle. The warm-up session is simple enough: a row of red cones are placed at the far end of the hall, and each kid has to run to one of them, bend to touch it and run back. Ilmaan who has CP is the slowest among them. He bends with difficulty but gamely accomplishes his feat.

Next, markers are placed in a matrix of columns and rows. The runner has to pause at each marker, crouch, and simultaneously jump up and clap their hands, and when they reach the cone they have to touch it and run back. Our eyes keep going back to plucky Ilmaan who is being helped to crouch and can barely jump but claps his hands, eager to follow what the rest are doing.

Then columns of markers are laid out in sets of three, and at each set they have to stand on one foot, hop and come down on two feet like in a hopscotch game. This is followed by pairs of markers spaced apart to form a 'gate' through which the kids have to first walk, and in the next round, dribble a ball through.

The floor is looking increasingly busy with every colour making its appearance and being randomly arranged. We can observe how this session has increasing levels of difficulty and involves all three elements of coordination, flexibility and endurance. Games are integrated into academics too – for example, identifying colours as in 'walk only through the orange gates' or 'dribble the ball only through the blue gates'.

We also observe how NT or HI kids are encouraged to lead or assist those with autism and CP. Ilmaan, helped by an older NT girl, kicks the ball gently through the markers whose colours he has been able to identify. Flushed and exhausted, he returns to universal applause and his mother's embrace.

Right through the proceedings, the Umoya team is helping the facilitators of the learning centre understand the principles so that they can later replicate the actions for the kids to continue the learning process. This happens at the other schools as well; Umoya visits each school two or three times a week. 'We customize and contextualize the sessions according to their requirements,' says Aditya. 'It's a two-way process.' Since the teachers will have paid close individual attention to their students, they help Umoya fine-tune the programme even more accurately to their needs. Teachers report on the changes they have observed in the kids in academics, social skills, motor skills and so on. The impact of the programme is monitored through qualitative and quantitative assessments.

Lokesh Jurel joined Aditya at Umoya after a common friend put them in touch, and he brought in an understanding of sports sciences. He graduated from Delhi University's (DU's) Indira Gandhi Institute of Physical Education and Sports Sciences (IGIPESS).

Growing up in Agra, Lokesh was a sporty kid. He learnt karate and in 2005, when he was in the third standard, he won a medal in judo at an inter-school competition. Thereafter he kept winning medals at every judo tournament he took part in, including one at the national level in 2008. He was also into football and gymnastics, and later represented his university in fencing.

Lokesh was in the eighth standard when he was selected for the school football team. Bubbling with anticipation on the night before his first game, he took his football and invited a friend, who wasn't selected, to play with him. They were walking out of the hostel when his friend (perhaps playfully) kicked him from behind.

The result: a spinal injury of the lumbar region. 'The doctor said I would never be able to stand. My brain broke,' Lokesh tells us.

Lokesh's father, who was in the potato business, consulted a string of doctors – all of whom told him an operation would be too risky and could result in total paralysis. 'I was in bed, flat on my back for two years. I couldn't even sit up,' he recalls. His father was his biggest source of strength. Every day he would sit by his son's side and give him words of hope – 'a good day will come' – and help him do his daily physio exercises until he was gradually able to sit up in bed. 'I was taking 24 medicines in a day. Total psycho!' he says. Two years later, putting both feet on the ground for the first time since the injury, 'I decided that if I can do it, anybody can.'

Even while he was bedridden he would read his school biology textbooks because he was curious to know more about this body of his and understand what made it tick. After the tenth standard his father, who wanted him to help in the family business, asked him to take up accounts. 'My heart wasn't in it,' he tells us. He managed to persuade his father to let him change his 'stream' to science. But the school rules dictated that if you changed your stream midway, you would have to pay for the new subject and the annual fees all over again. His father paid up, and Lokesh proved that the extra expense was not in vain when in the twelfth standard he got 83.6 per cent in his pet subject.

The time had come for him to decide where to do his graduation, and he began to meticulously research his choices, narrowing them down to two universities that offered Physical Education: the Lakshmi Bai National Institute of Physical Education in Gwalior, considered number one in India, and IGIPESS of Delhi University. He got into Gwalior but found it wanting in a crucial area of sport: Officiating. His research also yielded the name of 'the best professor of biomechanics and kinesiology' who happened to be the principal of IGIPESS, Dr Dhananjay Som.

Lokesh sought admission to DU, and scored 37 out of 40 in the entrance test and a perfect 10 in the interview. He threw himself into college life, attending his first international conference (on sports psychology, and later another one on exercise physiology), working with different sports organizations such as the Paralympics, fencing association and judo association, and 'gaining extra knowledge from Dr Som and all my professors wherever and whenever I could'. It was a demanding course with 36 subjects, and the 108 students selected knew they could be ordered to exit at any moment if they didn't perform.

As if the course wasn't taxing enough, Lokesh simultaneously did a few certificate courses at the Netaji Subhas National Institute of Sports in Patiala (NSNIS). He would go to Patiala on Friday night, attend classes on Saturday and Sunday, and be back for his Monday morning class in Delhi. During that time, one of his friends started a fencing club in Gurgaon, where he got a job as coach. After 5 p.m. when college ended, he would go to the club on his bike and it would be 1 a.m. when he returned home.

Lokesh says that the two clichéd career options that sports graduates seldom think beyond are coach and physical training instructor. After he teamed up with Aditya, he found that they had a common purpose: adapting sports to inclusive education. 'Umoya gives me a chance to implement my learning and knowledge in a new life that I am searching for,' he explains.

## Dancing Into Inclusion

Adults often need education more than children do, and mind you, we're not referring to what is commonly defined as 'adult education'. To be able to understand the differences between another human being and oneself, and to be able to connect to them is an ability lacking in many grown-ups. Through the example of sports we have seen how physical contact can forge human connections. The body can be used as a tool for inclusion in many ways, dance being one.

Avantika Bahl hasn't realized that 24 November 2018, the day her silent performance *Say, What?* premieres at Shoonya in Bengaluru, is Charles-Michel de l'Épée 306th birth anniversary. The eighteenth century Catholic priest from France is known as the Father of the Deaf because he laid the groundwork for French

Sign Language (LSF) – the official Sign Language, that is, for the Deaf had been signing long before that.

When Google acknowledges l'Épée on the day, Avantika's friends start messaging her and that's when she realizes how appropriately timed the event is. The collaboration between the 33-year-old dancer from Mumbai, Avantika, and well-known deaf dancer Vishal Sarvaiya is a first for India. Till now, there have only been performances where the deaf have taught the moves to the deaf, or the hearing asked the deaf to imitate them. Avantika, on the other hand, has learnt ISL to communicate with Vishal so that a genuine collaboration would emerge by which they could jointly conceive and create *Say, What?*.

Avantika has been dancing since her schooldays. Not the traditional dance forms, though. She laughingly recalls her only brush with classical dance. When she was seven, her mother had engaged a tutor to come home and teach her and her older sister Kathak. One day her sister told their mother, 'Ma, he's teaching us how to dance to *Choli Ke Peeche*.'[30] That was the end of their Kathak lessons; their mother fired the teacher the next day.

Avantika used to take part in dance programmes in school and college. She went pro in her late teens after she learnt jazz, salsa and ballet at Ashley Lobo's Danceworks, and joined the company. She was with them for six years, doing individual training in the morning, teaching in the afternoon and dancing with the repertory in the evening.

In 2011, she married her college sweetheart. A dancer? She shakes her head emphatically and responds, 'I wouldn't make that mistake!' When they moved to London for his job, she joined the London Contemporary Dance School. They returned to India in 2013 and moved to Mumbai, where they still live. In 2013, she

---

[30] A suggestive dance number from the Bollywood film *Khalnayak*. The refrain '*Choli ke peeche kya hai*' in the song literally means 'What's behind your blouse?'

staged her first production which she choreographed with four dancers. Called *Wonkot,* it was based on the fable of the six blind men and the elephant – the themes being knowledge, ignorance and perspective.

In 2014, she was part of the Gati Residency Programme in Delhi, where she created a solo work called *110048, M81.* This had been her address (Delhi pin code and house number) for the first 25 years of her life, the place she called home. The piece explored the question: 'What does home stand for?' In 2015, when she was selected for Attakkalari's FACETS International Choreography Residency Programme, she created her next solo named *Here*, which explored the meaning of the different spaces within the home. She also did several site-specific pieces after that. Her *Look Left, Turn Right* premiered at Serendipity festival in Goa in December 2018.

But 2015 was a turning point. She hit a road block. Her creativity evaporated; she found she couldn't teach or perform. One fine day she said to herself, 'I'm going to learn Sign language.' There was no apparent trigger for her decision; nobody in her circle was deaf. But buried in the dim past of her childhood was the memory of a book, a notebook in which she had written: 'I want to learn Braille. I want to learn Sign language.' Maybe some trace of that statement lingered in her when, at age 19, as part of her training at Danceworks she had to produce a Dream Book and on the first page she had stuck printouts of Braille. 'Destiny?' she now wonders aloud.

When she told a filmmaker friend of her desire to learn ISL, he joined her in signing up for classes. He dropped out after two weeks, but she stayed on.

After the course she asked her teacher if he knew any Deaf dancer, and he put her on to Vishal. Vishal Sarvaiya became a star among the Deaf community after he had studied under the famous choreographer Shiamak Davar and appeared on TV in the reality show 'Dance Premier League'. Avantika met him in 2016 with a proposal to join forces, and he 'was very interested in bringing together Sign and movement'.

She spent five hours a day working with Vishal and her Sign vocabulary improved vastly. At first, he found it tough because he was not used to looking within himself for more profound meanings and concepts, but gradually they evolved a shared language. 'It was important for me to create equitable ground, create a shared common experience between the deaf and hearing,' she tells us. The performance would privilege neither group. 'The social currency of sound is very high,' she says, pointing out that it is a rare experience for the hearing to watch, sit still and focus in complete silence.

At the premiere of *Say, What?* Vishal's reputation has preceded him and the Deaf, who comprise half the audience, line up after the show for selfies and autographs. Before the show, they stand in the foyer in tight groups of four or five, signing animatedly, while the average persons watch them from the sidelines with perhaps a mixture of admiration and envy. In the hall, deaf persons have to be reminded to switch off their mobile phones for the sake of the hearing. The performance is totally silent.

Communication is the theme, but ISL is not the medium – it is just an entry point into a language of gestures and movements that the two dancers have mutually discovered and developed. Each part of one body 'speaks' to the corresponding part of the other. The 'dialogue' is top-down, starting with the face and the head, with the focus shifting in stages to the chest, the legs, the feet and toes. The deaf, who are used to only using their hands to sign, are most entranced by the two pairs of feet that appear to frolic and tease each other.

In the initial sequence, the dancers move in similar patterns but rely on a few different gestures that set them apart. After many repetitions of the patterns, you notice that the differences are being ironed out and the gestures begin to resemble each other more and more until there is a smooth flow of perfect harmony.

During the discussion that follows, an elderly man raises his hand and shouts out his question: 'What is the story behind it?' A deaf man conveys: 'Neither the hearing nor the deaf understood it fully.' Avantika replies with a broad smile, 'That's the purpose.' A new language has been forged between the deaf and the hearing, and the interpretation is left to the audience.

Avantika says she intends to learn Braille next. 'I want to work with the idea of inclusion from now on,' she said, 'but inclusion for me isn't just about disability.' It is about different class groups as well, and those who cannot afford to access a ticketed space. She wants to create work that will be performed at traffic intersections 'where the richest and the poorest will share it for a moment as an intervention in their daily life'.

Physical connections do have the ability to spark emotional links that give birth to empathy and compassion. A world that includes everyone, regardless of class, creed, gender or disability, is the future we all look forward to.

# 12

# TWO PORTRAITS OF
# DETERMINATION

WE HAVE BEEN SPEAKING SO FAR ABOUT THE DIFFERENT
ways in which the question of inclusion has been approached by
various actors in India. We will now begin to meet some PwDs
themselves, and try to make sense of the different ways in which
they embody the battle for inclusion. In this chapter, we try to
answer the following question: What is it that makes the fire of
learning burn so bright in some people? The more cold water you
fling onto it, the fiercer the blaze.

Here are two young women with disabilities, who come from
personal and social circumstances that are polar opposites. Both
of them have managed to manouevre their way through the
mainstream education system and flourish despite it. The fire in
one was stoked by loving hands; in the other, it was kindled and
fuelled from within. But both have the power to ignite others.

—————

The Indian School of Business (ISB), in Hyderabad, is the kind of
place that automatically attracts the tag of 'prestigious'. Everything

is state-of-the-art at this institution, which boasts of having all the world class facilities a student might need.

Unless she happens to be blind.

When we arrive to meet Shravya Kanithi, we notice that the campus doesn't have tactile flooring, Braille signage or anything else that could make it accessible to the visually impaired. But Shravya, ISB's first blind student whom we have briefly encountered before in this book, intends to change all that. And given her drive, she probably would have by the time you read this.

When we meet in December 2019, Shravya is accompanied by her mother Sujatha who has been at her side literally every step of the way on campus, leading her from one class to the next, every single day for the entire year of the postgraduate diploma course! As a pioneer, Shravya has a clear aim: 'To see how I can influence this place to make it more inclusive, so that I can confidently go out and say to others like me, "ISB is all set for you."'

Confidence is her middle name. At ISB she is the President of the Women in Business Club (the Hyderabad wing), which has 440 of its 600 postgraduate students as members. She has 'made friends for life' here. In the college from which she graduated before ISB, she was the 'cultural captain' and the media coordinator for a commerce club for emerging entrepreneurs. A professional singer trained in both Hindustani and Carnatic music, she has sung on TV as well.

Right through her academic career, her mother saw to it that she was thoroughly engaged in extracurricular activities. When asked to talk about herself, Sujatha laughs embarrassedly and says, 'I did not do much.' An understatement if there ever was one. But what she means is that she hasn't achieved much in her own life if one goes by society's measure of 'achievement'. She was married at 19 to her aunt's son. Soon after, she contracted TB meningitis and was bedridden for three years. Just after she had recovered and regained her mobility, she conceived. Shravya was born blind; 'and then again the whole journey began'. She adds, 'I didn't feel it was a burden. I enjoyed the journey.'

But she cannot deny that it was rough going: accepting her daughter's disability, learning how to handle it and, worst of all, confronting social prejudices. 'The outside world was much worse 23 years ago, and when I saw people who did not accept her, relatives who didn't know how to behave with her, I went through a very tough time.' The many pinpricks she felt had to be suppressed; she says she couldn't express every little aspect of her distress to her husband.

When her husband's job took him away from Hyderabad for five years, first to Bengaluru and then to Sudan, she became Shravya's sole caregiver. 'I focussed completely, 100 per cent, on her and never stepped back.' Her single-minded ambition was: 'She should be a role model.' One wonders if she was thinking 'I'll show them all' to herself, thumbing her nose at a society that had caused her much pain.

The family moved to Hyderabad because it had mainstream schools that would admit children with disabilities. Shravya studied in Marica High School with the SSLC syllabus till the sixth standard. The school had Braille textbooks, and a home tutor taught her how to take down notes in class in Braille. In the seventh standard, when she joined an international school with the ICSE syllabus, the teachers there did not know how to handle a blind student; home tutors had to step in to fill the gap. There were no Braille textbooks so Sujatha started recording lessons, which Shravya would play back in order to revise what she had listened to in class. Or else the textbooks were scanned on a laptop and she would use the screen reader software to listen and memorize.

Besides Shravya being 'very good in studies', she had a talent for music that Sujatha considered even more important to foster. 'It is like god's gift; it does not come to everyone.' She would never miss taking her daughter to her music classes. Shravya says that since coming to ISB, she has been listening to music more than singing. Though trained in classical music, she enjoys listening to various genres: Bollywood film songs – both old and new, bhajans, Western music, and even Arabic music, to which she was introduced by her father.

For her eleventh and twelfth standard, Shravya went to Nasr School where she had 'really amazing teachers'. She used to go to the teachers' houses where, using objects and other tactile aids, they made sure she understood the concepts. For the board exam Shravya had a scribe – someone a year junior, according to government rules – and she got her teachers to teach the scribe which visual (graphs and so on) to draw at her command during the exam.

She then took up B.Com in St. Francis College. When it was time for campus placements, she had a clear aim in mind. 'I always wanted to get into ISB!' she says with a laugh. And to qualify she needed to have minimum two years' work experience. Many companies were straight up refusing to hire her because of her disability. Nobody said 'you don't have the required skill set', everyone was telling her 'we don't have the infrastructure to support you'.

She eventually got placed in Uber. Initially, Uber didn't know what role to give the first VI person they were hiring. At first she was on-boarding driver partners to the platform, and then she moved to the training team that focussed on upskilling employees to support drivers and riders better. She was programme manager for the training scheme, and after working in Uber for two-and-a-half years, she wrote the GMAT (Graduate Management Admission Test).[31] Twice. Since she was dissatisfied with her score the first time, she rewrote it. 'The second time I got a sort of decent score and I applied to ISB,' she recounts.

---

[31] The GMAT, or Graduate Management Admission Test, is a test for admission to a graduate management programme, such as an MBA programme.

In class at ISB she faced a peculiar problem: while she was keying in the notes, her screen reader software would begin to read aloud whatever she typed, its voice clashing with the lecturer's voice and creating a cacophony in her head. So she began to depend on friends' notes, which she would scan on her laptop. Lecturers also provide soft copy handouts, and some send their in-class presentations beforehand. She would go through them in advance so that she could familiarize herself with the material and get a head start during the class.

For the staff, dealing with a VI student was a new experience. If there was something she didn't understand, she would sit with the faculty who were 'really, really supportive' and work through concepts, especially those that were visual-heavy. The first term had subjects such as economics and statistics which involved plenty of graphs. 'In the beginning my dad used to make all the graphs with thread on paper [to help me follow]. Sometimes professors used to use [strips of] sandpaper,' she tells us.

When we meet, she has two more semesters to go but has already been selected through campus placement by Wells Fargo. Recalling the first four terms when she had plenty of exams to write, she says that ISB hadn't set examination procedures for a blind student. Obviously, the rule of the scribe having to be a year junior didn't apply because it's a one year course! 'In the first term we tried out interns, but it didn't work out because they weren't able to comprehend what I was saying. So from the second term onwards we started getting scribes from outside.' The L.V. Prasad Eye Institute, which she has been in touch with since birth, gave her the contact details of volunteer scribes.

'Since getting outside scribes is not always a possibility, we're trying to create a policy to have in-house scribes and train them. We're trying to work with the management and see if they can change the policy,' Shravya says. Sujatha has various suggestions for on-campus accessibility for the blind: the crucial tactile path,

Google Maps for easier movement, and Braille stickers to identify classrooms, bathrooms, lifts and other rooms.

Shravya had a trying time during placements. Although all companies claim to have D&I, the current fad, only some stood by their word, she says, 'Among the 300-odd companies that come to ISB, it would be useful to have a list of those that are genuinely inclusive and willing to take special needs candidates so that I can tailor my resume and application accordingly.' Wells Fargo was willing to make whatever policy changes were needed and give her the role she wanted. She was impressed with 'how collaborative they were right from the day of the interview', how they were 'not the kind of employer who says, "Oh listen, we're doing you a favour by giving you a job"'. She hoped to have a 'continuing dialogue with them' to see how they could accommodate her.

The long years of perseverance had paid off at last, although the journey goes on...

———

In the 1990s, a little girl played in the narrow lanes of East Delhi's Trilokpuri, a congested colony where those evicted in the 1976 'slum clearance drive' of the Congress government were resettled. The slightest fall, which would have given other kids a few bruises or a scraped knee, would break her bones.

Each time this happened, her father, who was a migrant from Rajasthan supporting his wife and three children on his daily earnings as a pushcart vendor, would take her to the All India Institute of Medical Sciences (AIIMS). Because hers weren't simple fractures; she needed surgeries. The doctors at AIIMS had told him she had a rare genetic disorder: Osteogenesis Imperfecta, commonly known as brittle bone disease.

If you had told him then that his daughter would one day become an assistant commissioner in the Indian Revenue Service, he would have laughed in your face and called you *paagal* (insane). It was a novelty for the children in his colony to even complete schooling, and for a child with a disability – especially one as debilitating as hers – it was out of the question.

But everyone isn't like Ummul Kher. Who knows how this intense desire to learn was born in her. Her hunger for knowledge overcame the hunger in her belly; it burned down every wall that tried to block it time and time again.

'I am extremely thankful to my father for taking me to AIIMS to get seven surgeries done,' Ummul tells us as she ticks off the medical interventions she has had so far: 16 fractures and eight surgeries, 13 steel rods in both her tibia and thigh bones. When we meet in October 2019 she has just been to AIIMS to check the condition of her crowns; OI has affected her teeth and many of them are false, while some had to be capped with metal crowns. 'It's all part of the package,' she says, laughing merrily as we head to the escalator that will take us to the food court on the top floor of Ambience Mall in Vasant Kunj.

At what age was she diagnosed? 'The fractures were the diagnosis,' she says simply. 'For whatever I have in my life, it is AIIMS that I should thank. Had I not got corrective surgeries done in time, I would have been like other people with OI who are not even able to stand.' Her disability only strengthened her resolve to keep doing what she had an innate aptitude for. 'The impetus to study further would come with every fracture, when I was confronted by my own vulnerability,' she explains. It was always the fractures that kept her focussed on academics instead of 'wasting' her 'time playing or chatting with other girls, or going into other people's houses to watch television'.

Her primary aim was to 'not be at the mercy' of her family. Her mother died in 2001, when she was barely into her teens, and her father remarried. Their family expanded to include, besides her older brother and sister, their new 'mamma' and the four daughters she had from her previous marriage. The couple later had a son together. Her mamma made it amply clear where her father's priorities should lie, she remembers. 'Whatever money my father earned was for my four sisters, not for me.' What riled her stepmother even more was that Ummul was flourishing in Amar Jyoti School, while her stepsisters were dropouts – none had studied beyond seventh standard. She begrudged her husband even the ₹20 monthly school fee that Amar Jyoti charged.

Therefore, when Ummul was 14, she started earning her keep. She used to take tuitions for the neighbourhood kids, charging them a modest ₹50 a month because it was all their parents could afford. After setting aside part of her earnings towards provisions for the family, she would spend the rest on textbooks, stationery and school fees. 'I was supporting my own education. The problem started when I reached ninth standard,' she says.

When Ummul completed her eighth standard her family considered her 'overqualified'. And when they found out that Uma Tuli of Amar Jyoti was securing Ummul's admission in a private school, Arwachin Bharti Bhawan Senior Secondary School, she tells us, 'My mamma said: "You will not go to school. What are you trying to prove to us?"' Ummul explains that her stepmother came from an extremely conservative Muslim family in the Jama Masjid area where women never studied, and the only skills desired were in sewing and embroidery. 'No blame can be attached to my mother,' she says magnanimously.

Ummul's mamma then put a stop to the tuitions. Ummul recalls, 'She said, "You will not stay in this house; we will not support you if you stay here." I wanted to say, "You are not supporting me even now!"' Pushed to the wall, Ummul requested their landlord for a space on rent to run her coaching class. It was a single room on the first floor of the same building where they stayed. He charged her ₹1,000; she would have to pay the electricity and water bills too.

Ummul had to start cooking for herself too – it was 'always rice, never chapathi', two meals a day. Her morning 'meal' was a bread pakora for ₹5, which she bought from the samosa stall around the corner. The pakora came with grated carrots and other bits of vegetables, which she would save to eat with plain rice at night. Her education was free at the time, because as a meritorious student she got a full concession.

Life was hectic. After school she would have no time to change her uniform before diving into tuitions. She taught kids of all ages in batches, back to back, until midnight. For seven days a week it was the same routine: 3 p.m. to 5 p.m. was for kindergarten and primary school kids; 5 p.m. to 7 p.m. for middle school; 7 p.m. to 9 p.m. for tenth standard students; and 9 p.m. to midnight for those in the twelfth standard. She had already reached the tenth standard herself, so she was teaching kids who were her peers and even older. 'Since I was not getting time to study, it used to be good revision for me...because when you teach somebody you learn much more than learning on your own. That's how I topped my class!' she explains. She scored 91 per cent in the tenth standard and topped the school in the twelfth, after which she got admission in the psychology honours course in Delhi University's Gargi College.

Her mamma once again put her foot down. Ummul says, 'To her, like in a Bollywood movie, college means boy and girl fall in love. She said, "You are bringing shame to us, people are already talking about you living separately upstairs. Now you will not live in Delhi, we are booking you a bus ticket to Rajasthan."' Ummul bluntly said no. Her parents came up to her room and a lot of shouting ensued. Her father said he had booked her bus ticket for the following morning.

This is where Ummul's life reached a turning point.

She used to listen to the news on FM radio on her basic mobile phone. She came across an interactive programme on *Meow* 104.8 (touted as 'India's first talk-based radio station for women'). Kiran Bedi, the Ramon Magsaysay award-winning Indian Police Service (IPS) officer and social activist, used to answer questions from listeners once a week on the programme. By coincidence, Bedi was on air that evening.

On an impulse, Ummul borrowed a more advanced phone from a neighbour and called the number for the programme. She explained her situation to Bedi in detail, emphasizing her financial independence. 'Education has become indispensable for me. I have been living in Delhi, taking care of my own needs. I want to continue living here. Tomorrow they are going to forcibly take me to the bus stand and put me on the bus to Rajasthan,' she told Bedi.

Bedi replied that she would be happy to help her and said that 'you are the daughter that every parent should have'. Then she presented an ingenious solution to the problem: Ummul should tell her parents she had filed an FIR against them in the police station. If this didn't scare them off, she told her to call back. Bedi assured her that she would send a couple of constables from the local Kalyanpur police station to come and stand in front of their house. Their menacing presence would settle the matter without the need for paperwork.

The next morning when her parents came up to her room, they asked, 'Why haven't you packed?' 'I said, I will not go. Mamma started mishandling me,' she recollects. That's when she brought out the threat: she said she had filed an FIR and if they beat her or forced her to go, there would be consequences. 'Then all hell broke loose.' Her mamma stood in the bylane outside the house and created a huge ruckus. All the neighbours heard her shouting and came running. She yelled at her husband, 'This is the day I was warning you about; I told you this would happen if you educated her. Now you will go to jail but I will not, because I want a divorce from you right now!' Once the curtains came down on the high drama, Ummul's parents agreed to let her continue living upstairs but said, 'We don't want to see your face; you are no longer our daughter.'

Reminiscing on the moment that changed her destiny, Ummul says, 'If I had not got that assurance from Kiran ma'am that day,

I would have gone to Rajasthan and my story would have been different.'

Travelling by government buses from Trilokpuri to Gargi College in the morning rush hour, she would be standing precariously at the entrance with a big bag across her shoulder. 'Every day there was a chance that I would not come back walking. I used to be very careful,' she says.

She continued home-tutoring to pay for her education, but she also found a new way to supplement her income. It was college festival season in DU, and there were plenty of debate competitions being held. Depending on how prosperous the college was, the prizes ranged from ₹1,000 to 2,000, which were big amounts those days. She calculated that if she managed to win 10–12 debates a year, she 'could earn ₹13,000 without any effort, by just speaking for five minutes'. She carefully selected the contests that offered the most cash. 'Some used to take part to impress others. I used to just go for the money!' she says.

She wanted to apply for a master's in psychology in DU. Her interest was in clinical psychology, but she'd have to do three or four months of compulsory internship in a hospital, which was impossible given her situation. Reluctantly giving up the subject she loved, she decided to take up something theoretical rather than practical. She zeroed in on international studies in Jawaharlal Nehru University – a degree in politics with a specialization in international relations. Although her Bachelor of Arts degree was in psychology, she cleared the entrance exam and was selected. '[Jawaharlal Nehru University] was another blessing for me because it had hostels,' she explains. The fee too was just ₹1,500, including food.

Ummul's activist self, which was already being shaped during her degree course – she had represented PwDs on a 15-day trip to South Korea – was fully formed in the lively political atmosphere of the university. The students had frequent run-ins with the administration and on one of these occasions, Ummul, a student leader then, went on a hunger strike with other protestors demanding, among other things, accessibility on campus for students with disability, especially the visually impaired. After three days of fasting, the vice chancellor (VC) agreed to meet the students. On the fourth day, they met the VC who assured them their demands would be met.

Ummul ate a few chocolates to break the fast and went to the canteen with her friends at lunchtime. She had just got up from her seat to get her food when she fainted. 'I fell and broke my bone of course. I didn't know that my bone condition was dynamic, that three days of fasting would have an impact on my bone strength and it would become more brittle,' she recollects. It was time for surgery number eight.

'The Almighty was extremely kind; I was getting fractures in very safe places, at the right time. Thankfully it happened when I was in [Jawaharlal Nehru University], where I had friends to take care of me,' she says. She contacted her older brother who was running a business in Rajasthan and requested him to send her money for surgery and medicines. He sent her ₹5,000 monthly for more than a year. She had to use a wheelchair for nearly seven months and crutches for a year and a half till her bone was strong enough to bear her weight.

Ummul has been a vocal advocate for disability rights on campus. She organized a protest against the registrar for not filling the vacancies reserved for candidates with disabilities; it resulted in interview calls to 10 candidates with disabilities and posts being filled. Ummul had met the legendary Javed Abidi at the NCPEDP office in 2012 during the infamous 'Nirbhaya case' – the brutal gang-rape and murder of a young woman in Delhi that caused nationwide outrage and a change in the anti-rape laws. Javed *bhai* made her India's representative of the Youth Wing of Disabled People International (DPI) during the two years that he was President of DPI. She presented a paper in South Korea on 'Issues of Women with Disabilities in South Asia'.

After her MA, she was selected for an MPhil integrated with PhD. She secured a Junior Research Fellowship that brought her a monthly stipend: ₹16,000, which was soon upgraded to ₹25,000. But her latest fracture made her seriously rethink her doctorate plan. She decided that after completing her MPhil, she would write the Union Public Service Commission (UPSC) exam to fast-track her career. After one year of her MPhil, she went to Japan for a one-year international leadership training programme, where she gained deeper insight into disability. She returned in July 2015, worked day and night on her dissertation and completed it in December 2015. From January 2016 onwards, she started preparing for the UPSC exam.

Ummul cleared the exam in her first attempt – a rare feat indeed. In a mischievous quirk of providence, her rank was 420. The term '420' being a colloquialism for 'a cheat' (since the punishment for cheating is laid down in Section 420 of the Indian Penal Code). Ummul says, 'I was very embarrassed; I was asking the Almighty: "Why have you given me this number?"' With her excellent rank, she would normally have easily got into the IAS but there was another PwD that year with a higher rank, and she got into the IRS (Indian Revenue Service) instead.

Ummul is an officer trainee at the National Academy of Customs, Indirect Taxes and Narcotics (NACIN) in Faridabad when we meet. She is awaiting her posting the following month. After on-the-job training for a few months, she will return to the Academy for a refurbisher course and then take independent charge, she says.

We are sure that wherever Ummul Kher's career might take her, disability and gender will always remain her prime concerns. 'Girls with disability should be encouraged to study to any extent they wish,' she says passionately. And in those concluding words, we once again see that little girl who wanted to learn – come hell or high water – and would let nothing get in her way.

# 13

# UP, DOWN...AND UP AGAIN

WHEN WE SEE PWDS IN THEIR MOST SUCCESSFUL *AVATARS*, when we see them flourishing in their jobs, winning awards, or reaping medals in sporting events, it is easy to forget what they must have gone through to get where they are today.

Inspirational figures can be pretty demoralizing for someone who is struggling with a disability every day. Some PwDs we met were born with a disability and some acquired it at a later stage, but all of them have experienced crucial moments of despair. In this chapter, we are going to dwell on the worst phases of their lives.

The worst is not when they've been laid low by circumstances. The worst is when just as they're beginning to believe they've gained a foothold, the rock is suddenly dislodged and they go plummeting down the mountain. The down after an up is the hardest to get past, to get over.

Before we get to the lows, here's how Jerry White, speaking at the India Inclusion Summit 2018, describes the stages a PwD might go through. Jerry, who is co-recipient of the Nobel Peace Prize and co-lead of the International Campaign to Ban Landmines, was 20 when he travelled to Israel and a landmine ripped off his right leg. His recovery and activism thereafter led to the Landmine Ban Treaty of 1997. 'Losing our limbs is not the problem; losing our place in society is,' says Jerry as he outlines how one could move from being a victim to a survivor. He says that victimhood is being stuck in the past, filled with self-pity and resentment and blaming others for your condition. You start surviving when you face facts, choose life, reach out and get moving. Instead of just taking, you start giving back.

———

Nipun Malhotra was born with arthrogryposis in 1987 on Ganesh Chaturthi, a day in honour of the divine remover of obstacles. Obstacles kept rolling up in Nipun's life, but there was one human who tried her best to knock them aside one by one – his mother Priyanka.

Nipun was diagnosed as 100 per cent disabled, which was later generously amended to 'above 80 per cent'. The 'wooden doll' prognosis of the doctors was 'very traumatic', says Priyanka, but then her 'protective instincts' kicked in. The inspirational stories in *Reader's Digest* were all she had to motivate her. Through surgery, a few muscles in his right hand could be retrieved. Right from the start, she made him adapt to a regular environment. She improvised instead of giving him 'special' equipment, got him to drink through a straw and steady his hand with an upturned bowl that would serve as a table while he ate. No adaptive computers; he had to learn to use regular ones.

The nightmare of school admissions began right at the playschool stage. One of the playschools said it would only take toddlers who were able to walk, and they made an exception only after Priyanka repeatedly pleaded with them. Later, she was determined to get Nipun into a mainstream school, so she knocked on eight or ten doors but was always met with the same response: 'We are not equipped for the disabled.' She was standing at Chowpatty one day, crying. On top of a hillock she saw a *trishul* (trident),[32] and she prayed for help from 'whoever you are'. It happened to be Babulnath, an ancient Shiva temple on top of the hillock. The next school she went to, St. Mary's, agreed to admit Nipun. 'So I became an ardent believer,' she says with a half-laugh, 'Faith kept driving me.'

Priyanka used to drop him to school every day. 'The first year, the classroom was downstairs. Next year, it was upstairs so I requested them to shift his classroom down. And they said we won't even do it for the prime minister's son. So I used to keep one wheelchair on the ground floor, one on the first and carry him up.'

Nipun had completed the fourth standard when his parents moved from Mumbai to Delhi. 'Luckily the Apeejay School chairman had had polio as a child and I was aware of that, so we applied,' says Priyanka. 'They had ramps.' She was a constant presence in his school life. 'Till Class 10, I used to go to school every day to copy notes. And when exams were on, I would almost beg people to help turn pages,' she recollects. Young Nipun did not appreciate his mother hovering around. 'He was like, "Why are you here?" So our battles also started.'

Nipun says students didn't know how to interact with a child with a disability, 'Throughout my school life, I did not have a single friend.' But he was 'pushy' by his own admission and wanted to be part of every extracurricular activity. In one play he was a tree. Wasn't he being dismissed as a mere prop? 'I loved that!' he protests. 'I kept fighting with the school till they gave me that role.' On sports day, he used to barge into the principal's office and say, 'Why don't you make me the master of ceremonies?' He loved cricket and dreamed of becoming a sports commentator. 'I interviewed Harsha Bhogle for the cover story of my school magazine. I still remember a line that he told me I think I'll remember for the rest of my life: Don't try to be Harsha Bhogle because you'll only be the

---

[32] The trident is one of the principal symbols of the divine in Hinduism.

second best Harsha Bhogle. Try to be the first Nipun Malhotra,'
he says.

Nipun's confidence and independent spirit seems to have no
bounds. In the tenth standard board exam he scored 87 per cent
and he told his mother, 'This is just the start. By 12th you'll see me
on the first page.' And in twelfth standard he did indeed top the
country in business studies, and it made front page news.

'After school I started taking control of my own life,' he says.
When his parents, finding that no college in Delhi University was
accessible, sent him to a private college, he rebelled, 'It wasn't any
college of academic excellence. I quit and decided to apply to Delhi
University. It was the first time in my life I was taking a decision.
My parents thought I'd gone mad, and my mother gained weight
because of stress.'

They needn't have worried because Nipun got into St. Stephen's
College. The principal said that this is a heritage building and we
cannot make changes to it, so are you ready to go every day to the
classroom on the first floor? Nipun agreed. He used to take two
people with him who would lift him in his wheelchair up the stairs.
It was really precarious, because if one of them slipped and fell it
would grievously injure all of them. For four days he ascended like
that, and his persistence moved the college authorities to shift the
classroom downstairs.

At Stephen's, he made friends for the first time in his life.
After graduating he applied to the Delhi School of Economics for
his master's. He sat in his room and slogged for one-and-a-half
months for the entrance exam. He got the 52nd national rank and
admission to the Delhi School of Economics in the general (not
disability) category.

Looking back, Nipun says, 'For me it was an academic peak
that I reached.' Once that peak was scaled, once he began to feel
invulnerable, reality punched him in the face.

In the 2011–12 academic year, when he applied for placements

like everyone else in his class did, he was rebuffed at every turn.
No company was willing to hire him. 'I saw first-hand the kind
of discrimination that PwDs face. One company didn't hire me
because they didn't have a disabled-friendly toilet – and this was
after seven rounds of interviews. Another rejected me because they
doubted whether I could sit in a wheelchair for eight hours a day;
they wanted me to do a physical test. A third company said you're
faking your degrees, so get a letter from your college saying you've
actually graduated. So in 2012 I was depressed, I was humiliated;
I locked myself up in my room for a month. I even wrote my
obituary. I wouldn't say I was suicidal, but I had given up on life.
I did not know what to do. I've gone through tough phases in my
life after that, but I don't think I've ever been as low as I was then,'
he recounts.

He used to believe in god, but 'the Nipun Malhotra who got out
of that depression' did not. 'People kept throwing religious tools
to me, saying, "*Iss swami ke paas jao* (Go to this holy man), go to
this church, whatever." They thought religion should be the crutch
on which I should stand. But then I got so angry with various
religious beliefs that I became an atheist! The funny thing is that
until then I wasn't an atheist. Usually during a tough time people
become a believer. For me it was the reverse.' Since then, he says, he
had evolved a defence mechanism that he lacked those days, 'I've
developed this kind of inner arrogance; I think that protects me.'

Nipun joined his father's business. Soon after, he started the
Wheels for India movement, which connects donors of wheelchairs
with deserving recipients. With his mother, he co-founded the
Nipman Foundation which works towards accessibility, attitudinal
change and providing affordable assistive devices. The annual
Nipman Foundation–Microsoft Equal Opportunity Awards go to
entities that promote the employment of PwDs.

Explaining that arthrogryposis is not a progressive disability
like MD or MS, and that his lack of muscles will save him from the

aches and pains that the 'able-bodied' experience with age, Nipun says, 'The good thing about my life is that I can plan my life; I know what condition I will be in at the age of 50 or 60. You've seen the movie *Unbreakable*? In that sense I am sort of unbreakable.'

———

Vishwas K.S., the youngest of three siblings, was born in Bengaluru but soon after his family moved to the village of Kalahastipura, about 10 km from Kolar. In the fourth standard he was 'even more mischievous than 10-year-olds usually are', he says, speaking in Kannada. 'I was disobedient, uncontrollable and just scraping through exams.'

Their house was under construction; the upper floor had exposed beams and the concrete roof was getting cured. One afternoon, Vishwas was pestering his visiting cousins during play when his father said, to divert him, 'Go and pour water on the concrete on the terrace.' He went and started fooling with the hosepipe, spraying water on himself and on his cousins below. Amid his antics, he slipped and fell off the roof. His fall was broken by a power line that ran dangerously close to the compound.

The boy was slumped across the wire, dangling by his shoulders, with fire sparking off his body. His father came rushing up to save him, grabbed a pole and leaned over to start prodding his son to disentangle him. The father lost balance, falling to the ground and dying on the spot. Vishwas kept hanging there for an interminable time before his body fell to the ground, minus both arms.

At the hospital, Vishwas didn't regain consciousness for two months. While he recovered, he wasn't told about his father's death because they didn't want to pile on one shock after the other. His friends broke the news to him only when it was time for him to be discharged. They were the ones who helped him study, while his mother attended to all his needs at home. He cleared the fifth and sixth standards by answering exams orally – the class teachers would ask him questions – but for the seventh standard public exam, he had to get a scribe. 'I used to have two crude plastic arms, weighing a total of four or five kilos – totally useless, couldn't even lift a sheet of paper with it,' he says.

The family moved to Bengaluru at the turn of the century. He finished his 10th and pre-university and took up B.Com just because his friends too chose the subject. He struggled with statistics and accountancy, he recollects, 'Drawing graphs – how to do? It became a big Ramayana (saga). There were no objective type questions; everything had to be written.' During exams, the invigilators would give him no extra time at all. When he questioned them about it, they told him the rules for PwDs applied only to the blind! Instead, they advised him to speed up his dictation to the scribe so that he could finish on time.

When Vishwas was in the fifth semester, his mother died. Her health had been failing for a year. She had been the mainstay in his life; she used to feed him, dress him, get his books ready for college – literally wait on him hand and foot. Her death sent him into a tailspin. He failed the final year B.Com exams, but rewrote it and passed in 2013.

'I tried to find a job, I attended job fairs for the disabled, but had no success. I simply did not know what to do. I was stuck,' he says.

He felt ashamed to go out of the house and was afraid of neighbours and acquaintances asking him the usual question: What are you doing these days? 'I can tell them once that I'm looking for a job, but I can't keep telling them the same thing one month later, two months later, a year later,' he explains. He had no money to go out with friends, so he would stay at home. Doing absolutely nothing.

'No mobile, those days. All I would do was watch TV. I would not sleep at night; I'd be staring at the TV till almost 3 a.m., jabbing the remote, hardly aware of what channel I was watching. My target was to sleep for 12 hours and get up only at 2 p.m. or 3 p.m., so that most of the day would be over by the time I got up,' he remembers.

It was classic depression. He would cry aloud, but for how long could he cry? He would ask why god had done this to him, but the heavens sent him no reply. Steeped in self-disgust, he didn't even bother with his personal grooming. His friends would advise him to get up early in the morning and be active or his mental health would suffer. He would say 'yes, yes' to them and do exactly the same thing the next day – watch TV mindlessly and get up late.

What happened next is what he calls 'the miracle'. Something inside him wanted to live, to do more than merely exist. He searched in his mind for a way to banish his lethargy. Out of nowhere came 'a really silly option': swimming. It was his laziness that put the idea into his head, he says. The bizarre logic was: For this activity he needn't bother to put on clothes; he could swim in his underwear! He didn't have the courage to ask anyone if they knew someone who could teach him swimming. They would laugh at him or think him crazy, he thought to himself. The only thing he knew was that the Sree Kanteerava Stadium was a venue for sporting events.

He had a bus pass, so he took a bus to Majestic (an area in the city). From there, he found his way to the stadium. Someone there gave him the contact number of S.R. Sindia, then head of the Karnataka Swimming Association. The Sindia swimming pool was miles away, in Nagarbhavi, and classes started before dawn, but Vishwas was undaunted. He took up a room on rent nearby and stayed there for two years, getting up at 4 a.m. to make it to his 5 a.m. class every day.

Swimming lifted him out of his depression. 'My mind became active. Creativity flowed, because I was learning new things,' he says.

One can only imagine Sindia's reaction when a young man with no arms approached him for swimming lessons. It took Vishwas six months to move from a depth of three feet to six, but over time he mastered the swimming strokes. He says Sindia is his 'godfather for swimming'; later he was coached by Sharath Gaekwad.

Bitten by the swimming bug, he now wanted to extend himself; besides, after his early morning class, he had nothing else to occupy him for the rest of the day. In order to improve his skills, he wished to strengthen his lower body and give extra power to his legs, which were his core asset. Kung fu came as the answer.

He set himself a busy schedule that stretched across the whole day: swimming, Kung fu, gym and fitness classes. On some days, just as he was getting ready to go swimming, it would rain. 'After getting ready, to go back to bed was torture. So I thought, "What activity can I do at home on such days?"' This is how dance entered his mind. He looked for a teacher until one finally agreed to coach him.

Vishwas has now become a professional swimmer. 'No winter or summer seasons for me, every season is swimming season!' he says. He has won 17 swimming medals in national and international Paralympic events. Dance is an equally important part of his life. He says that these days he charges ₹15,000 for one of his spectacular performances; it's how he makes a living, along with public talks. 'Speech is income,' he quips. For delivering a speech in English he takes a week to 10 days to memorize and practice it. But if it's in Kannada, he says, 'I go like bullet, *dhoom–dham–dhamaka* (bang–bang)!' He really enjoys speaking about his achievements to schoolchildren, he says, far more than at employee sensitization programmes in workplaces.

The human body is a wonderfully adaptive mechanism. When it is missing a part, it recruits another to serve the purpose. Vishwas's legs function as his arms; they even gesture emotively when he speaks. As we sit in his tiny rented flat he points out that he lives independently. He needs no help to keep the place tidy or to see to his basic physical needs. He can effortlessly take a bath, shave, cook, wash vessels and clothes, comb his hair, boil an egg, change the refill in his pen...whatever it takes.

About having won the 2018 National Award for Best Role Model, he says, 'All these medals, prizes, (and) certificates – it's all momentary. If, by my getting the national award, it inspires someone else like me, I would feel it has fulfilled its purpose.'

# 14

# CHANGE THE WORLD OR CHANGE ONESELF FOR THE WORLD?

THE COVID-19 PANDEMIC HAS GIVEN MOST AVERAGE individuals a bitter taste of how 'locked down' thousands of PwDs in India have felt throughout their lives. We have experienced a minuscule fraction of 'their inability' to get out of their houses and move around freely. The reason for their lack of mobility is so blindingly obvious it doesn't need repeating, but we'll say it anyway: The outdoors are pretty much inaccessible to PwDs in our country.

How many public spaces are accessible to those with orthopaedic impairments? How many have Braille signage for the VI? How many welcome those with sensory disorders? You can add any number of disabilities to the list and get the same answer: Barely any. Before we talk at length about the various types of access required for different disabilities – both indoors and outdoors, and about what Indian government has done (or not) to provide it, let's focus on physical access and listen to a few PwDs describe how they have navigated the world around them.

There are activists among them who cry, 'The world must change for us.' There are realists who say, 'Since the world isn't going to change, I must adapt to it.' There are still others who say today, 'Why should I bother to step out into a world bristling with physical barriers when technology can bring the world to my doorstep?'

## Barriers All the Way

People with mobility issues need phenomenal reserves of tolerance and persistence to deal with the endless hurdles in their path. Ummul Kher, whom we have met previously in this book, has been swimming upstream for much of her life. She remembers how, after studying till the fifth standard in a special school, she went to a mainstream school for two years. She was then a wheelchair user and her classmates used to lift her and her wheelchair to the classroom upstairs. 'I never used to drink water in my school. It had no washroom. I used to go home and pee. What to do? We can't put education on hold till the toilets are made,' she says.

When Anita Sharma, who is mobility impaired, was a student at the Indian Institute of Management (IIM) Indore, she found the campus '60 per cent accessible' and was determined to notch it up to 100. She went around taking photos of all the areas that were inaccessible and presented the evidence to the director, who simply sat on it. Then, a new director took charge – Rishikesh Krishnan, who was responsible for making IIM Bangalore totally accessible. He was obviously more receptive and created a committee of which Anita was the student representative. V-Shesh stepped in from Chennai for consultation and by 2014 the entire campus was made accessible.

Wherever Anita went, she lobbied for accessibility. When she joined IIM Amritsar as a teacher, it was situated on a transit campus while the permanent building was under construction. 'It was completely inaccessible,' she says. The classroom where she was to teach was on the third floor. There was a ramp but no handrails, making it impossible for a person in a manual wheelchair to go up.

They gave her an alternative: a first floor classroom to which the only access was a staircase. She was assigned an assistant who was not on call because he had other jobs to do on campus. She would have to summon and wait for him to haul her in her wheelchair up the stairs. When she asked for a lift, the response was: Why spend so much when we will be anyway moving from here to the new building? They were reluctant to even spend on a handrail.

Now, the director of IIM Kozhikode had come to mentor IIM Amritsar and help set it up. He had a knee problem and found it difficult to climb the stairs. In seven days the handrail was constructed! But by then Anita had persisted in and won her demand for a ground floor classroom.

The world dismisses PwDs with 'We can't afford to cater for all your needs' and then trots out a helpful suggestion: 'Why don't you just stay indoors and make it easy for all of us?' A charitable explanation for such an unfeeling statement could be that it springs from misplaced concern for the 'handicapped' person. Hansa Ramasubban contracted ALS (Amyotrophic Lateral Sclerosis, or Lou Gehrig's disease) and is a wheelchair user without vocal speech. Her daughters Vidhya and Priya make it a point to take her out in her wheelchair to movies and other outings. She texts me via Priya's phone to say: 'When I go out people used to say, "These sorts of people shouldn't go out."'

## Creating Your Own World

Well, some PwDs have taken the 'why don't you sit at home?' sentiment at face value. Siddharth Jayakumar who has CP that restricts his mobility tells us, 'I am happy to be at home. I have killed my desire to go out.' This might appear defeatist, but one has no right to challenge his personal solution to negotiating an uncaring environment. He says that instead of enduring the hassle that going out to a cinema involves, he watches whatever movie he wants on his computer or his tablet; there are enough and more subscription channels. If he has to take the family out, he catches hold of an auto driver and hires them for ₹150 an hour to take them to all their destinations, because he knows it will be a struggle to find different autos to go from point to point.

Disability evangelist and national award winner Dhanya Ravi, who has OI, also rarely goes out but manages to stay productive. 'My room is my world,' she says. Her brother Rajesh Ravi taught her the use of the computer. Everything she needs is at her fingertips. She has a busy social life online, is a part of a musical forum since early 2000 (music is an abiding passion), and spreads awareness about rare diseases including OI. She has appeared on chat shows and reality shows on Malayalam TV channels, gives motivational talks and actively involves herself in the annual Inclusive Walkathon in Bengaluru.

Dhanya, who sustained her first fracture when she was 56 days old, says she has 'more fractures than there are bones in my body' and describes the ICU as 'my second home'. Her neighbour 'Victoria aunty' dedicated one hour every single day for 10 years to teaching her the regular school curriculum, which is how she passed the tenth standard. Much later she did a bridge course through Indira Gandhi National Open University (IGNOU) and reached pre-university.

Sitting in her room, she has informally counselled parents, connected people to one another and helped raise funds. No wonder she says, 'A friend asked me, "Why don't you go out?" And I told him, "Why should I? I am quite content."'

When she occasionally does venture out, she has her 'BMW' (her name for her powered wheelchair), but she doesn't balk at asking for help whenever necessary. 'It is okay to seek help. Why be ashamed of dependency? Everyone is dependent on others,' Dhanya says and scoffs at the concept of 'losing dignity' on being lifted and carried. If the most comfortable option in a certain situation was being pushed in a stroller, she would take it, and she wouldn't care if people thought it infantilized her, she says.

## Adapting to the World

The determination to adapt to the present, rather than wait for future change, is what drove Major Devender Pal Singh to become India's first amputee marathoner in 2009 and India's first blade runner in 2011. 'Do not wait for infrastructure and ideal situations to come to you,' he says. 'Just start working towards your goal and things will fall in place.' He rejects the cliché 'fought against the odds' and prefers to say 'I have risen above the odds' because then the odds are below him and appear small.

DP (as he is popularly called), who had a shattered right leg and 50 pieces of shrapnel in his body after a mortar landed near him in the Kargil War, is someone who loves to keep changing the goalpost. The moment he nears one, he moves it farther away, and from the ground it has soared up to the skies. For many years he had wanted to go skydiving; he seized his chance when he became a brand ambassador for the year 2018, which was declared 'year of the disabled in the line of duty' by the Indian army. He joined the training course in skydiving at the Army Adventure Wing in Nashik on 18 March. And on 28 March, he accomplished his first solo accelerated freefall (AFF) sky dive.

Here's where you have to keep your school physics lessons in mind. When you are freefalling, it is vital to balance your body. If a part of one leg is missing (DP had to remove his prosthesis for the task), air cuts through faster there and you start spinning. So you have to manoeuvre your body to maintain equilibrium. During his fifth trial jump, his instructor let go of his hand too early and he started spinning like a top. But he wasn't bothered by it. 'I was enjoying this. I knew that after checking the altimeter at 6,500 ft you are supposed to pull the parachute, and I did,' he says.

After eight jumps, he felt he was ready to go solo AFF. He leapt from the helicopter at 9,000 feet. 'The moment I opened the parachute, suddenly it was pin-drop silence; it was bliss!' He sums it up philosophically: 'In those 40 seconds of freefall you realize that however high you may fly, finally you will have to land on the ground.' The lesson he gathered from the experience was: Be grounded, don't let your ego overpower you.

Although DP takes the world head on, he doesn't think of himself as an activist. 'You will not find me in any disability conference,' he says. He believes in 'leading the change by example'. And through his NGO, The Challenging Ones, he rallies other amputees to push themselves to their limits by running marathons. The example he sets them is also to expose their prostheses to the public eye. 'You can hide your amputation and survive like that your whole life. So that becomes a reason for staying in a comfort zone and not exploring yourself. The first and foremost step is to accept your reality, accept your shortcoming and know your strengths,' he argues.

DP says he was aware that 'disability is sometimes used by PwDs as a tool to gain sympathy'. He quotes his grandfather who used to say, '*Jiska kaam chale, kheti kare kyo?*' It translates as: If I can be a victim and other people can do my work, why should I work? Ability is finding a way to overcome a difficult situation, he adds.

While each PwD has their own unique way of coping and thriving, one cannot deny that there is a pressing need to focus on accessibility by rethinking design, architecture and transport. In the popular imagination, though, accessibility means just ramps. Many buildings in India boast of being PwD-friendly just because there's a ramp at the entrance – and never mind that the gradient is too steep. One wheelchair user drily describes a common experience: 'You will find in front of the ramp decorative pots, or two steps, or a dumping yard, or a parking place, or a locked wicket gate that will be opened only when someone in a wheelchair has come and the key will be with someone who has gone for lunch!'

DP has a pertinent point to add about restricting the idea of physical accessibility to only ramps. His prosthesis is more suited to stairs than ramps. 'You should have stair-climbing wheelchairs, and make them easily available and affordable. Both things are required, ramp[s] and more efficient wheelchairs. You should not make accessibility an excuse to stop living,' he says.

We will return, in the next chapter, to the question of how the world can be changed and made more accessible so that there are no more excuses for hindering people from living life on their own terms, but before that let us conclude this one with a final reflection on the divergent outlooks of PwDs.

Mohan Sundaram of Artilab helps us understand and reconcile the divergent attitudes of PwDs – changing the world or adapting to the world. It is not an 'either-or' question; we must see them as short–term and long–term perspectives. He says, 'It is important to accept the world for what it is, for otherwise you won't come to terms with the life that you are leading. In the short term, the world can't change, and I'll have to learn to adjust. But I must not give up my intent to change what exists, if not for me [then] for the next generation. I am not fighting for an inclusive today; I am fighting for an inclusive tomorrow.'

Mohan says that 'only activism' doesn't help; activists must rally around those who create solutions and push for adopting those solutions. He is optimistic about the future: 'There is enough good in the world. We should leverage the goodness. Let us be collaborative, not confrontational.'

# 15

# ACCESSIBILITY – THE BIGGEST HURDLE

THE FIFTH SMART CITIES INDIA 2019 EXPO WAS BEING held in Delhi's Pragati Maidan. On 24 May, the last day of the Expo, Nipun Malhotra of Nipman Foundation was supposed to speak about accessibility in public transport for PwDs in smart cities. But the managers of the event weren't that smart. They had not provided a ramp for his wheelchair to access the stage!

The average person seldom thinks about the physical aspects of disability. Even more so in the case of non-physical aspects of accessibility, for example accessible information and communications in the electronic media – web content in simple language for easy comprehension of those with ID, audio descriptions of visuals, websites and Apps designed for VI users, or closed captioning (subtitles plus other relevant information) for the HI to access TV programmes and online videos.

To provide accessibility across all its aspects and across all disabilities, 'Universal Design' is a useful concept that developed nations have been using for decades. Although it has its roots in architecture, it refers to the barrier-free design of not only buildings and environments, but also products that can be used by everyone regardless of age, ability or situation. 'Design for All' is an offshoot: it targets the use of products, services and systems by as many people as possible.

## Universal Design

If you design something for PwDs, it benefits all of society. In fact, you use many products without realizing that they were originally designed keeping in mind the ageing and disabled population.

When you watch a movie with subtitles, listen to an audiobook while driving, turn the lever of a door handle instead of twisting a knob, hear floors being announced in a lift, or tap the large, flat light switches in a hotel room, you never consider how essential they are to the VI, the HI and those with impaired motor skills.

You are grateful for the automatic door in a supermarket when both hands are laden with shopping bags, but that door is an absolute necessity for a wheelchair user. The Velcro on your sneakers, the long-handled lever on your washbasin tap that you push with your elbow when washing your soapy hands, the convenient 'strolley' (roll-along suitcase) – think of how vital they are when the muscles in your limbs are impaired from old age or disability.

Universal Design has yet to find a home in India, though. It made a brief appearance in 2006 in the National Policy for Persons with Disabilities, which suggested that Universal Design be included in curricula of architecture and engineering colleges. It gets a fleeting mention in the RPwD Act, which speaks of the need to ensure that 'electronic goods and equipment, which are meant for every day use, are available in universal design';[33] and the

---

[33] RPwD Act, Chapter VIII, Section 42 (iii).

need to promote the production and distribution of 'universally designed consumer products and accessories'.[34]

The Indian government launched its Accessible India Campaign (Sugamya Bharat Abhiyan) in December 2015 and set various deadlines for making 50 per cent of all government buildings, government websites and railway stations accessible. Since the deadlines were being systematically missed, they set a new deadline for all the initiatives: March 2020. And along came the global pandemic.

## Accessible Buildings

Meanwhile, the RPwD Act gave a bold new thrust to the law on the built environment. Section 44 mandates that *every new building* constructed in India must be in accordance with the accessibility guidelines laid out in the National Building Code (NBC) 2016 – and this applies to both government and private buildings.

You probably remember having seen dozens of new private constructions since then, none of which were accessible. What's the catch? Enforcement resides with local authorities. If individual states don't modify their building bye-laws to take into account the revised accessibility standards, the Code will remain on paper.

On paper, the NBC 2016 is a milestone, achieved in no small measure through the persistent interventions of the cross-disability advocacy organization, NCPEDP and recommendations by the Diversity and Equal Opportunity Centre (DEOC), which specializes in accessibility.

To devise a clear and all-encompassing national building code for India was no joke, given that different standards were merrily co-existing. Try and follow this chain of events:

The United Nations Economic and Social Commission for Asia

---

[34] RPwD Act, Chapter VIII, Section 43.

and the Pacific (UNESCAP), Central Public Works Department (CPWD), NBC 2005 and quite a few other entities had set building guidelines of their own. To solve the problem of multiple standards for accessibility of the built environment, the Ministry of Urban Development (MoUD) developed the 'Harmonized Guidelines and Space Standards for Barrier Free Built Environment for Persons with Disability and Elderly Persons', 2016. Quite a mouthful, so it is usually referred to as the 'Harmonized Guidelines' or 'HG'.

The RPwD Rules were notified in 2017, a year after the Act came into force. The Rules stated that all buildings had to conform to the HG. Now even as the HG was in the making, the NBC was being revised.

The NCPEDP found that there were discrepancies between these two standards – HG and NBC. The NBC was found to be more comprehensive. The NCPEDP succeeded in slamming the brakes on it, and commissioned the DEOC to review it and come up with recommendations.

The result was the NBC 2016 we have today. Accepting most of the DEOC's recommendations, it has foregrounded accessibility for PwDs in the Foreword and in all relevant chapters. Many chapters emphasize the fact that facilities open to the public should adhere to accessibility standards. Most importantly, the Code includes 'Accessibility and Universal Design Specialist' as part of the list of professionals in the design/construction team and provides for periodic accessibility audits of public buildings.

There is a need to create a cadre of competent access auditors who can inspect and certify buildings. Nipun Malhotra told us what a senior bureaucrat had revealed to him: When the government put out ads for access auditors while inviting tenders for 50 government buildings to be made accessible, several chartered accountants applied! Few people knew what the term meant.

Nipman Foundation has audited the Srinagar High Court, the Jammu airport, Rajghat in Delhi and several private sector companies. 'How do you become an access auditor?' Nipun asks rhetorically, pointing to the absence of training for this skill, and then adds, 'It's almost like a guild where you work under somebody else and learn the ropes.'

V-Shesh has done access audits for 225+ buildings, its co-founder Shashaank Awasthi says, even as his partner P. Rajasekharan adds, 'None of us are engineers or architects.' They just go by their deep understanding of the challenges involved and their audit team's 'eye for detail' when setting benchmarks – for the width of the door, the design of the latch and its height on the door, and numerous other details to which meticulous attention must be paid. 'We always have a PwD in our team to do the quality assurance, navigate the space and give feedback,' says Raja, while Shashaank chimes in, 'We have a problem with one of our favourite volunteers – because he's so good with his wheelchair, he can manoeuvre into any space! We tell him, "Think of somebody who is not as flexible, as adept as you are."'

## Accessible Public Transport

The RPwD Act addresses the question of public transport for PwDs.[35] All modes of transport should conform to the design standards for accessibility, and old modes should be retrofitted. The government should provide accessible parking spaces, ticketing counters, ticketing machines and toilets for PwDs at bus stops, railways stations and airports.

More than fare concessions and reservation quotas, what the travelling PwD needs is access – to the mode of transport as well as the space that accommodates it. Airports are relatively accessible today compared to railway stations and bus terminals with both the latter having undergone largely cosmetic changes, if any, to

---

[35] RPwD Act, Chapter VIII, Section 41.

accommodate passengers with disabilities. No wonder only 15 per cent of Indians with a locomotor disability use public transport, as compared to 65 per cent in affluent countries.

Take the 'disabled coach' that we've begun to see in many trains. This is the single, specially designed coach in each train, marked SLRD (Seating-cum-Luggage Rake, with D indicating disabled) and reserved exclusively for PwDs and their escorts if any; it has wide entrances, a roomy interior and modified toilets. But blind lawyer Sudheendra Kumar puts it bluntly, 'If you don't pack food and water, you'll starve on long journeys.' That's because the SLR coach is at one of the train's extremities, either just behind the engine or just before the guard's van. Since platform vendors never bother to walk all the way to the end of the train, the SLRD coach is never served. Wouldn't that deter PwDs from travelling independently, and oblige them to lean on escorts to fetch and carry for them?

In the 1980s, when top-ranking percussion artist Ghatam Suresh was a young man, he could not do without an escort when taking trains to other cities for concerts. Besides having to expend extra energy and effort to walk and climb steps, he also had to carry his fragile instrument: the clay pot that is the ghatam. An escort, usually a family member, would have to set aside their other commitments to make time for him. And concert organizers would be reluctant to book him when they realized they would have to pay for two people's fare and accommodation. 'I have lost many concerts because of that,' says Suresh. The fewer concerts he played, the less frequently his name would occur to organizers. 'Out of sight, out of mind,' as he puts it.

Suresh's wife Sumathy, whom he calls his 'strong pillar', was the one who encouraged him to travel independently. On railway platforms, he would actually scan the faces of passengers trying to identify people who 'looked the type' who might appreciate classical music, so that when he asked them for help carrying the ghatam to his coach they would understand the importance of handling it with care. Once seated, he couldn't simply push the ghatam in the space underneath because some suitcase might knock and break it. He would have to place it on his lap throughout the journey. His distress was heightened when (often) he wasn't allotted the lower berth and he'd have to clamber up the iron railing to the topmost one.

When it comes to expediting measures to make railway stations accessible, the Indian government has been trundling along like a goods train. But social entrepreneurs and disability activists have been trying to fast-track the process. Anuprayaas, a social organization focussed on disability and inclusion, has been taking the lead in easing rail travel for the blind and VI in particular. Since 2014, when the young couple Pancham and Shakti Cajla founded Anuprayaas, they have converted an impressive number of railway stations into VI-friendly spaces.

Pancham's association with disability dates back to his college days when he used to volunteer as a scribe for blind candidates. During his job at Infosys in Mysuru (where he also met Shakti), he took active part in social initiatives involving cancer patients and PwDs. When a blind friend told him how he had missed the train to his hometown the previous night because he had waited on the wrong platform, Pancham 'couldn't sleep that night'. Impulsively, the next day he went to the Bengaluru City Railway Station, later named the Krantivira Sangolli Rayanna (KSR) railway station.

The Divisional Railway Manager would have never expected a 27-year-old wearing Bermudas and a T-shirt to barge into his office and ask why railway stations couldn't be made blind-friendly. If he was taken aback, he didn't show it. Instead, he countered: 'Why don't you do it?'

Well, that set the wheels turning in Pancham's head. The Railways was only too keen to encourage him, and so he roped in friends and persuaded architects, research professionals and designers to lend their expertise. This was how Anuprayaas completed its first project: the launch of India's first VI-friendly railway station in Mysuru in November 2015.

Partnering with the Indian Railways and, later, with different companies through their Corporate Social Responsibility (CSR) initiatives, they completed a series of VI-friendly railway projects in rapid succession. This included India's first VI-friendly Mysuru–Varanasi Express, and the following VI-friendly stations: KSR, Borivali (Mumbai), Coimbatore, Dehradun, Chandigarh, Salem and Karur. Ongoing projects include the New Delhi railway station and three more of Mumbai's local train stations: the Chhatrapati Shivaji Maharaj Terminus, Lokmanya Tilak Terminus and Andheri. They introduced guidance booklets in Braille at the counters, and Braille tactile maps indicating the location and distance to and between platforms, eateries, toilets and other facilities; Braille indicators and signs across the premises including platform numbers on railings, portable ramps; and restaurant menu cards in Braille. VI persons are thus easily able to commute without assistance.

Anuprayaas also does projects in blind schools, and holds disability awareness programmes in offices and educational institutions. Under the label Braillemate they sell merchandise such as T-shirts, posters and wall décor – all of which sustains their work and generates awareness.

Rather than striving to create a name for themselves, they let their work speak for them. The result is that most VI commuters and railway travellers are surprised when they find out who is responsible for creating all these accessible spaces. Strangers call them to appreciate their work, says Shakti, and this is their greatest motivation to keep going forward.

When it comes to bus travel, PwDs in India face a grimly inhospitable environment. Forget travel between villages, towns and cities, even commutes in metropolitan cities are not PwD-friendly. Nipun Malhotra has been fighting for accessible buses for the nation's capital, for a start. He has taken the matter to the courts so many times that, he says, 'in the disability sector I am famous as the PIL [Public Interest Litigation] guy'.

In 2015 the Delhi government announced its 'odd-even scheme' of trying to reduce pollution by permitting cars with odd-numbered and even-numbered plates to enter the city on alternate days. The PwD was not on the government's long list of exceptions to the rule. Nipun wrote letters to all the officials and representatives concerned but to no avail. Eventually the transport secretary invited him for a meeting at an inaccessible venue. Nipun wrote an article about this and tried raising awareness through videos, but nothing happened.

Fed up, he filed a PIL in December 2015 in the Delhi High Court asking for exemption for PwDs from the odd-even scheme, citing the inaccessibility of Delhi's public transport that forced them to depend on their own vehicles. The Delhi High Court not only heard the PIL, but also asked the Delhi government what precautions they were taking with regard to PwDs. It was only in 2019 that the government finally exempted PwDs from the scheme.

In 2017, Nipun filed another PIL asking for a disability access audit for Delhi's public spaces. When it came up for hearing in January 2018, the high court directed the government to make all government offices, public buildings and public transport in Delhi accessible.

Meanwhile, in 2017, the Delhi government announced its decision to spend ₹300 crore to procure 2,000 buses that were not of the low-floor, accessible kind. Nipun filed a PIL seeking to stop the purchase. 'It took two years; it was exhausting. I used to go to court for every hearing myself,' he recollects. He had a lawyer friend fighting along with him against the Delhi government's battery of senior advocates. And what was the government's defence? Too expensive, and only 10 per cent of the buses need to be accessible. Nipun recalls: 'Acting Chief Justice Gita Mittal asked a beautiful question: If only 10 per cent of the buses are accessible, will PwDs have a timetable?' PwDs would have to order their life according to the bus schedule and change their life, office hours and shifts to suit the timings of 'accessible' buses.

In March 2018, the Delhi government floated a tender to procure another 1,000 standard-floor buses. So Nipun filed yet another PIL. In March 2019, the Delhi cabinet approved reimbursements for fitting hydraulic lifts to the standard floors of 1000 buses to make them more accessible. The lifts came, but the retrofit failed initially because the drivers were not taught how to operate them! In July 2019, the Supreme Court ruled in favour of mandating low-floor buses in Delhi and across the country.

---

You might imagine that well-heeled PwDs have it easy. On the face of it they appear to glide through swanky airports with ease, but there are various invisible traps beneath the surface.

The International Air Transport Association (IATA) has evolved a set of Special Service Request (SSR) codes for the different kinds of assistance a PwD might need while flying; every airline must follow them. The four-character codes are assigned depending on the disability and nature of assistance required. For example BLND is for the blind, and DPNA (short for Disabled Persons Needing Assistance) is for those with ID and DD. There are separate codes for wheelchair users depending on the level of assistance they need. A completely immobile person would have a different code from someone who needs help while climbing and descending steps. On the other hand, a VI person should be assisted all the way up to the cabin seat.

Neha Arora of Planet Abled comments that most PwDs who fly are not aware of their rights or the relevant IATA regulations. She observes that many airlines in India have just the one assistant on their staff, and no matter what the disability – whether BLND, DEAF or DPNA – they thrust the PwD into a wheelchair. She has witnessed the misuse of wheelchairs for Non-resident Indian (NRI) kids travelling alone; they have a different SSR code but the assistant is the same – the one assigned to wheelchair service.

Airlines are not supposed to charge PwDs for their ADs; they can have up to two of them for free. However, a domestic Indian airline charged one of Planet Abled's clients excess baggage for his wheelchair. Neha wrote to the airline but got no response. Then she took to social media and shamed them, finally managing to get a refund.

There have been multiple instances of airport security staff across the country being insensitive, inconsiderate or downright rude to PwDs. Checks are particularly problematic. Asking someone to remove their prosthetic limb to check for explosives or asking a quadriplegic to get up from their wheelchair is simply unpardonable. When Nipun Malhotra was humiliated in this manner by a Central Industrial Security Force (CISF) officer at the Bengaluru airport in 2016, he and other activists lobbied with CISF to ease security procedures for PwDs at airports. In October 2017, the Bureau of Civil Aviation Security (BCAS) decided that X-ray scanning would be used only as a last resort for those with prosthetic and orthotic devices, and PwDs could be checked with a handheld explosives trace detector.

Ghatam Suresh had a few unpleasant experiences travelling abroad for concerts in the 1990s. This was before he got a customized box made for the ghatam to go as cargo. A particularly harrowing experience was in 1989 on his second trip to Australia, when he was just 23. He was carrying two ghatams and no other musician in their ensemble would assist him. He slipped on the polished floor, both ghatams broke and a family member had to send one from Chennai by post. 'It cost more than what I earned at the concert!' he exclaims.

In the rigidly hierarchical world of Carnatic music, the senior artists of the ensemble would expect the juniors to be at their beck and call. Since Suresh couldn't fulfil that role, he was seldom their ghatam player of choice. When he became a senior artist, he started going as an independent performer instead of as part of an ensemble. He explains, 'I wanted to prove that I could travel alone.' At airports, he would pointedly refuse a wheelchair, but he says he has often seen people far more agile than him ask for wheelchairs just in order to jump the queue and be the first to board the plane.

Suresh says his disability has cost him many a lost opportunity to play at festivals abroad: 'It was like an iron curtain blocking me. I had to break that curtain.'

# 16

# AFFORDABLE, INDIGENOUS ASSISTIVE TECHNOLOGY

TO FUNCTION IN AN ACCESSIBLE ENVIRONMENT, PWDS must first be equipped with personal ADs that aid their mobility. Assistive Technology (AT) is an umbrella term for assistive, adaptive and rehabilitative devices for PwDs or the elderly. It could be hardware, software or both; it could be low-tech, mid-tech or high-tech. It includes everything from your ordinary reading glasses to the exoskeleton for the mobility impaired and wearable technology for the visually impaired.

Without appropriate ADs, it is difficult for PwDs to participate in education, the labour market, and social life. The World Health Organization has listed 50,000 assistive products, of which 50 are considered essential. According to the organization, over a billion people need AT, but less than 10 per cent of PwDs in the world and only 3–5 per cent of them in India have access to it.

Indigenous AT that is high-quality yet affordable is not a pipedream for India. The country's first ever national conference on 'AT for All' by 2030, organized by Mobility India, provides a glimpse into ingenious and game-changing ADs developed in our national institutes and innovation hubs. What stands out at the conference, held in Bengaluru on 2 and 3 August 2019, is how the domains of research, academia, engineering, design and medicine have networked to develop cutting edge AT.

But have these imaginative innovations travelled from lab to home?

There's a yawning gap that many have called the 'Valley of Death'. You soar from idea to Research and Development (R&D) and then working prototype, but you bite the dust unless you make the leap to the marketplace. There exists no robust ecosystem to convert every prototype into a product.

At the conference, Sujatha Srinivasan who is professor of the Mechanical Engineering department at IIT Madras asks, 'Why aren't innovations becoming products? We can have simple solutions that make an impact while suiting Indian needs.' India has the most number of engineers in the world, there is plenty of engineering talent in academic institutions, and there is no dearth of funds either, she says, adding, 'But the ecosystem is underdeveloped across the supply chain.'

Patanjali Dev Nayar of the WHO South-East Asian Regional Office (SEARO) comments on the discrepancies in access to ADs in India. He explains that we have over-priced, high-quality, higher-end ones for the few/rich, and cheap, low-quality, simple ones for the poor/larger population.

How do we provide ADs to all at a price that everyone can afford? This is the challenge that our IITs and other national science-and-technology institutions have been attempting to overcome. One way is to take an imported AD, and adapt it to suit Indian geographical and social conditions. Another, is to refine an existing device by identifying and removing its glitches. Examples of both were showcased at the conference.

Since the 1980s, the government of India, under its scheme called ADIP, has been distributing heavily subsidized or free ADs to low-income PwDs. The implementing agencies for this scheme include national institutes, local bodies, NGOs and the

Artificial Limbs Manufacturing Corporation of India (ALIMCO), a government undertaking. ADs manufactured by ALIMCO, such as canes, crutches, wheelchairs and motorized tricycles, are a common sight in both urban and rural areas. But they are not exactly top-of-the-line.

Arvind Suresh Ambalapuzha of IIT Delhi describes the problems faced by users of axillary crutches, most of which are manufactured by ALIMCO. 'The crutches have an extremely old design and are not tuned to the users' lifestyle,' he says. His team surveyed 124 users and the respondents complained that the crutches were not suitable for muddy, rocky or snowy terrain; they also found that the crutches deformed the spine, and gave users calluses, shoulder pain and underarm abrasions, besides soiling their clothes.

The biggest problem users faced was that the rubber tip degraded within a month or two, says Arvind, 'What happens now is that a user gets a crutch from an NGO, discards it after two months and gets another free one from another NGO. The new user is therefore deprived of a chance to get a free crutch.' Think of the wastage that could be avoided by simply replacing rubber with some long-lasting material that will firmly grip any kind of terrain.

Similarly, physiotherapist Bart Geilen found that many PwDs in rural areas discarded their wheelchairs. You don't just give a PwD a wheelchair and expect them to be fully functional, he explains, 'It's not one size fits all.' The wheelchair must suit the person's needs, environment and lifestyle. Support services are crucial; a trained professional/technician must see that the wheelchair is comfortable and provides proper fit and postural support, identify and remove pressure spots, and give the user training in how to repair and maintain it.

When we speak to APD president and wheelchair-user Mohan Sundaram, he gives us a novel solution to the maintenance problem: 'Take every cycle repair shop all over the country and train them to repair wheelchairs, because every wheelchair is made up of cycle parts.'

Sujatha Srinivasan, who also heads the TTK Centre for Rehabilitation Research and Device Development (R2D2), says that by WHO estimates, one per cent of the over 30 million Indians with locomotor disabilities need wheelchairs. But the existing ones are either low-cost, primitive and rejected by many, or exorbitantly priced, hi-tech and not always suited to our environment.

Why don't users of unsuitable ADs complain? Perhaps they don't want to look a gift horse in the mouth. Also, the AD comes at low or no cost, so it's easier to throw and replace. The result is that there is no feedback and no demand for improving the device.

At R2D2, they are looking to improve basic ADs such as the calliper, or Knee-Ankle-Foot Orthosis (KAFO) as it is referred to. The regular calliper, used by over 10 million Indians, has sharp edges that cut into the leg when the user sits and tears their clothes too, says Sujatha. 'We came up with a lever-operated drop lock for the KAFO. It creates greater flexion, and you can sit cross-legged or kneel with ease.'

One of R2D2's innovative AT solutions that actually made it to the manufacturing stage is the Standing Wheelchair. Entirely mechanical and operated by the user's arms, it is therapeutic; it gives relief to the back and bottom and prevents the secondary health problems that tend to develop when users sit for long periods. 'The team made several iterations before making this model. What costs $15,000 abroad can be made available for just ₹15,000!' Sujatha exclaims.

To develop the prototype to commercialization, R2D2 and industry partner Phoenix Medical Systems were funded by the Wellcome Trust, a United Kingdom Foundation. The funding provided for all aspects of the development – R&D, human resources at both R2D2 and the industry, travel for extensive user trials, prototyping, testing, tooling for production and initial dissemination. Such a comprehensive and flexible grant enabled the final price of the product to be affordable, since the manufacturer now only has to recoup operating costs with a reasonable profit for sustainability. The product named Arise was launched in November 2019.

The latest product to roll out of R2D2 in 2020 is a vastly improved wheelchair from NeoMotion, a start-up spun off from the lab and incubated at IIT Madras. The self-propelled NeoFly priced at ₹35,000 is compact so that it can squeeze through narrow spaces. Stylish and lightweight, it is ergonomically designed with 18 customizations to ensure comfortable seating. Since it is also swift, efficient, and minimizes physical effort, it has won praise from users who are wheelchair marathoners and sportspersons. For travellers, there's the electrically powered NeoBolt for ₹50,000 which easily attaches to the NeoFly. It is rugged and tailor-made for the rough Indian terrain, whether city streets, or rocky or slushy mud-tracks in villages. These R2D2 products are crying out for a mass market; they need to go from hundreds to tens of thousands. If only every successful prototype could vault smoothly over the Valley of Death.

Commercializing an AD is as painful an ordeal as climbing steps with lopsided crutches. For a start, innovators are not entrepreneurs. 'Most of the technology development happens in academia, which does research but doesn't have the business sense to translate it into products and take it to the marketplace,' says Mohan Sundaram of Artilab, India's first incubator to focus exclusively on disability. 'It's not a problem peculiar to India; it happens the world over,' he adds.

Large corporations are eager to fund research when they see its commercial potential. Are they reluctant to support research into ADs that they believe will be confined to a niche market? Manufacturers too seem to think it's a niche market, but are they mistaken? Are thousands of potential buyers simply 'invisible' to their blinkered eyes? These are questions worth pondering.

## Smart Tech to Devise Aids

Another rare success story, one that emerged from IIT Delhi and was supported by GCE-I and Wellcome Trust, is the Smart Cane. A similar foreign cane costs upward of $300, while this is available for just ₹2,500. The white cane used by the blind has an additional electronic device fitted on top that detects obstacles above knee-level and conveys information about distances to the user through vibratory patterns, so they can avoid overhanging branches and protruding objects such as signboards, parked vehicles and open windows.

Digital technology and artificial intelligence (AI) are coming to the aid of many innovators of AT in India. Not all of them have crossed the boundaries of the laboratory, though.

Professor Dibakar Sen of the Indian Institute of Science (IISc) describes the intelligent prosthetic limb that his department at IISc has come up with. It has software that is mind-controlled, with biosensors to detect neurological signals. Dr Manimozhi Theodore, director of the Defence Bioengineering and Electromedical Laboratory, says they have developed an intelligent wheelchair and are doing research on a cognitive-controlled wheelchair that can sense its surroundings.

A 3D scanner and 3D printer can revolutionize the fitting of prosthetics for amputees – especially in rural areas, says Soikat Ghosh Moulic, associate director of Technical and Quality Systems at Mobility India. You scan the amputated stump of the limb from all angles and after modifications, get it 3D-printed. A prosthetic can be printed in 18 hours; a foot is done in nine phases and it takes about 20–25 hours only, says Soikat. They've done a pilot and are waiting for ethics approval to start clinical trials.

Then there is Arun Joshua Cherian's promising invention, the Rise leg, which has braved the Valley. It's a fraction of the cost of a regular prosthetic leg for below-the-knee amputees, because it is made of cane. The talking point in the media may be the unique use of cane, but the digital manufacturing technique is what provides the perfect fit for the user. Many artificial leg users suffer pain, discomfort and sores when they wear it for long periods, because the ill-fitting socket starts rubbing against protruding bones. The Rise leg is digitally scanned and the socket, digitally machined. The user is fitted with the leg in record time, two and a half hours from scan to fitting – while the regular process takes a week.

The Indian Army, which has six Artificial Limb Centres (ALCs) that make prosthetics for soldiers who have lost their limbs in combat, was so pleased with trials for Rise legs that it wants them for all its soldiers. Rise measures soldiers at the ALCs and then fabricates the legs at its unit in Bengaluru, but the Army plans to go one step further by adopting this digital technology to manufacture Rise legs in all six ALCs.

## Showcasing Innovation

Like the Grand Challenges, there are events and contests where innovative projects are recognized and rewarded. Hackathons and Makeathons are gaining popularity in India and disability, when it's not the primary focus, often finds a place at them. To name a few, there's the Innovation Challenge Design Contest for engineering students held by the Department of Science and Technology, and Texas Instruments, the Enable Makeathon by the International Committee of the Red Cross, the medical devices hackathons that IIT Bombay conducts regularly and the NCPEDP-MPhasis Universal Design Award. Disability also often features in the Aarohan Social Innovation Awards by Infosys and Titan's Design: Impact Awards for Social Change.

A realm where indigenous AT can play a vital role is medical devices. As Dr Subramani Kanagaraj of IIT Guwahati points out, India imports $6,50,000 worth of biomedical devices every year. IIT Guwahati has garnered patents for their innovative biomedical devices, while IIT Bombay's Biomedical, Engineering and Technical Innovation Centre (BETIC) has over 50 award-winning product patents.

Speaking at the AT for All conference, Professor B. Ravi of BETIC explains that their projects start with the doctor or surgeon who defines the problem. The researcher then develops and delivers a solution to the end user. They conduct medical device hackathons and the winning entrepreneurs are given a one-year fellowship, helped to exhibit and test their products, and put in touch with consultants.

As part of IIT Bombay's diamond jubilee celebrations, a Medical Device Expo was held where 20 novel devices were exhibited. Among them was a KAFO (Knee-Ankle-Foot Orthosis) invented by Aneesh Karma, 36, who has polio and is a native of Bulandshahr in UP. He had failed his twelfth standard, but his innovation showed such promise that BETIC took him on as a project technical assistant to develop his idea into a product. He patented it and later won the NCPEDP–MPhasis Universal Design Award 2019.

One can discover native genius in the most unexpected places. Dr N.K. Sridhar, Dean of Faculty of Commerce and Management at Bangalore University, and a wheelchair user, speaks about non-formal ADs – homemade devices that are conceived by the average person. 'Using indigenous brains, [while] sitting at home, [or] in the office, people are developing devices,' he says. 'We should create a research portal that will trigger formal organizations to innovate and develop these devices.'

One such individual is Dilip Patro who designed a device to ease bladder and bowel movement for spinal cord injured patients

(SCIPs). Being a SCIP himself, he pinpointed the basic, everyday barrier of going to the toilet that they face, and worked on a solution.

'There are 1.5 million persons with spinal cord injuries in India, and 20,000 are added every year,' Patro says at the conference. 'About 70 to 80 per cent of SCIs are from road accidents, and 95 per cent of SCIPs do not come out of the house.' In 1997, Patro was involved in a road accident in Mumbai that rendered him quadriplegic. In 2007, he started The Ability People (TAP) in Vishakhapatnam to provide rehabilitation services to SCIPs and spread awareness about road accident prevention.

Patro takes individual orders (online and offline) for his device, which is in the form of a kit. Accessible to all and customized for the user, it is bio-compatible and suited to the Indian climate. The kit comes with aids such as flexible mirrors, inspection mirror, knee-spreader with mirror, catheter inserter, digital bowel stimulator and so on. 'It is one-tenth the cost of a similar foreign product,' he says. He tweaks his design when users phone him with feedback. TAP's mobile mentors teach them how to use the kit via the mobile. It can be mass produced, but a service delivery mechanism needs to be put in place, he says.

When innovations don't find backers, most people hang on to their patents and hope for an opportune moment, while a few magnanimously put it out in the public domain and allow it to attract support. 'In Artilab, we open-source anything that we can't take to the market,' says Mohan Sundaram. 'Let people build on what we have done.'

# 17

# ASSISTIVE TECHNOLOGY START-UPS STEP INTO THE MARKET

MOHAN SUNDARAM, EXECUTIVE DIRECTOR AND co-founder of Artilab, explains the difference between accelerators and incubators. The accelerator sets the start-up a tight deadline – just three to four months – to scale, and typically works well with web applications. The incubator gives the start-up a lead time of 12 to 18 months to develop. 'Our engagement is for 36 months,' Mohan says. 'We have to build the ecosystem; we need a longer term of nurturance.'

Pointing to the uniqueness of Artilab, which is the only incubator (not accelerator) that focuses singly on assistive technology, he says that they fill the gap between academia and the market. They are now picking up projects that address the WHO list of 50 essential assistive products, shortlisted based on worldwide demand. Since what works in India will also work in other developing nations, Mohan suggests that India start innovating, test products here, fine-tune them and get them out into the world.

Product-testing in different conditions is much easier to do in India, he says, giving the example of Handicapped International, an international NGO that was making a prosthetic hand. It took two-and-a-half years for them to test the hand with 26 subjects across Kenya, Uganda and Yemen. 'If it had come to us, we would have done 100 subjects in a year! If you take a particular disability, you get enough number of people here to test it out on, to fine-tune the product and get it working,' he says.

Artilab, which is accredited and funded by the Department of Science and Technology (DST), sees a lot of potential in bright ideas that emerge from various challenge-based events. Mohan has plans for the future in relation to this. He says, 'We also intend to run our own challenge events, invite people, get them to build products, set them specific challenges. If it's a pan-Indian event, DST will fund it.'

One of the projects Artilab has picked up to incubate is Web-e Systems, which develops technology that will make Science, Technology, Engineering and Mathematics (STEM) education accessible for blind and VI children. This is an initiative of Vision Empower (VE), co-founded by Vidhya Y. Typically, after class seven, blind students are actively discouraged from taking up math and science, and pushed towards the arts – sociology, law, anything that doesn't need visuals. VE's core objective is to create accessible content to assist the teaching and learning of STEM subjects for VI children.

Every stage in the life of Vidhya, who is blind herself, was a battle to convince others of her abilities – and the 'others' included the Indian Institute of Information Technology which she entered and graduated from as a medal-winning topper. The combat resumed when she started applying for jobs. She couldn't get any because the by-now familiar story was playing out: employers questioned her capability, asked whether she could use a keyboard and so on. She wanted to do something to change this situation for everyone else, and it led to the birth of VE which she co-founded with managing trustee Supriya Dey and mentor Professor Amit Prakash.

VE identified a plethora of drawbacks in education for the blind.

With one Braille book for the teacher and none for the child, she has to listen and take notes. In some cases, teachers are themselves blind but they themselves haven't had math and science education, so how do they teach these subjects? There is a paucity of tools to teach the visual component. For instance, one would have to substitute tactile diagrams or audio for visual descriptions. VE has a content partner that combines forces with a set of teachers to build accessible content for the VI child.

## Braille Devices for Self-learning

Braille might be considered old school in this digital age, but knowledge of Braille is of vital importance for the blind when they go outdoors. A device called Annie designed by Thinkerbell Labs enables children to learn to read, write and type in Braille on their own.

When we meet the Thinkerbell team in 2019, they have just made their first sale to the United Kingdom. The inventors of Annie are all in their twenties. Aman Srivastava, Sanskriti Dawle and Dilip Ramesh, who were classmates and computer science graduates from Birla Institute of Technology and Science (BITS) Pilani in Goa, made the innovation along with Saif Shaikh, a junior from the same university with a background in mechanical engineering.

Annie, named after Helen Keller's teacher Ann Sullivan, satisfies lovers of Braille and lovers of audio by combining the two, says Aman who gives us a demonstration. We sit down next to a blue-and-white device that looks roughly like a modem or a set-top box. There are six large raised keys in the middle, and in the top left corner a matrix of six holes like the side of a die. 'Jumbo Braille,' says Aman. You learn the alphabet on this mega-sized version and practice it on regular Braille with its tiny bumps (raised dots) on the top-right corner.

Our fingers aren't sensitive enough to make out the standard Braille dots, but we can feel the raised projections in each hole of the Jumbo. The numbers are read from top to bottom: the first column being 1, 2, 3 and the second, 4, 5, 6. Simple enough for a beginner. 'The combination 1, 4, 5 makes the letter "d",' Aman tells us.

If you press down the projections one by one in the right order, Annie's voice tells you that you're right. If you press down the same combination on the keys one by one, like before, Annie will regretfully inform you that it's a mistake because you're supposed to press them all together. When you do it correctly, she congratulates you. As you move on to a simple game where she dictates letters, it's easy to get hooked. It's certainly a healthy addiction for a child to have.

Writing is another ball game altogether. Aman explains how Braille writing works. You use a stylus to punch the appropriate dots on a sheet, turn it over and read the embossed letters. What you punch, therefore, will be a mirror image of what you read. Here, instead of paper there's a groove with holes in the same set of six, and a stylus – a thick pin with a wooden grip. You have to poke what would be the obverse of 1, 4, 5 to type 'd', that is, 2, 1, 4.

And so on, one letter at a time. You don't learn the alphabet from A to Z, but in assorted groups starting with letters that are easiest to learn and then moving through increasing levels of difficulty. After Grade One, which is on the basic alphabet, you move to Grade Two, and this involves around 200 contractions and abbreviations that usually take till Grade Six to master. There are numbers and punctuation marks and words... Enough to keep a child occupied and self-motivated too.

The problem with Braille writing in an ordinary classroom situation is that the teacher can't monitor the pupil as she punches the sheet with the stylus, but has to wait till the sheet is complete and pulled out, after which she reads the raised dots. 'In a class of 25 to 40 there's no way she can check their work while they're writing,' Aman says. And if the teacher gives the child homework to practice a letter many times, the child may have made a mistake repetitively but the teacher will find out only the next day in class.

Annie, on the other hand, can also be connected to the teacher's computer. The teacher can access all the Annies and monitor the children's progress on a dashboard called Helios connected to the local server, to which all data is synced. When the data gets onto the cloud, Thinkerbell can view it. 'Helios allows you to monitor multiple Annies in multiple locations,' says Aman. 'If we have 2,000 Annies out there in the next two to three years, we'll be able to see which region of the world is doing better. Which lesson plans are working well? What kind of teacher intervention is best? Can we reduce the dependence on special educators, and where they are available can we increase their impact?'

Aman shows us on-screen data for the Rajyakrit Netrahin Madhya Vidyalaya in Harmu, Ranchi – one of the many blind schools in India that use Annies. (The prime minister mentioned this school's Annie-enabled 'smart class' in a public address in January 2021.) On the screen we can see the names of the school's active users. The teacher can see how long each user has spent on it per day, what lessons they've done, what mistakes they're making and an assessment of their level of performance. The objective is to measure the accuracy level of each child in the three skills of reading, writing and typing.

The level that follows literacy is vocabulary. The teacher can measure how many words the child has learnt. There are vocabulary trackers for different languages if they are learning more than one. Annie can be programmed in other languages, although they'll still be learning the English alphabet. Bharatiya Braille consists of phonetic mappings of Braille in *desi* languages, approximating the sounds of English.

In dictation, which tests listening, the content must be

comprehensible and match the child's context. In lessons, the words the child has learnt will be incorporated into a narrative. The stories, the voice artists and their accents and even dialects have to be changed according to the cultural context. 'It's an immersive, interactive experience,' Aman sums it up.

The idea for Annie popped up over breakfast one day in BITS Pilani in 2015. Sanskriti, Dilip and Aman had just attended a workshop where they learnt about the Raspberry Pi (RP) Foundation in the United Kingdom. The RP being a full-fledged $35 computer was revolutionizing access to good computer education in poor countries. Sanskriti wondered aloud whether the 'linear actuator', the projections that pop up, could be used to teach Braille.

They did some digging and found out that Braille literacy in India is less than one per cent, which is among the lowest in the world. Their first prototype, a Braille dicta-teacher that teaches one alphabet at a time got an unprecedented response from blind schools. The Professor Suresh Ramaswamy grant got them 'a bit of cash' and unlimited access to all the labs in their college. After they graduated, they started working on a prototype of Annie. The first one, which came out in January 2016, won the Tech Rocketship Awards, an initiative of the United Kingdom's Department for International Trade to identify India's top young entrepreneurs and help connect them to investors. That year, the Duke and Duchess of Cambridge launched the awards in Mumbai and Sanskriti taught them how to type their son's name 'George' in Braille.

In June 2016, they set up Thinkerbell in Bengaluru, and the following July they got their first round of funding from Anand Mahindra and the Indian Angel Network. The Department for International Trade organized visits to the United Kingdom and provided 'a soft landing' for them. Today Annie is being used in schools abroad – in the United Kingdom and Dubai when we checked in 2020 – besides several Indian states. It took a series of prototypes for a sophisticated Annie to evolve, and samples of each version – from the first crude one to the finished product – are displayed at the Thinkerbell office. They serve as a visual reminder of how far this spunky young team has travelled.

## Robotics for Autism

Research has shown that children with autism are especially attracted to robots. The kids are drawn to them because they are inanimate and their expression doesn't change. Humanoid robots are being used abroad in therapy, to improve the child with autism's 'triad of impairment' in behaviour, communication and social interaction.

However, many children with ASD also have poor psychomotor skills. The child has to be taught literally hundreds of skills involved in performing routine acts such as holding a cup or opening a door. This is why ADLs such as eating food or brushing teeth become so difficult for them.

Robotics had not addressed this aspect of the child with autism's impairments until Dr Ramya S. Moorthy conducted her pioneering research. She is the brain behind Nimaya Innovations, which designs robotic devices for training kids on the spectrum with impaired psychomotor and cognitive skills. The company has already launched six devices and there are plenty more in the pipeline.

Ramya makes it clear that Nimaya's Skill Training Units, which are proven to be 'up to 60 per cent more efficient than the current learning system', are not meant to replace the occupational therapist. She says, 'We are not a competitive training but a complementary training. There is accelerated learning. We wanted to make it easier for the therapist and for the child, to make it simple and fun.'

Ramya had graduated in electrical and electronic engineering but her keen interest in robotics drove her to switch to mechanical engineering for her masters; in fact she and her father share a hobby, buying off-the-shelf kits for robotic devices and assembling them. After her M.Tech in robotics as a university topper, she joined Sastra University in Thanjavur and worked on her PhD thesis on 'applying social robotics to acquiring psychomotor skills for children with autism'. When she started her research, meeting special educators and therapists and reading 'thousands of papers and journals' on the subject, she found a total absence of baseline studies in this area.

Ramya found that people abroad were effectively using humanoid robots to improve the child's social skills, but she rejected the method outright because (a) humanoids cost three to six lakh rupees and was therefore out of reach for the average Indian family, and (b) the robot would give commands to the child, whereas she firmly believed that it should be a human being who did the training. Her idea was to take each activity and the skills associated with it, and break down each skill into tiny parameters which the child could learn step by step. She designed and developed six devices addressing different psychomotor skills and ADLs – the varying grasps one uses to hold a ball, hold a pen, grip a stick, turn a key and so on. The devices also addressed their cognitive skills, vestibular action and other factors. Many children with autism have vestibular issues that affect their equilibrium. 'Using one of our devices a child was able to walk backwards,' she explains.

Designing a task specifically for autism was another mighty challenge, because there was no available literature to guide her on the appropriate design. Kids with autism are sensitive to sounds, colours and textures. Everything has to be just right: the line of sight, the shape of the lever the child operates, the colour of the device and so on. If the lever is spherical, they will simply fiddle with it without pulling it; if it is a cube, the sharp edges will feel abrasive to their sensitive palms. The size must suit them and they should be given a choice of colours. She believes, 'There is no one concrete device that works for all children with autism.'

Ramya tested her devices on a control group in a school in Thanjavur and a target group in the Academy for Severe Handicaps and Autism in Bengaluru. Comparing the equipment they regularly used for occupational therapy with her devices, and with the same number of days, parameters, number of trials and training sessions per day, she could measure the effect on the children. She did pre- and post-assessments of both types of training – with and without her devices – to measure the child's level of competency. It can take six months to a year for a child with ASD to master the skills needed to open and close a door, says Ramya, 'We were able to teach the children in two to three weeks!' The biggest advantage was they were able to apply their learning to everyday life and open any kind of regular door since they had learnt the skill. She was able to establish that her devices accelerated learning by 60 per cent.

Even as she wrote her thesis, she discussed the idea of starting a company with her father. But then in 2017, she had 'a major life-changing event'. A week before her PhD thesis submission she was sleeping over at a friend's house when it caught fire, and carbon monoxide poisoning almost took her life. She lost her voice for six months; an equally crushing loss was that of her 350-page thesis when her laptop went up in flames. The backup was also in the laptop bag, she recalls, 'I lost three years of data in one minute.'

After taking such physical and emotional battering, Ramya might have admitted failure but for the turning point: a phone call from a teacher at the academy. In August 2017, the teacher called to share her excitement over the progress of a two-year-old whose therapist had declared she had 'zero psychomotor skills'; the girl used to keep her hands permanently and tightly clenched. In August 2016, Ramya had been astonished enough when the girl learnt nine out of 13 psychomotor skills on the robotic devices in less than two months, but now the teacher was telling her that the girl remembered those skills a whole year later and was responding in class.

'That is when I said, I have to do this now; I have to take it to the children; I have to get back in the saddle and finish this.' Despite her parents' protests she returned to college that very month and slogged over her thesis, working over 18 hours a day, collating raw data and redoing 900 to 1,000 graphs. Her guide and her senior Hari provided 'amazing support'. She finished her thesis by the end of November 2017, defended it in July 2018 and got her PhD that September.

It was time for the birth of Nimaya. The design team consisted of her, a software engineer, a hardware engineer and a manufacturer. Nimaya is both a product-based and a service-based company; it's an end-to-end process that comprises training and evaluation. Since the existing concepts that therapists use have been adapted to the psychomotor Skill Training Units (STUs), each requires just two or three days of training.

In October 2019, Ramya launched six of the 13 STUs they have developed so far, and in Phase Two she plans to launch more than 50 STUs in a staggered fashion until the end of 2021. The units start with tackling a set of ADLs that involve basic grasps – to put on shoes, wear a shirt, open the door and so on – and then teach complex grasps along with rotary motions and hand-eye coordination. Phase Two will teach ADLs such as potty training, brushing teeth and eating.

The STUs are cloud-monitored, taking in data from the child which will be available to the therapist and the parents, both of whom can keep track of the sessions. It works on a subscription model, and the target users are special schools, special educators, government health institutions and parents of special children.

In 2021, Nimaya received a financial boost – a ₹6 lakh grant from the Atal Incubation Centre Association of Lady Entrepreneurs of India, Hyderabad, and a women entrepreneurship programme fellowship of ₹3 lakh from the Pernod Ricard India Foundation. Nimaya has also developed a new technology known as Cognitive Augmented Interactive Display System. The first version of the product is used to teach preschool children the English alphabet without the use of pen and pencil, and builds excellent eye-hand coordination. The product series is called Tactile Immersive Learning System (TILES), and a tailormade version of TILES is used to train children with dyslexia, ADHD and other learning disabilities.

# 18

# THE EMPLOYMENT SAGA

EVEN IF PWDS MANAGE TO NAVIGATE THEIR WAY THROUGH the various accessibility related challenges, using ADs or without them, whether they can flourish is still a big question mark. One of the major hurdles they face on the road to independence and security is unemployment.

After Ashwin Karthik graduated in 2005, for instance, he found that nobody would give him a job. Ashwin has a form of CP accompanied by quadriplegia (paralysis of all four limbs), which renders him a wheelchair user. Being turned down for a job might not sound remarkable – after all, we have millions of disappointed graduate job-seekers in India. Except that over two years, Ashwin attended a jaw-dropping 45 unsuccessful job interviews!

He isn't kidding, he assures us. It was his mother who pushed him to keep answering interview calls. He landed a job in MPhasis after his 46th job interview. When he quit after eight years of working there, many companies were still hesitating to employ him despite his work experience. It was time for another interview marathon. He attended 20-odd interviews before striking it lucky at Australia and New Zealand Banking Group (ANZ). He says the process of switching to Dell (where he is working when we meet him) wasn't so tedious, and adds, 'Or maybe I didn't feel the pinch because I realized that patience is a virtue.'

The questions he was asked at interviews were similar to what Nipun Malhotra (and hundreds of other PwDs, doubtless) faced. Can you sit for eight hours in your wheelchair? How will you go to the toilet? If we have to send you out of the office for site visits, how will you go? A human resources executive actually told him, after he had successfully answered all her questions, 'If you can get up and climb those two steps, the job is yours.'

In 2013, when Ashwin was to receive the President's Award for Best Employee, he noticed a familiar face. It was the same human resources executive waiting in line to accept the award for Best Employer for her company.

She looked at him curiously and asked, 'Haven't I met you before?' And he replied, 'Yes, six years ago, we had a bittersweet conversation!'

## An Uphill Journey

Ashwin's 45 isn't a record-breaker in failed interviews, though. That 'honour' possibly belongs to Harish Raghavan, who clocked 70 unsuccessful interviews in the 1990s despite having an MBA in marketing. Incidentally, he is Shanti Raghavan's brother who inspired her and her husband Dipesh Sutariya to set up Enable India after he lost his vision from the degenerative eye disease, retinitis pigmentosa.

If you thought education for PwDs was the Hill of Difficulty (to give John Bunyan's allegory *The Pilgrim's Progress* a disability twist), the next stage of the ordeal – employment – could well take them through the Valley of Humiliation and the Slough of Despond. Both government and private establishments haven't gauged the full measure of PwDs' capabilities. They are only now waking up to the term 'reasonable accommodation' which stands for the adjustments and modifications that have to be made (in this case in the workplace) to ensure that PwDs enjoy equal rights.

As you can imagine there is severe unemployment and underemployment among PwDs in India. Of the 2.68 crore PwDs in India, according to the 2011 Census, 1.34 crore are of employable age, but the majority among them – 99 lakh – are either unemployed or marginal workers.

The private sector was let off easy by the RPwD Act; its regulations apply only to government establishments. For instance, it says that no government establishment shall discriminate against PwDs in matters relating to employment, and government establishments shall provide reasonable accommodation and a barrier-free, conducive environment.[36]

However, the 2016 Act was followed by the RPwD Rules issued on 15 June 2017, which made it clear that they were also applicable to 'a private establishment employing 20 or more persons'. Private firms too are therefore prohibited from discriminating on the grounds of disability and must publish their equal opportunity policy, which includes a list of posts suitable for PwDs, provisions for a barrier-free and accessible environment, and facilities that 'enable them to discharge their duties in the establishment'.

Now the RPwD Act mandates the government to reserve 'not less than four per cent' of all its jobs for PwDs,[37] but it goes easy on the private sector, only mentioning that the government should 'provide incentives to employer in private sector to ensure that at least five per cent of their workforce is composed of persons with benchmark disability'.[38] This sort of gentle nudging is not going to create an appreciable increase in PwD employment in the private sector.

A study by Corporate Responsibility Watch on the 'Status of Corporate Responsibility in India 2019' analysed the Business

---

[36] RPwD Act, Chapter IV, Section 20.

[37] RPwD Act, Chapter VI, Section 34.

[38] RPwD Act, Chapter VI, Section 35.

Responsibility Reports of 300 randomly selected private and public sector companies from the top 500 Bombay Stock Exchange (BSE) listed companies. The companies, spread across 16 sectors, together employ approximately 55 lakh workers.

The study found that *over 70 per cent of the businesses had either zero or less than one per cent of employees with disabilities*. And although public sector units (PSUs) fall in the category of government establishment and are supposed to appoint PwDs in at least four per cent of its posts, only three of the 47 PSUs that were part of this study had three or more per cent of employees with disability.

Madhumitha Venkataraman of Diversity Dialogues, a collective working on inclusion, is a wheelchair user with left-hemiplegia (paralysis of the left side so she cannot use her left limbs). Speaking about her 11-year career with corporates at the annual Intuit India Accessibility Summit on 17 October 2019 in Bengaluru, she lists the reactions she had received from employers who had rejected her as well as those who had taken her in:

- Mistrust: 'You must have faked your degree.' (Precisely the same reaction that Nipun got from an employer.)
- 'Can you type with one hand?'
- 'You can't do this, it's too hard for you.'
- Avoidance: Skirting the subject of disability.
- Inspiration porn: 'Wow, you can actually do this?' when she performs a simple act.
- 'Be grateful we've employed you.' And the unspoken, 'Don't expect promotion or benefits.'

The theme of the 2019 Summit is 'Employment opportunities for PwDs' and the speakers are clearly discussing jobs in the corporate sector for those who had degrees under their belt. When it comes to the underprivileged and less educated, however, government jobs are their first and often only hope.

## Government Post List

Back in 2001, MSJE's Department of Disability Affairs had got an expert committee, helped by three sub-committees, to identify a list of government posts suitable for PwDs in the Group A, B, C and D categories. The categories are ranked according to their pay scales in descending order – from Group A, comprising those in high-ranking and administrative jobs (such as scientists, bureaucrats, judges, top officers in the armed forces and civil services), down to Group D comprising unskilled and semi-skilled workers (ayahs, cooks, gardeners, attenders and so on).

Scanning the list of 1,100 government posts for PwDs (from a total of 3,000) is an illuminating exercise, to say the least. One can witness the good old Indian bureaucratic tradition in all its glory. It also seems as though many of the designations haven't been altered in a hundred years – but we'll come to that in a minute.

Each post in each Group is divided into columns stating (i) designation, (ii) physical requirements, (iii) the categories of PwDs suitable for the job, (iv) nature of work and (v) working conditions. And boy do they go into detail!

Physical requirements encompass the abilities to sit, stand, see, hear, communicate, read and write, manipulate with fingers, crawl, climb, bend, jump, kneel and crouch, and pull and push. Requirements vary depending on the job and they are abbreviated in typical government-of-India style: PP for pulling and pushing, MF for manipulation with fingers and so on. Categories of disability of those eligible are also given initials, such as OA (one arm), OL (one leg), BL (both legs), LV (low vision) and LC (leprosy cured).

There are elaborate descriptions of the nature of work – for instance, there's a veritable lesson on how to embalm a corpse. The designations under Group D are particularly noteworthy and give us a sneaking suspicion that they originated in the colonial era. We learn how an Anti-malaria Coolie differs from an Anti-malaria

Mazdoor, and a Sweeper (Dry) from a Sweeper (Wet). We fervently wish they would amend the job description of the last mentioned, a part of which is a criminal offence today. A wet sweeper is a 'scavenger' who, besides cleaning bathrooms, and lavatories and so on, 'removes night soil using spade and broom, and carries it to [the] dumping ground in hand-cart'.

And then you have the Khalasi, Lascar, Jamadar, Mistry and Bawaheer (the last being one who repairs and preserves glass objects, we are told), besides the *Dakiya* or Runner who delivers letters to remote areas and 'may carry with him spearhead stick fitted with small bells to ward off wild animals'. A government post for Billiard Marker brings to mind sahibs having *chota* (small) pegs in Whites-only clubs. Bureaucratic tradition dictates that each 'unskilled' job must be divided into as many parts as possible so that more poor people get employed. Therefore you have Rug Cleaner and Spot Remover, Mat Trimmer and Carpet Clipper. The Chair Re-caner repairs cane chairs by weaving new cane to replace broken old cane.

The expert committee hasn't bothered to amend the designations or, god forbid, eliminate any of them because that would bring down the number of posts available. Much simpler to hire someone for a certain post and, in practice, alter the nature of the work. We're rather keen to meet a HH (hearing handicapped) person who has filled in a vacancy for Paste Maker and see what job has actually been assigned to him.

Some of the jobs are fast vanishing if they haven't gone extinct already. Some remnants from the past include telegram sorter, typist, stenographer, telephone operator and Gestetner operator. The standard sentence 'Incumbent should be functionally able to complete the assigned task efficiently with aids and appliances, whenever necessary' has been tagged onto almost every entry in the 'working conditions' column.

Across the four groups, those with orthopaedic disabilities

have a clear edge over those with hearing and vision impairments, while intellectual disabilities (as per usual) are barely represented. The government needs to update not only its job list but also its knowledge of the capabilities of the blind, VI, deaf and HI for a start. For example, in Group A, in a progressive move, the physical requirements for a judge/magistrate allow for B and LV (blind and low vision) candidates to apply. The Supreme Court allows blind candidates to take the exam for judges, but many states deny this. So far only Rajasthan and Delhi have allowed blind candidates to write exams for judges.

## D&I Among Corporates

The buzzword among corporate firms, D&I, has not been satisfactorily translated into action in India when it comes to PwDs. There is no point in playing the numbers game; creating an inclusive ecosystem at the workplace is of the utmost importance. As Vidya Rao, Global Disability Lead at Wipro, says during Intuit's 2019 Accessibility Summit, 'Don't focus on just filling quotas by hiring a large number of PwDs. Provide reasonable accommodation, personalize it for each one's needs, and integrate them into the system.'

Reasonable accommodation is actually affirmative action, Madhumitha Venkataraman says at the same summit. The reasonable accommodation policy must have a broad scope and not be limited to the 21 officially listed disabilities. It must be left to each organization to define 'reasonable'. Going one step further, she says that caregivers of PwDs also need reasonable accommodation at their workplaces.

Vidya Rao, who is visually impaired, speaks about how to on-board PwDs through training (pre-job and on-job), some hand-holding, and creating a conducive work environment by providing amenities and sensitizing colleagues. 'It is like peeling the layers of an onion,' she says. 'The first layer is acceptance, the second is integration.'

Acceptance becomes easier once you become aware of your own biases, Vidya says, referring to a 30-minute online 'unconscious bias module' that her company uses for its employees. It has also launched a pilot project of 'reverse mentoring', as part of which a PwD is attached to a senior leader who has a series of personal interactions with them. This would include, for example, going to the cafeteria with a person who is blind or has a locomotor disability and ordering lunch. The leader then has a de-briefing on these interactions with Vidya.

To get an idea of how comically (or is it tragically?) unprepared a company can be to employ a PwD, you have to listen to Sivapriya's story. Sivapriya, who is visually impaired and in charge of the centre for visual impairment at Youth4Jobs (Y4J) Hyderabad, narrates her experiences at a corporate firm she formerly worked for. It was the company, more than her, who 'literally learnt on the job' when it came to accommodating her. Theirs was a 'course-correction as you go along' approach, she says.

On the first day Sivapriya was welcomed by everyone at her workplace, and everything seemed fine. But on the second day, the hurdles commenced right from the gate. Her approach was first stalled by security, who hadn't been informed about her needs. The female guard, whose assistance she had sought to be led to her desk, was puzzled since Sivapriya looked 'normal' – no dark glasses or cane – and asked her whether she needed help because she was pregnant or was about to faint. She had to wait till someone was free to lead her all the way to her work station (it was an expansive campus like that of most corporate firms). This became routine, and there were days when she took 20 minutes to reach her desk from the entrance.

Sivapriya says that neither the company nor she herself had anticipated these and other barriers that cropped up one by one, and most of her time was spent not on her work but overcoming hurdles caused by her disability (or the company's ill-preparedness to accommodate a PwD, rather). She had to ask to get a screen reader – that most basic requirement of a VI person. She had to then also ask for a magnifier, and she did not get the camera mouse she asked for. She discovered that the screen reader did not read pdfs, and portals were inaccessible.

Sivapriya's experience reminds us of another that dates back several decades – even as solutions are found for challenges that PwDs face, newer problems crop up. From the first chapter you may remember that Neha Arora had told us about her mother, a wheelchair user and the only woman working in Agra's Office of the Registrar of Property. Her mother's chance of promotion was hampered purely because the office had no lift. The new post would involve her having to work on the first floor, so the 'solution' found by her seniors was to keep her stuck in the same post in her ground floor workspace throughout the 32 years of her career.

Vidya underscores the importance of sensitizing the support staff, including security staff, library staff, cab drivers and canteen managers. Neha Arora shares with us a novel idea that she has for corporates who, in order to fulfil their D&I mandate, hire trainers to conduct sensitization workshops for their employees. Wearing a blindfold for a few hours (a common exercise during such training sessions) does not really have a long-term impact, she observes. Why not instead spend the money set aside for these workshops to get their staff to become travel buddies of PwDs on inclusive tours? Neha suggests, adding, 'In this way they can learn firsthand the challenges that PwDs face and what living with a disability is like. It would change their mindset about inclusion, and influence attitudes in the workplace too.'

Vidya's point about the need to sensitize support staff was echoed by Jeevan B., a software engineer with OI. Speaking at the summit he also refers to the basic need for accessibility, recalling that at the biggest tech park in Kerala, when he went for a job interview, 'there were so many steps that [even the] people who were carrying me got tired'. There was no accessible toilet there either.

Accessibility (to be discussed in a separate chapter) includes removal of not just physical but also online barriers. The Indian government had grandly announced in February 2009 that all government websites shall be made WCAG-compliant (the Web Content Accessibility Guidelines have been developed by the World Wide Web Consortium, W3C). Leave alone government websites, the technology sector itself has not bucked up and rendered all their sites universally accessible. Both Vidya and Dennis Wilfred – the latter is Head of Talent Acquisition at Intuit India – point out that many job portals are not accessible to PwDs and don't have a disability window.

## Smoothening On-boarding

'Interviewers should learn the right etiquette in hiring…know how to ask the right questions,' says Vidya, adding that Wipro employees do the Interview Certification Programme (ICP) which familiarizes them with various interview scenarios related to diversity. Sivapriya says, '[The human resources department] must ask the candidate what they need and customize the interview process accordingly.'

Pratap R., a Senior Business Analyst at JP Morgan Chase who has CP, suggests that employers 'do their homework' before interviewing a PwD candidate to figure out what s/he is capable of. He says that he appreciates the attitude of the person who interviewed him for his current job, 'I was very nervous. He waited 10 minutes for me to settle down.' However, it took Pratap two years to settle into his job.

Dennis Wilfred states that each interviewer in Intuit is trained in how to assess each candidate depending on their disability. 'Hire a candidate with potential; skills can be acquired,' he says. 'Look for "coachability", someone who would be eager to learn.'

Vidya calls for flexible policy procedures to ensure a smooth transition from training to workplace. The Deaf are often left out, and they must be included in in-house meetings and client meetings, she says. Interpreters as well as sign-to-text and speech-to-text Apps to help communication will enable managers to work with the Deaf. 'For other disabilities, the methodology differs but the principle is the same,' she stresses.

Invisible disabilities often slip under the radar. Mental illnesses and other forms of disability that are not immediately apparent are often ignored. The EAP (Employee Assistance Programme) of a company should include mental health and create 'a safe and secure environment' for everyone with invisible disabilities, says Vidya. Employees may fear losing their job, being bullied, or not being invited to meetings if they reveal their disability, so they may hide it.

That is exactly what Gagandeep Chandok did. At the summit he describes how, after college, he got rejected during three job interviews on declaring that he has thalassaemia. The fourth time he hid his condition and got the job. His form of invisible disability, Thalassaemia Major, poses its own distinct challenges. Persons with this condition, being severely anaemic, need regular blood transfusions. After each transfusion, the injection needle is left in the arm for 10 to 15 hours, causing a swelling. When Gagandeep was assigned the graveyard shifts, his health started deteriorating. He had to have a transfusion every 15 days and sometimes even sooner if his haemoglobin count dropped as the result of a cough or cold. There were days when he went to work wearing a full-sleeved shirt to hide his swollen arm. His need for frequent leave did not go down well with the company. He resigned after barely seven months.

Gagandeep then joined a British firm, once again without revealing he had thalassaemia. Unfortunately, a traffic accident hindered his career further. He was happy when he finally got a job in a firm that accepted his condition, but it too eventually used his poor health as an excuse to fire him when it was downsizing. 'Psychologically, I was broken. It took me three months to recoup mentally,' he recollects. Finally he joined Accenture where he has now been working for nine years; only three years into the job, he 'unofficially' revealed the fact of his thalassaemia to one of his managers.

As president of the TSCS, Karnataka, Gagandeep says that he found many 'thals' hesitating to disclose their condition for fear of not getting jobs or working with the constant fear of losing their jobs. His advice to employers is this: 'Be aware of our disability. Make us comfortable during the interview. After on-boarding, six months later do a follow-up to see how we're doing.'

## Stalled Careers

There is no career growth for PwDs, Madhumitha says. Stagnation is common. Appraisals can become problematic, since a large part of the appraisal has to do with assessing communication skills. 'How do you do performance appraisal for the Deaf?' she asks. She recommends that career growth be planned a year in advance so that one can train the PwD to be in that position.

TEDx speaker and senior bank manager Siddharth Jayakumar believes that the lack of empowerment hinders PwDs from furthering their careers. 'There's low ambition – they're very happy they have a job with some money coming in. After they get employed, five years down the line they're doing the same job. And because there is no promotion, there is a backlog in filling vacancies. If you employ 2,000 PwDs and even if 200 of them are promoted, there will be 200 more vacancies to be filled by PwDs,' he says.

Pavithra Y.S. of Vindhya e-Infomedia where over 62 per cent of the workforce comprises PwDs, lays down a few guidelines for companies that want to hire PwDs and encourage their growth:

- Ask the potential employee what challenges they might face.
- Once they're employed, keep tabs on them – keep the connection going.
- Ensure basic physical needs such as ramps and accessible lifts, toilets and so on are in place.
- Ask them, 'What do you want? This chair? This language? This manual?'
- Have a buddy system.
- Don't 'help' – I don't believe in that word. Support them.
- Their learning curve is longer so give them time and additional support.
- Only work on their abilities; adapt the job accordingly.
- Groom them. Identify their strengths. Give them responsibility to help them grow.
- Create an ecosystem; make everyone aware.
- Banish preconceived notions. Don't make assumptions just because a person looks or behaves differently from you.

# 19

# TOWARDS EFFECTIVE AND
# RELEVANT SKILLS TRAINING

BEFORE YOU PLANT A SEED, THE GROUND MUST BE READIED. But even after softening the soil and watering it, the seed needs a little coaxing. It must be encouraged to put out a shoot, extend it upward and outward, and rise towards freedom. Similarly, before you create a conducive work environment, you have to prepare PwDs for the job. The process begins with rehabilitation and pre-vocational training.

The RPwD Act, in its chapter on skill development and employment, enjoins state governments to include PwDs in all its mainstream vocational and skill training programmes, as well as provide such programmes exclusively 'for those with developmental, intellectual, multiple disabilities and autism' with 'active links to the market'.[39]

One of GOI's earliest ventures was in 1968 when it signed a bilateral agreement with the United States to set up two Vocational Rehabilitation Centres (VRCs). There were 21 at the last count, situated in urban areas and 11 Rural Rehabilitation Extension Centres. Here, adult PwDs are evaluated and assessed, given the

---

[39] RPwD Act, Chapter IV, Section 19.

necessary rehabilitative assistance, and either guided towards suitable jobs or helped to secure loans for self-employment. Seven VRCs have skill training workshops attached to them where, after assessment, PwDs are trained as painters, tailors, mechanics, carpenters and so on.

The 21 VRCs are a mere drop in the ocean, and most PwDs barely know they exist. Besides, there is an absence of structured, formal training and a clear, seamless link between training and placement. How can skills training be made effective, widespread and relevant?

The answer came to us via the National Skill Development Corporation (NSDC), set up on a Public-Private Partnership (PPP) model. To bridge the gap between industry demands and skilling requirements, the NSDC in 2015 identified 38 sectors that suffer a skill shortage – everything from the aviation, automotive, food, tourism, telecom and textile industries to the agriculture, beauty and wellness, domestic worker and healthcare sectors. It then set up Sector Skills Councils (SSCs) that would define job roles and design skill training curriculums. One of the SSCs was the Skill Council for Persons with Disability (SCPwD) which would offer PwDs meaningful industry relevant skill-based training.

The SSCs don't run the training programmes themselves but reimburse the entities – mainly NGOs – that set up the training centres. So far, approval has been granted for 160 PwD-exclusive training centres. The skills are drawn from all 38 sectors, but the method of imparting them obviously needs to be modified and made accessible to PwDs. However, so far, those with intellectual disabilities have been barely served, and the schemes are mainly for those with physical disabilities. We're a long way away from training those with ID, DD, autism and multiple disabilities, as mentioned in the RPwD Act.

One shouldn't forget that skills training must encompass both professional and social skills. Many PwDs who are mired in dependency and helplessness need to acquire life skills and soft skills training, so they can come out of the victim mode and join the work culture. Employers must be sensitized, but so must potential employees. It takes two hands to clap.

'We found people not able to take the rigours of the job,' says Shanti Raghavan of Enable India, which has trained and placed tens of thousands of PwDs in hundreds of reputed companies. She asks: If family and society place no expectations on them to achieve anything, how can you expect them to meet a target at work?

Vidya Rao of Wipro emphasizes the necessity for PwDs to go through the rehabilitation process in order to integrate into a work environment. 'Jobs seekers with disabilities who apply to a mainstream organization should be ready to deal with competition,' she says. 'No special treatment. They cannot expect additional support all the time. For example, the blind have to learn how to take notes in a meeting and can't expect someone to do it for them always; a wheelchair user cannot expect someone to do the pushing and instead could apply for a loan to get a motorized wheelchair.'

'One has to be open to skill training,' says Prateek Kaul of GiftAbled. 'Discipline, commitment, deliverables – all these matter. People with multiple or profound or intellectual disability must be given support for extended periods but others must learn to adapt.' He observes that many PwDs were 'brought up in their own silos', and the attrition rate is high particularly among those coming from rural areas to cities.

## Skilling Rural Youth with Disabilities

Few people have experienced the challenges of employment training for rural youth with disabilities more than Meera Shenoy, who founded Youth4Jobs (Y4J) in Hyderabad in 2012. Meera, who had set up India's first skilling mission in 2004, had imagined that since her team was already working in the rural areas, they simply had to top it with their understanding of disability. As she puts it, 'We thought, no great shakes, we can do it.' But when they set up their first training centre for rural youth with disabilities they found it 'incredibly difficult' for a number of reasons: the youth had low self-esteem, parents were set in their belief that their children with disabilities could not work, trainers were difficult to get and the best of them had gone abroad, and companies had to be convinced that it would work.

Back in 2004, the proactive government of Andhra Pradesh was the first to act on GOI's announcement of a Skill India Mission and had picked Meera to head it in the (then undivided) state. As a private sector person, she could think beyond the run-of-the-mill government schemes and design something that ensured job placements for uneducated or less educated rural youth. The mission was a World Bank-funded project called the Employment Generation and Marketing Mission (EGMM). She started with a budget of ₹1 crore; six years later when she left, she had taken it to ₹300 crore. What made EGMM an award-winning success were two things: they could create pilots and template it, hardwire the processes and scale them; and they could change mindsets.

By converting the unused government infrastructure into training centres, Meera set up 200 of them across the state. To convince the pessimistic bureaucrats that the model would work, she deliberately picked remote tribal areas so that once she demonstrated its success there, no one could doubt its efficacy elsewhere. The mission was mainly in, but not limited to, the service sector. The next challenge was to change the mindset of industries about hiring rural youth, and prove that degrees were not essential for retail sector jobs that entailed, for example, packing and stacking items.

Once the mission was on track and the bureaucrats had taken ownership of it, Meera moved on to consult with UNDP and World Bank across South East Asia, and then finally decided to work in the disability sector. The three-member team that had supported her in her government work came on board to make up the core team of Y4J. Meera says she set it up for two reasons: no one at that time in India was working on scale for rural youth with disabilities; and since 80 per cent of the world's PwD population is in developing countries such as India, a scaling model she created for India could be applied globally.

By the end of the first year the Y4J team had hardwired the model, fixed the template and were ready to start. Before they could approach funders their first funder approached them instead. Axis Bank, which had heard of their reputation in the government, came to them in 2013 and asked, 'What is your dream?' Meera recalls: 'The four of us looked at each other, and I just picked a number – I thought eight plus one is lucky – and I said 18 centres. And they said, done!'

Y4J created a plan to set up 18 centres over four years. Today they have 27 training centres in 18 states across the length and breadth of India and have won both national and international awards – for example in 2019, they were the Asia winners of the MIT Inclusive Innovation Challenge and also the winner of the prestigious QIMPRO Gold Standard Award in the Education category. They are also setting up satellite centres which will go even closer to the rural poor and link them with jobs in the local economy wherever possible.

They gradually increased the level of disability, altering the curriculum and strategy accordingly; starting with those with locomotor disabilities, they moved to the SHI and then to the VI and the blind. Although there are also persons with CP and DS who enrol at their centres, about half the youth are HI; they've placed about 650 of them in Amazon (mainly in Inventory and Warehousing) and 100 in Google.

Y4J encourages companies to measure the impact of their work. Their mantra has always been: 'Don't hire because of empathy or sympathy; hire because it helps your business.' Meera narrates how a business head of Amazon called them and said that if in a typical Business Process Outsourcing (BPO) firm an employee is able to do 50 to 60 forms in a day, Y4J youths are able to do 70 to 75. There are two of them there whom they call Centurions.

With around 20,000 rural youth with disabilities trained and 13,000 placed in a dozen sectors that include manufacturing, retail, BPO, hospitality, banking, travel and healthcare, Y4J's strategy has been to take one company from a fast growing industry, hardwire the processes and share that case study with other companies. The automobile industry was one of the first they broke into. When the chief executive officer of a French company asked them for a receptionist with a disability at their plant, Y4J went several steps further. The company sensitized the entire team at the plant, did job role mapping and took 25 Industrial Training Institute-qualified SHI persons for the shop floor. They made adaptations for safety: alarms with lights flashing, translucent jackets and so on. Three months later the company found that overall productivity had increased by 15 per cent. When one of the company managers moved to Pune, the first thing he did was hire people from Y4J's Pune training centre. After showcasing this example at various auto forums, 15 to 20 automakers came on board.

In the last two years, they have found jobs for 500 graduates with disabilities. But many rural youth have very little education. It is for them that Y4J devised a free, residential programme. The Work-Integrated Skills and English (WISE) programme trains them for two months in soft skills, English, computers, and through sector-specific modules. They are rolled out 'like in a conveyor-belt', Meera says; WISE turns out 10 employable youth every single day. It's a short term approach where they are put in entry-level jobs but are encouraged to enlist in IGNOU, the open university, to become graduates and move up the ladder.

But we know well by now that the number of PwDs who

enrol in colleges is pitifully low and even if they graduate through IGNOU, their chance of finding a job is about as high as finding the proverbial needle in the haystack. Y4J decided to embed themselves in universities and colleges through their Youth Connect initiative. They pioneered the concept of the Smart Inclusion Centre (SIC); the first in the series was set up in Kalasalingam University in Virudhunagar, Tamil Nadu. The SIC showcases assistive technology, assists PwDs in enrolling in college, sensitizes faculty and other staff, and encourages visiting companies to look at their talent pool of PwDs. In this way, not only are more rural PwD youth helped to enter college but they are also given job-linked skilling and customized training so that they are directly connected to employment.

Meera does not follow the train-the-trainer method. 'You may train the trainer and assume there's going to be a ripple effect, which may not happen according to your calculations. For me, the joy comes with working with each human being. I work 24/7; I just love what I do. I believe in what Mahatma Gandhi said: The only way to find yourself is to lose yourself in the service of others,' she says.

## Changing the Hiring Mindset

When we pull up our chairs for an interview with P. Rajasekharan and Shashaank Awasthi in Chennai, there are three other people in the room. They are sitting within arm's reach, concentrating hard on their computer screens. Wouldn't we be disturbing them? Raja says smoothly, 'They're deaf, so no problem.'

V-Shesh, the jobs company they founded in 2009, trains PwDs for employment and primarily works with the deaf and HI. Four in 1,000 children in India are born deaf, and V-Shesh's pathbreaking bridge English curriculum has already changed the learning dynamics for HI schoolchildren. Towards employment, they run courses of different durations where trainees are taught soft skills, interview skills, English and communication skills, and of course the skills in the domain in which they will work – whether it be in the hospitality, retail, Information Technology, or banking and finance sectors.

Shashaank points out that the three deaf individuals in the room are working live because their training was work-trial-based. In their 90-day training programme, they practiced this process which deals with balance sheets and financials, and now they were working for a potential employer. The person from the employer organization, who was at first doubtful whether deaf persons could do the job, saw their performance after 45 days and gained confidence in them.

The game changer here is the method of assessment. 'They've not been put in a room and asked, what is a balance sheet?' Shashaank says, underlining the need to find new ways of hiring PwDs. Raja adds, 'We're always challenging the convention when it comes to [human resources] practice and mainstreaming. Work-trial-based is the most effective way of selecting the candidate for a job. It's a simple yet superior way, but it's a struggle to get [the human resources department] to change their selection mode.' They stick to the same old 'funnel approach' with a standard test for every post, after which candidates are whittled down with Group Discussions and a series of interviews. 'Here the candidates are already filtered because they've done the job for you!' he says.

Shashaank and Raja, old friends working in the private sector who both wanted to enter the social sector, say they are 'in the behaviour-cum-mindset-change space'. Forty per cent of their team turned out to have some form of disability, and this happened 'very organically', Shashaank says. V-Shesh claims that their trainees are the highest paid in their education cohort, among persons with and without disabilities in this country.

When they have their initial meeting with their prospective

client, the hiring company, they don't know which way it will go. 'We are now completely prepared that it will be a blockbuster success, or it will end there and they will never call us again. Many times they say: Why don't you talk to our CSR? I say: No, I want you to hire.' With experience they've learnt not to begin by speaking about inclusion and sensitization, although they are important aspects. They 'get down to the nuts and bolts', says Shashaank.

For example, a client may tell them that their financial operations will be too difficult for a PwD to handle. Instead of arguing with him, the V-Shesh team will agree but then say, 'Just so you know, we have "x" number of banks who are our clients, and there's somebody we've trained who does trade finance processing there.' They follow this up by saying, 'We'll send you a list of 10 job descriptions they can handle.' The client, who had expected them to ask for charity, suddenly finds they're selling them an asset instead.

Richa Bansal, founder of Saarathee, has learnt the hard way how to pitch a business prospect to a client. Saarathee, a small Delhi-based company that supports its clients in their business development and customer engagement needs, consciously employs only PwDs – mainly VI. In the beginning, when she had a business development meeting, Richa would introduce Saarathee as a social impact organization that works with people with disabilities. 'But the first impression you would give everybody was that you are an NGO. Or that you will end up giving them sub-optimal work,' she realized.

She recalls the time she had gone to meet the largest company in the private home loan sector in Tier Two and Tier Three cities. The higher-ups had already discussed the business modalities with her and she went for her final meeting, which was with the business managing director – just a formality, she thought. The managing director asked her to tell him about Saarathee and she delivered her line about social impact and disability. 'Interesting,' he said, 'very nice, you're doing a good job. Let me sleep over it.' Richa told us wryly, 'He is still sleeping over it. Deep sleep it became!'

One of her friends helped her work on her pitch, and from then on she would say: 'We are moving towards digital transformation and losing the human connection. Saarathee is here to bridge the gap. We take pride in creating the human connect for your customers on your behalf.' The focus was solely on the value she provided and not on having hired PwDs. She took a 'don't ask, don't tell' approach. Not that she was hiding the fact; if the client found out and asked her why she hadn't mentioned that her employees were VI, she would reply – quite rightly – that it was just an incidental detail.

Shashaank says that over the decade, since they founded V-Shesh, two things have not changed. They still occasionally get the 'we will let you know' brush-off and – this is their pet peeve – almost everyone claims that 'we are an equal opportunity employer' despite having 'no access, no Sign Language, no nothing'.

'Our aspiration is for people to recognize PwDs as equals,' he says, 'with equal opportunities, equal rights, as equal participants with the same abilities and the same desires, to be served in the same way.'

# 20

# THE SELF-EMPLOYED AND THE WELL-PLACED

PWDS DO OFTEN HAVE A HARD TIME NAVIGATING THE world. But there are many who can manage to rise against all odds and prosper. There are individuals and organizations that help some of them achieve their full potential.

Many of these individuals and organizations have arrived at the following insight and work with it: A salaried job in a city may be the ambition of many an educated PwD, but what about those living in far-flung regions of the country who may not have academic qualifications? Self-employment can be a lucrative avenue for them.

There are many NGOs that develop the job skills of such PwDs in rural communities, and GiftAbled is one of them. What makes GifttAbled special, though, is that rather than focus on skill-training for the existing job market, they conduct region-specific and disability-specific skill training for women with disabilities and their caretakers in rural areas. These are vocational training centres with a difference. The skilling is followed by design and development to create products that are then marketed both online and offline. Local women handle end-to-end operations from sourcing material to product delivery.

'Gift made by PwDs' is generally a tag that's meant to tug at the heartstrings and open the purse strings. But that's not how GiftAbled operates. 'The charity model for products has completely vanished,' says co-founder Prateek Kaul. While the women are trained in basket weaving and making toys, bags and fridge magnets and in various other skills, product design and development become crucial since GiftAbled is competing with mainstream vendors. GiftAbled gets professional designers on board when required in order to refresh the products every six months, by coming up with new contemporary designs while strictly maintaining quality. To optimize the supply chain, they source raw material at the lowest price possible and aggregate as much as possible. 'Instead of one organization making 1,000 bags, we distribute raw material to 10 different organizations, ensure that quality is checked at their and our level[s], and give companies what they need. Over 80 per cent are repeat clients,' he says.

Marketing goes hand in hand with building brand awareness. GiftAbled leverages cost-effective technology as much as possible, because it has to be scaled up. For instance the e-commerce platform has to be accessible globally, so that anyone anywhere can view the products and their background details. At the back end, they use inventory management, collaborating and connecting with partners spread across the country. 'We have to minimize cost by using platforms, not only ours but what is available in the market. We have around 150+ unique products and had 500+ artists/artisans in 2018; this year (2019) we have1000+ artists,' Prateek explains.

GiftAbled, which is headquartered in Pune, Maharashtra, started by creating livelihood centres in Karnataka and now has a presence in six states. They hope to spread out to 10–15 states in the next three years to reach the most backward 50 to 100 districts in the country. 'Once the green shoots start emerging in those states, I'm pretty sure there will be a cascading effect and within

five years you will see the whole narrative has changed,' Prateek
says confidently. 'Sensitization should happen in those areas whose
names we are not aware of, where PwDs have zero possibility of
employment, government support is pitiful, and they are not even
sure of getting their pittance of a monthly pension of ₹200.'[40]

Their strategy is to partner with grassroots organizations that
have been around in the sector for decades and who have the assets
and the network but have yet to create a deep and broad impact.
'They're spreading themselves too thin,' says Prateek. 'When we
come in, things will start moving faster; what takes 10 years will
happen in two years.' His ultimate hope: 'GiftAbled may not be
required. Other entities will emerge and take over.'

Ideas flow irrepressibly from Shanti Raghavan's brain and before
you've had time to catch your breath, she has brought one to
fruition and come up with the next. This is the reason we find it
hard to slot Enable India, which she co-founded with husband
Dipesh Sutariya, into a single, fixed category. Is EI a pre-job
training centre for PwDs? Does it develop entrepreneurship? Is it a
placement agency? Yes and no, because it's so much more.

EI started with visual impairment and now covers 14
disabilities. With its footprint in 28 states, it works with 229 partner
organizations in 27 countries. On the website of this multi-award-
winning organization that has impacted over 2,20,000 PwDs and
their stakeholders, more staggering numbers are revealed – the
number of companies that have employed PwDs (600+ across 27

---

[40] This amount varies from state to state. Although the current Indira Gandhi
National Disability Pension Scheme stipulates a pension of ₹300–500
depending on the PwD's age, individual states may choose to give matching
grants or decide to give an extra amount through some other scheme
initiated by the state.

sectors), of PwDs who have been helped towards self-employment and entrepreneurship (1200+ trained of whom 65 per cent started their own ventures in 70 trades), of the leaders and managers who have been coached and mentored to foster inclusion in their companies (10,000+).

Training, whether short- or long-term, includes not just life skills and performance feedback but a community-service module. The idea is that once the training has instilled enough self-confidence, one must think beyond oneself and about the larger community. The power of volunteer work is, as Shanti puts it, 'When something is bigger than you, you rise to the challenge.' It builds resilience and you become a problem-solver. She gives the example of Haseena, a survivor of an acid attack who got placed in the Defence Research and Development Organization (DRDO). When Haseena first came in for training, she was so reticent that she would hide her face. As her confidence grew, and the time came for her to serve others, she went out to solicit donations for Bihar flood victims, standing in front of an unfamiliar audience proudly revealing her identity. 'We're building an alumni network,' says Shanti, 'a pool of people with the right calibre who can be change agents, self-advocates, and who will help us when we scale.'

When it comes to employment, the 'ayyo-paavam' attitude should not be a reason to take in a PwD, she says, adding sharply, 'And also, not because "he will be loyal". Is he a dog or what?' Of course, scores of forward-thinking companies who collaborated with EI have by now realized the capabilities of trained PwDs who have not only retained their jobs but progressed in their careers once a supportive job environment was created. 'Employers started using our word, workplace solutions,' Shanti says. Besides 'workplace solutions', 'includability' is another term coined by EI; in fact, they have copyrighted Includability Quotient (a measurement tool like IQ and EQ). They have brought out a job compendium identifying nearly 300 roles (to which more are being added), matching the disability to the job role – a ready reference for employers and potential PwD employees alike.

EI has always believed in pushing the envelope. They went to 25 visionary companies who were already employing PwDs and asked them, 'Are you ready for more? Take the severely disabled now.' The companies signed up for Mission 1000: to create 1,000 job opportunities in 1,000 days for those with severe, multiple and developmental disabilities. 'In the last one and a half years, we have created more than 630 opportunities for these companies to develop, incubate and then employ candidates,' Shanti says. 'More than 300 have got employed now, persons with intellectual disabilities like autism, Down Syndrome, the deaf-blind, etc.'

EI has customized programmes for PSUs and government departments to enable inclusion of PwDs recruited under the reservation quota. It has been connecting with universities to build skills of graduating students with disabilities, allying with NGOs and the government to scale employment and inclusion, and spreading awareness in the community by getting volunteers to go on treks or watch movies with VI persons and dance or play sports with PwDs.

A novel and award-winning idea of EI is Enable Vaani, their rural social networking platform, through which over 28,000 PwDs in 16 states are networking with a simple mobile phone. It's called Namma Vaani in Karnataka and Hamara Vaani in Hindi-speaking states. You just give a missed call to the number provided, and you get a call back from an IVR system, after which you choose from the menu to listen to or share information. PwDs, NGOs, companies, parents and other enablers use the platform for information on opportunities, employment, entrepreneurship, education, disability-related schemes and assistive aids. People leave questions to be answered, crowd-source solutions, post motivating stories and so on.

Then there's Enable Academy which offers courses, resources and publications online. What next? House of Change, Triveni the training and research institute... Shanti is brimming with ideas again!

———

It is Pankajam Sreedevi's last day as chief executive officer of ANZ Grindlay Bank when we meet her in 2019. Pankajam, who is the managing director of the Commonwealth Bank of Australia in India, was primarily responsible for kick-starting ANZ's employment of PwDs.

It was in 2009 that Raja of V-Shesh approached her and asked if she could employ five or six SHI graduates. Pankajam, who had always believed that corporates have a social responsibility (way before CSR became a buzz word), seized this as her first opportunity to fulfil it. Instead of formally putting up a proposal to the management, she decided to see for herself what V-Shesh was doing. So she simply upped and left for Chennai in her car.

Impressed by their work, she offered to hire a few SHI individuals 'as an experiment'; she ended up taking six into Institutional Operations. Since this was virgin territory, she had no idea of the modalities involved in making a work environment disabled-friendly so she sat down with Raja and his team and mapped out the life of an employee – from the moment they entered the office through the multiple aspects of their working day. They looked at how to sensitize other employees, from security and canteen staff to business continuity management, not forgetting the crucial fire drill.

Training the SHI employees was a challenge, Pankajam says, 'We had to build a vocabulary for them. For example the word "sanction" has no equivalent in Sign, and it is a crucial word in the banking industry! We hired a Sign expert who worked inside our premises for a month and a half. That was the start.' Then the entire organization pitched in. The current chief executive officer, who was then the head of institutional operations, was moved by the stories of how the SHI employees took pride in working here and removed the hiring freeze that existed then.

Three years earlier, ANZ had laid out the purpose of the organization: to shape a world where people and communities thrive. Pankajam latched onto it and said: This is our purpose; PwD is a community, and we need to have a replica of this community inside the organization. She got together a core team of employees, including managers who were 'passionate about community service', and decided that 10 per cent of those they hired would be PwDs – with CP, locomotor impairment and a few with autism. She was confident that the group she built would take the mission forward even in her absence.

Today the Bengaluru headquarter of ANZ has over 140 PwDs – one of the highest among corporate companies, says Pankajam, but she is not entirely satisfied, for it's a drop in the ocean after all. 'The pipeline is very small, of employable PwDs. All the organizations are after the same set of people who're employed,' she points out. Striking the same, rather pessimistic note, she says, 'Disability won't be a boardroom agenda, because it is not considered the most important thing for India, which has so many issues.' But she clarifies that her own stance is quite different, 'It is a major issue, to my mind. Every person has the right to be treated the same as others, [and] have the same benefits as others.'

———

On the surface, the employment for PwDs can bring nothing but benefits. As Raja of V-Shesh describes it, 'With every person who gets a job, we see the transformation. They move from being hungry for a job, to being grateful that we've opened our doors and given them training, to their becoming confident, and immediately their family also becoming confident. We see our trainees have their own bike, some of them are on TV, they get awards, get married, have children, support their parents.' Meera Shenoy of Y4J observes in a similar vein: 'A job for a youth takes the entire family out of poverty.'

But family relationships are never that simple. For PwDs in our country, the family tends to play a big part in their achievements or lack thereof. And since human beings come in many shapes and shades, one can see families responding in diverse ways to their newly employed members with disabilities. There could be tremendous support and pride; but there could also be selfishness and emotional blackmail.

When GiftAbled opened their first training centre in Bagalkot, parents were initially hesitant to send their daughters with disabilities there. Prarthana Kaul explains that it was not because they were worried about safety. 'Who will do the housework?' was the question. Domestic drudgery was all that the women were considered fit for. GiftAbled coaxed parents to 'just send her for two days'. And when the daughter made a purse and took it home to show her parents, they changed their minds. 'Now they encouraged her, you go and learn. Because they knew if she learnt she would also be able to earn her livelihood,' Prarthana says. And they would be able to contribute to the family income too, no doubt.

As often happens when PwDs move towards self-reliance, they feel an added sense of responsibility towards the family, which increases their self-esteem but can also be subtly exploited by family members. Meanwhile, there can be many twists and turns in their path to employment. An individual might be trained for a job and later realize that it is not the right fit. They might get a job and be unable to stick on, struggling to adapt to changes in their environment.

It's a mixed bag. PwDs have to learn to deal with the complexities of life and relationships, like anyone else. And nobody is entitled to pass a judgment on them or their families. As Shanti Raghavan puts it, 'Every PwD has their own journey of becoming independent. Every parent has their journey towards letting go.'

# 21

# THE SMALL BUT BIG EMPLOYERS

IT IS NOT ONLY COMPANIES THAT HAVE REALIZED THE capabilities of PwDs. There are individuals who, for varying reasons, have started ventures to consciously employ only or mainly PwDs.

Delhi-based Richa Bansal is someone who discovered the coolability of blind and VI individuals; she feels it's their sense of empathy that makes them successful telecallers. She set up Saarathee in December 2017 as a social enterprise to provide a livelihood to PwDs, but soon realized that the VI employees were filling a vital need in the market. In BPOs there's a disconnect between the customer and the brand, and Richa felt that PwDs would bring in a natural empathy and human connect to each conversation with the customers. Of Saarathee's 22 employees, most are VI, but there are also the HI and the orthopaedically disabled.

Richa spent nine years working for Vodafone, where she headed the telemarketing channel in Delhi. In between 2009 and 2010, her counterpart in Mumbai set up a telemarketing centre in the National Association for the Blind in Mumbai, which won accolades. He decided to take the initiative forward to other cities, and Richa was given the mandate of hiring 20 people with VI by tying up with the NAB India Centre in Hauz Khas. She received no guidelines, so she started from scratch, setting up a centre with 10 blind employees at NAB and deputing two or three VI employees each in other existing call centres in the city. Her measure of their success was based on the 'myopic view' that if an average person was able to do 12 to 15 closures in a month, VI employees were able to do at least 10.

Eventually Richa moved to the social sector and worked with Child Relief and You (CRY) for three years. She heard from the NAB director Shalini Khanna that the VI project was fizzling out. Then Richa took a break for personal reasons and started consulting for NAB, where Shalini included her in their day-to-day activities and encouraged her to find out for herself why the VI project had failed. Richa began to 'see the other side'. The VI employees had been given a job opportunity but was it accessible? Was the right environment provided? Did they feel they belonged? The answers were all 'no'.

Richa decided to take the plunge and start out on her own. Shalini introduced her to Pavithra Y.S. of Vindhya, whom she met in Bengaluru to seek her counsel on how to set up Saarathee. 'She was very kind, spent a full day with us and from that day onwards she became my advisor and mentor. The first eight months were a huge struggle. There were a lot of out-of-pocket expenses,' she says, recounting how she started with six to seven people. But there was attrition. While she was interviewing them, they would ask her questions in turn, for they didn't trust her and were suspicious of her intentions. Their attitudes ranged from a sense of entitlement to extremely low self-esteem. Pavithra was a huge support in those difficult times.

'I don't look at them as "*hai bechaara*"', says Richa, who hired people in whom she saw 'a hunger to grow'. She started rotating them through the different processes involved in a call centre. Customer service is the easiest, since it only requires speaking to the customer in a courteous manner; in the lead conversion process, you not only educate but convince the person; more complex processes involve hiring the seller, managing the customer's account and so on. Soon after hiring them, she would throw them in the deep end, allowing them to stumble over the most complex processes. Then she would make them handle the easy processes, and they would sail through with soaring confidence, ready to be groomed into team leaders. The trainer does a mind mapping of the trainee – a one-on-one where their emotional state is assessed with questions about their earlier life and aspirations for the future.

'When you spend time with people you understand their competencies and their skill set, and it allows you to place them accordingly,' she says. For instance one has to allocate appropriate responsibilities after identifying who works best individually and who is a good team worker. The organization's manageable size is an advantage; another is that since everyone is a PwD, they feel part of a community. To further the sense of belonging, Richa takes them for new business development meetings and client review meetings, and organizes a *baithak* (meeting) on the first of every month (a concept she picked up from Goonj and is on the lines of 'Coffee with Pavithra'). From 9.30 a.m. to 11 a.m. they all get together and each one shares a minimum of two things happening in their lives, beginning with Richa. Then they discuss work; she shares with them news about any businesses they are about to lose or close, and this transparency makes them feel included.

'I want more and more people to use Saarathee as an example,' says Richa. 'I intend to create a model which can be replicated by corporates to create the right environment for PwDs to work.'

---

One of the few remaining small industries in the bylanes of Adugodi in Bengaluru is Ganesh Mani's Jehovah Jirah. It's a 20 ft x 20 ft space (with another 20 x 20 as a mezzanine floor) where he employs PwDs – men and women with various disabilities that he rattles off, 'polio, mental retardation, cerebral palsy, blind, spinal cord injury after accident, one-hand-user.' He has 15 on the rolls but has work for only five when we visit; he has given the others a temporary break because no work was coming in for them. 'I call it summer holidays!' he jokes. He also gives piecework to 25 other PwDs in the vicinity of Adugodi and Koramangala.

Ganesh, who contracted polio at age five, had no schooling to speak of. After both of his parents died early and his siblings got busy with their own families, Ganesh realized he would have to fend for himself. For eight months he travelled to the Peenya Industrial Estate every day, knocking on the doors of various industries for a job and returning empty-handed. Finally he struck it lucky with the owner of a precision tools industry.

Since Ganesh knew no skill, he told his employer he was willing to try anything. He learnt his job through observation and imitation. In fact he was such a good student that he became an expert tool-and-die-maker. 'I was operating CNC (computer numerical control) cutting machines,' he reminisces. He would slog for 10–12 hours a day, often carrying on until midnight. His boss gave him a room to stay on the premises, and he would come home only on weekends. He earned enough to start building a house of his own five years ago.

Ganesh worked in the precision tools factory for five years and his last salary was ₹25,000 a month. Then he announced that he wanted to leave. His boss kicked up a huge fuss because he obviously didn't want to let go of such a dedicated workhorse. We ask Ganesh the reason why he decided to give up such a well-paid job. He says it was because he had become the cynosure of all PwDs in his neighbourhood. They kept asking him: Can you find me also a job like yours?

Ganesh quit only to attempt to help others like him stand on their own feet. He started the Koramangala Angavikalara Okkutta (an organization for those with physical disabilities), finding sponsors for school fees for children with disabilities, helping PwDs find employment, conducting life skills awareness programmes, procuring subsidies through the MLA fund, getting disability vehicles sanctioned by the government and so on. He was president of the organization for one year, after which he handed it over to other PwDs.

In 2015, Ganesh started Jehovah Jirah, which means 'God will provide' in Hebrew. 'I started my industry with two feet by two feet,' he says, and when we look quizzical he explains that in the beginning he had bought a single die machine which he installed in his house (in the 2 x 2 space) and taught others to use. Mobility India, which had been a great source of help all along, helped him find clients, and pretty soon he had moved to his current space. He bought other kinds of equipment and diversified to screen printing on cloth bags, making packing covers, moulds for wooden heels for the Jaipur Foot for amputees, areca bowls and plates, and so on.

Today, through the Swabhimaan Trust, he distributes monthly rations for the old and disabled, and provides free food every day at lunchtime and dinnertime. As we speak, surrounded by bags stuffed with old clothes collected from nearby apartments and waiting to be distributed to the needy, three employees sit on the floor and sort out and fold chocolate wrappers – Ranjitha (20) and Lakshmi (25) have a physical disability, and David has ID. There are 25 others making paper bags (from old newspapers) in their houses and earning ₹10,000–15,000 a month by selling them.

Ganesh has a meeting with Dell the following day to set up a car wash arrangement called Car Care, where PwDs could earn by washing the cars of company employees. (The proposal met with success, we later learnt.)

'Dignity, not charity' is his last word on the subject.

———

Pavithra Y.S.'s is a rare story of having made the impossible possible through pluck, drive, a kind of naive enthusiasm and the best of intentions. She firmly believes that if she and her husband Ashok Giri had listened to level-headed business advice and drawn up a carefully thought out plan in 2006, they would never have started Vindhya e-Infomedia, a company that today has an annual turnover of over ₹25 crore and a 1,600-strong workforce, most of whom are socially disadvantaged and/or have different disabilities. When Pavithra says they are all members of the same family she is not mouthing the sort of platitude often displayed in corporate ads. 'I think I know most of their names,' she tells us confidently. 'I know their backgrounds, their likes and dislikes, their hobbies.'

Sitting in her office, all four of its walls plastered with framed awards, we listen to the fascinating story of how Ashok wooed and won her over. Their families were reluctant to give the nod to an inter-caste union, but they finally came around. After her marriage, she knew she wanted to 'do something' but she had no idea what. Doting husband Ashok, who was in sales, said he would back whatever plan she came up with. For a while she held summer camps for children at home, but at the back of her mind was the notion of 'helping someone', which she says she probably imbibed from her doctor-mother who used to run a small clinic in a slum.

Meanwhile, Pavithra became a mother herself. Their daughter Vindhya ('She is my first daughter, the company is my second daughter!' Pavithra says) was a few months old when one evening, as she and Ashok were standing in the balcony of their house, she saw a man with crutches struggling to cross the road. 'I remember it was raining. I saw him and I said: I want to help that man,' she remembers, even as she insists that it was no grand epiphany; it was a simple thought that sprang spontaneously to her mind.

Ashok said that he had money to buy a car. She told him to give it to her instead. Carrying her infant, she scouted for office space in Basaveshwar Nagar (the neighbourhood in Bengaluru where they have been living and working till date) and found one on 4th Main, a stone's throw from their current premises. She confessed to the amiable landlord that she had a limited budget, so he lowered the rent knowing that she was going to use it for a good cause. 'It was on the first floor, (had) no lift, with stairs outside the building – for the disabled – imagine! I knew nothing about disability,' she admits. She put up a banner that announced jobs for PwDs, and people began to trickle in.

In July 2006, she started with two employees with physical disabilities doing data entry. Many among the core team have remained with the company. E. Veerabhadra remembers seeing the banner and waiting at the foot of the stairs for Pavithra to arrive. She came, carrying three-month-old Vindhya, and asked him if he would be able to go up the steps. He scooted upstairs ahead of her. Yashodha, who is deaf, is another veteran employee who recalls (in Sign, interpreted by one of the employees, Sripriya) that when she joined the company Vindhya was a babe-in-arms. 'And now she is taller than me!' she remarks. Yashodha and Pavithra initially communicated by writing on slips of paper, but they knew it wouldn't work for long. 'So I told her you teach me my job, and I'll teach you my language,' Yashodha says. Pavithra says she started with the alphabet, moved on to the 'shortcuts' and was able to pick up the basics of Sign in 10 days. From then on, all new employees were taught Sign; today, most of them know enough for basic communication.

In the beginning, Vindhya got a few data entry orders through word of mouth. Their first large order was from a neighbourhood florist who asked Pavithra to convert his list of 5,000 clients into a database. 'Database?' she had asked him. 'What's that?' She now frequently breaks into laughter while tracing her own learning curve for us. She sourced trained personnel through the government vocational training centre and a few NGOs. In two years the company's strength had increased to around 15.

But then she faced a crisis. Orders started drying up. She could no longer afford to retain the employees on their monthly salary of ₹2,000. But when she shared the news with them, they unanimously declared that they would stick on until business improved. They continued to come to office every day, and she would conduct skill-enhancement sessions for them. Pavithra brought them food from home, and at lunchtime all the employees would share whatever was in their lunchboxes. The hard times they shared created deep personal bonds, and that's how the feeling of 'one family' seeped into everything she did later.

During the crisis, Pavithra began to shoot off letters to foundations and one found its way into the inbox of Wipro's chief training officer (CTO), N. Balasubramanya. Coincidentally, the company had just planned to outsource the data entry of its employee records. The CTO said he would send Vindhya 200 files of their employees' records, for a start, and if they did a good job he would send 1,00,000 files. Pavithra could hardly believe her ears. It was the turning point she had dreamed of. Obviously, she would need to hire more people – something that she gladly did.

Since the Wipro breakthrough, Vindhya has never looked back. Today it is located across three floors each in three buildings and provides a spectrum of services – data entry and management, call centre support, onsite deployment and accessibility testing – and caters to industries that range from banking, finance and telecommunication to manufacturing and healthcare. Over 62 per cent of its workforce comprises employees who are missing limbs, deaf, blind or deaf-blind, have polio, or are with disabilities such as CP, borderline autism and dwarfism. 'They complement each other, become aware of one another's disabilities,' Pavithra points out, recalling former employees who were acid attack survivors and women with hirsutism (hair growing all over the body, including the face). Since none of the employees stare or make others feel awkward, they feel completely at home here. Besides Pavithra's daily exchanges with employees, she meets them over the monthly 'Coffee with Pavithra' sessions. Around 30 people, a mix of old and new employees, sit on the floor in a circle and 'open up, share life journeys, inspirations, [and] ambitions'.

Another major thrust that Pavithra gave the company was the recruitment of PwDs from rural and/or underprivileged backgrounds. It all started in 2007 when she visited a rural government college and found people looking for employment. To test the waters, she and one of her managers who was from Shivamogga went there to hold a PwD employment camp, and people turned up in such large numbers that she knew this was the way forward. From then on, Vindhya has been systematically networking with NGOs in villages across India to hold rural camps and hire PwDs. Human resources and operations team managers have gone recruiting not only to towns and villages in the southern states but also to 'Assam, Punjab, Jharkhand, West Bengal, Odisha, Maharashtra, [and] Gujarat' – Pavithra runs out of names and ends with 'every part of the country!' This is why you will hear call centre operators in Vindhya speaking no less than 11 languages as they handle inbound and outbound calls, validating bank account details, welcoming new customers, upgrading data packages, conducting feedback surveys and doing a host of other operations.

'Ask them what they need' is Pavithra's mantra. A young woman with OI would find it impossible to work during her period, so she was given five days off every month. 'Today she is working for ANZ,' we are updated. One woman with dwarfism found it difficult to reach her desk; an extra cushion on her chair helped.

Pavithra noticed that new mothers got no support after delivery so she started a crèche that operates on the terrace of one of their buildings. Vindhya also reimburses the school fees of one child in each employee's family, provides interest-free loans and assistive aids. 'Close to 50 are getting educated this way,' Pavithra informs us.

'We will never say no to two things: any kind of job that comes our way, and anyone who walks in for a job,' Pavithra says. Does the man have only one hand? He can do scanning. What about the man with no hands? Vijay was one such. He told her, 'But I have feet, ma'am.' And today you can see him dexterously operating the keyboard with his feet and toes.

Pavithra describes her plan to set up India's largest campus for PwDs. People can get trained, get employed and benefit from assisted living – all in one place. They've been offered space by the Andhra government in Hyderabad and they're 'in execution mode now'. 'Lot of dreams,' she says gently with a smile. The smile hides a steely determination, though, and so one is fairly certain that her dreams will have no choice but to meekly follow her orders and be transformed into reality.

# 22

# THE EMPLOYABILITY OF MINDS
# WITH DISABILITY

INDIA HAS NOT FULLY MINED THE VALUABLE RESERVES buried in those with intellectual and developmental disabilities. When it comes to employers – and particularly the country's biggest employer, the government – they provide them with only limited and unimaginative job options. For example, most of us in India treat persons with ID (MR, to use the inappropriate but official term) as if they can't think for themselves and their opinions don't matter. Therefore we are fixed in the 'they should be grateful to get any kind of job' mode and don't bother to ask them: 'Are you happy? Are you satisfied?'

When I (C.K. Meena) ask Rajesh H.R., a 34-year-old who has ID, whether he likes his hospital job, he unhesitatingly replies that he is happy there and has made friends at work. I meet him at his old school, Sahas in Madikeri, in 2019. He is eating a samosa when a teacher asks him to speak to me. Immediately, he hastens towards the empty chair opposite mine. I urge him to finish eating but he sits bolt upright, plate in hand, unsmiling, waiting for my questions which he tackles earnestly as if he were answering an oral exam.

His father, S.D. Raghava, used to work in an automobile service station and then opened a provision store. Rajesh is the oldest among his siblings. His sister is a nurse in a local hospital, and his brother works in the panchayat Block Development Office (BDO). After school, Rajesh worked for a while in the Nambike shop started and run by Meena Cariappa. He says that he had been employed for the past five years as a ward boy in Ashwini Hospital where he starts work at 7.30 a.m. and knocks off at 6.30 p.m.

What does his work involve? He ticks off his duties one by one: collecting out-patient slips at the OPD, ferrying patients in wheelchairs to the X-Ray room and other points where they need to go, helping carry them in stretchers, putting 'tablet and syrup' (medicines) in paper covers and stapling them at the pharmacy, helping with 'dressing' (bandaging wounds), switching the generator on and off when the power goes and comes... He seems to be a general factotum, and his former teachers tell me that he is the most popular and 'wanted' person in the hospital.

His weekly day off used to be Friday, but now it's Wednesday, he informs me. And what does he do on his day off? He likes playing volleyball. He used to play it in school. Cricket too. As an afterthought he tells me that he has won a gold medal for volleyball. I cry out involuntarily, 'Where? You should have told me about it right in the beginning!' Then I bite my tongue, because it is a stupid statement – the kind that is made by those who value typical 'achievements', the ranks and awards and promotions that average people boast of. The gold medal is in his house, he says. He won it in 2007 playing volleyball at the Shanghai Special Olympics.

More valuable than a medal, for Rajesh, was the job that gave him dignity and satisfaction.

## The Dandelion Model

Persons with a DD such as autism are completely alien territory for most of us. The situation isn't vastly different in the West when it comes to autism. Take the pioneering Thorkil Sonne who founded Specialisterne (in translation, The Specialists) in Copenhagen, Denmark in 2003. 'I had never met an adult with autism with a job,' he says. Employers were averse to hiring those diagnosed with ASD, 'and if you tell a recruiter you have ASD plus ADHD, he'll be scared as hell'.

Thorkil's own journey with autism began when the youngest of his three sons, Lars (who is now 24), was diagnosed with infantile autism when he was just two and a half. Thorkil began to read up on the subject, but he gave up after reading 'one and a half books on autism' because the books could only explain what a kid cannot do, not what he can. Thorkil likes how the Chinese refer to people with autism as 'self-closed people'. The root of autism is auto and ism, self and direction. And they are certainly self-directed.

Thanks to the welfare state, Lars went to a special school, but the system also allows PwDs to live on welfare, says Thorkil, and he didn't want his son to lead an unproductive life. He would focus on what persons with autism could do, rather than what they couldn't. Specialisterne's logo is a symbol of coolability: the dandelion. It is a weed in the wrong environment, but a nutritious and medicinal herb in the right one. The four-member team running Specialisterne began to identify the coolabilities of persons with autism and employed them as consultants in mainly software testing, programming and data entry for both corporate and government sectors.

After Thorkil read *The Power of Unreasonable People* by John Elkington and Pamela Hartigan, he came to a realization: 'I am an unreasonable man!' Only such a man would start The Specialisterne Foundation with the goal of creating 1 million jobs for persons with autism. Now there are 13 Specialisternes worldwide. In fact, Specialisterne has inspired several corporates to hire people with ASD, including IBM which aimed to hire 300 people with autism globally by 2020. Thorkil says that over 100 big and small companies are keen to hire persons with autism and over 100 different jobs had been identified for them – including pig farming, since many of them love being with animals.

How does he identify their coolabilities? Thorkil explains the process of matching skills with jobs: It's a four-week programme to learn about the individual and see beyond their medical 'description'. To hire eight people, 10 potential candidates are selected as a group and given tough tasks.

In the first week, they get used to the workspace. They find their individual comfort zones. 'Parents are confined to the lobby!' Thorkil explains. In the second week, the team finds its comfort zone; they have to work together. In the third week and fourth weeks their personal business profiles are identified. Each is given a mentor or buddy – someone to go to for doubts and questions. They get a safe line to a professional who knows about their anxiety and issues. They are assessed on their

- motivation,
- work ability,
- professional skills (related to the job description; for example, computer skills),
- specialist skills (one 'coolability'/set of skills is expected from the candidate) and
- shared skills (a playful environment is created so that people with ASD can also work in teams).

'We want to mainstream this model,' says Thorkil, '[and] expand the spectrum of normality.'

A *New York Times* article in 2012 on Thorkil and Lars had the headline: 'The Autism Advantage'. In 2018, The Specialisterne Foundation collaborated with the United Nations Department of Public Instruction (UNDPI) to organize the Autism Advantage Luncheon at the UN Headquarters in New York. The aim of the event was to promote the employment of persons with autism (PwAs) globally and encourage employers to provide an inclusive work environment.

The Autism Advantage Luncheon 2019 was held at SAP Labs India in Bengaluru following the annual Autism at Work Summit. The Luncheon was attended by over 30 employers, as well as NGOs, teachers, parents, government representatives and other stakeholders.

Thorkil inspired V.R. Ferose to start the AaW programme at SAP Labs India in 2012. It was made global in 2013, and there are now 160 PwAs in SAP worldwide. In the programme, ability is matched to a specific job. After training, each PwA is placed with a buddy, a mentor and a job coach where necessary. The manager is a key to the process. Speaking at the Autism Advantage Luncheon 2019, Ferose says, 'We should make the success of the AaW programme a management tool to assess managers. Managers should be incentivized. They should be both compassionate and outcome-driven.' As Thorkil mentioned earlier, rather than an employee with autism being fired for not performing, the question should be why they haven't performed. The manager who handles PwAs develops skills that are a means to assess how well his/her department functions.

Through a pre-recorded video played during the luncheon, Professor Rob Austin emphasizes how employing PwAs makes good business sense. 'Solutions for neurodiversity benefit all employees,' he says. Creating a meaningful workplace for neurodiverse people makes the workplace meaningful for all employees.

Vibha Krishnamurthy of Ummeed Child Developmental Centre in Mumbai speaks of 'Working towards the workplace', how youngsters with autism can be trained early on in life to enter the workplace by addressing three areas: self-help, self-advocacy and self-awareness. Developing independent living skills (broken down into smaller steps) is important in the self-help journey, she says. Household chores can teach them executive function skills such as planning, organizing, managing time and completing tasks.

## Providing the Right Environment

Other than tech companies, there are a few large companies in India, such as Lemon Tree Hotels and the Big Bazaar chain of stores, that have won awards for actively employing PwDs including some with autism. But Merry Barua of AFA in Delhi, says, 'The vast majority of PwAs currently in India are in sheltered or supported employment because the environment is not ready for them.'

Merry, who founded AFA over 20 years ago, and is primarily responsible for making autism a talking point in the country, observes that there aren't enough sheltered workplaces to meet the needs of the population. There is supported employment where PwAs have job coaches and are eased into their jobs with continued support. AFA does sensitization with organizations and also provides some on-the-job strategies not only for PwAs but for their coworkers and others at the workplace.

Employers want those who don't have any 'behaviours' (their word for anything that doesn't gel with 'normal' office decorum), says Merry, and there have been cases where these 'behaviours' have cost PwAs their jobs. 'It cannot be just the PwA who has to change. Society and the environment also have to change. I don't mean only acceptance; they must provide the assistive survival strategies that PwAs need, just as you provide ramps for wheelchairs and tactile pathways for the VI,' she argues. Once you've employed them you have to provide the supports they need, she points out, 'You can't just say: "You have to be quiet, you have to sit and work." Give them the vision to know how to do it, and they'll do it. Put them on jobs they have an aptitude for, let them work for the hours they are able to perform.'

Merry has also noticed a kind of herd mentality when it comes to employers. It's a 'follow the leader' approach, she says. 'SAP is IT so everybody in the IT sector wants to employ. Not every kid with autism is IT savvy. In Delhi, because Lemon Tree has been employing PwAs (we've been working with them for four years), only the hospitality sector here wants to employ them.'

―――

A small player in the PwA employment arena with relatively modest aims is CanBridge Academy in Chennai.

When Kavitha Krishnamurthy realized that her 17-year-old son Ananth Kavitha Ganesh would be leaving his autism school (We Can) within a year, the question 'what next?' begged for an answer. She looked around her and came to a conclusion: 'There really is nothing.' There were places that offered vocational training for those with multiple disabilities, but they did not successfully cater for those with autism, especially so for the children and adults at We Can who were on the severe end of the spectrum and mainly non-verbal.

At We Can there were no academic 'levels'; the students were not geared towards exams and even NIOS subjects were beyond their depth. Ananth's seniors had either dropped out or, at ages 18–22, were just sitting at home. Kavitha astutely observed that since middle class parents like her don't expect their children to start earning at 18, and they put them into at least four more years of regular education, it shouldn't be any different for kids with autism.

CanBridge Academy was set up by Kavitha and a group of other parents with the goal of offering 'a bouquet of training opportunities'. 'We say it's a college,' Kavitha says. Their four-year programme is 'a preparation for life rather than just a vocation'.

They started with two skills: cooking and weaving. Weaving is a carryover from We Can, which had started teaching this skill in collaboration with Shuttles and Needles, a small enterprise that sources imported table looms and imported yarn to popularize weaving. Many kids and adults on the spectrum seemed to take to the fairly simple and repetitive technique of weaving, and the colours and patterns held their interest. CanBridge brought in the professional element by ensuring quality control and tying up with a designer who would use the woven material to design products. 'A skill that the school was teaching them got translated into a viable employment opportunity,' Kavitha says. The weavers, who comprise students at We Can and two other special schools in Chennai, are paid by the yardage and at the end of the year they get a share of profits too.

CanBridge has four students in 2019 when we meet Kavitha. None of them are verbal, and three are keen on cooking – not least because they are all foodies! We Can had given them the prep skills – the chopping, grinding, grating, etc. – but they were only used to microwave cooking, making sandwiches and other dishes that could be assembled. 'We're taking them to the next level – stovetop cooking. We started with popcorn and now they've started making their own lunch – dal, rice and veg – and take turns to do each so that each learns them all,' Kavitha explains. One boy who has great cooking skills is interning with a *maami* (the Tamil word for an old aunt) who is in the catering business and lives two houses away from him.

Students are given one hour of the arts each day: music, movement, theatre and visual arts. 'We find that expressive arts are helping them a lot in managing themselves. It acts like a pressure valve, [it] brings equilibrium,' she says. Fitness is a major component, so they are taken to the gym too. CanBridge is also building a communication programme with computer-based learning. The kids are allowed to explore and find their level in each of these components depending on their interests and abilities. Kavitha says that one boy loved running so CanBridge would get him someone of his age to act as a buddy and run with him on the beach twice a week. Another boy enjoys movement and music so he gets individual sessions; even if he doesn't take it up as a profession, it will at least be something that keeps him engaged for a period of time.

CanBridge's goal is to give students seven to eight hours of meaningful activity every day. They choose from four or five options in fitness, a vocation of their choice which they work at for two hours a day, and an hour of whichever expressive art they choose. It's a small beginning, but then, small beginnings have led to sizeable results in the past.

## Making a Living through Art

Anima Nair, who co-founded Sense Kaleidoscopes with artist Akshayee Shetty, says firmly: 'We are not an art therapy centre. It's a vocational centre where persons with autism can earn a living through art.'

Akshayee, a graphic designer who has a master's in art, design and architecture in education from the University of Glasgow, teamed up with Anima, the software professional we have met before in this book, to start Sense Kaleidoscopes in Bengaluru in 2013. (Anima's son Pranav was diagnosed with ASD.) And they've certainly been going places of late. Artworks by its students have sold for handsome sums in the open market and have been invited to international exhibitions.

The curriculum at Sense Kaleidoscopes is geared towards children with autism. In one stream, they receive basic academic training in math, English and science. The other has creative arts and vocational training. Arts practitioners come in to teach the students specific arts: painting (including oils on canvas), screen printing (marbling and other techniques), pottery, sculpture and carpentry, besides theatre and yoga.

The students' art was first exhibited in local venues and then got a tremendous fillip in 2019 when the works of nine students were exhibited at the Outsider Art Show supported by the Kochi Biennale Foundation. There's been no stopping them since. The premier international Outsider Art Fair got wind of them and invited them to the exhibition in Paris in October 2019 and New York in January 2020. In Paris, 22 works by Rohit Anand (19), Ayush Bhambhani (20), Kalash Cariappa (17), Adarsh Shetty (23) and Pranav Nair (19) were exhibited, but they couldn't exhibit in New York for lack of funds.

Facets of the autistic personality such as sensory processing disorders, obsessive-compulsive nature and non-linear thinking inspire the students to create vibrant, highly imaginative, breathtakingly detailed paintings. Anima said emphatically that they didn't want '*ayyo paavam* pity sales'; the art must be bought for its quality. Renowned artist Bose Krishnamachari bought a painting by one of their students. Playback singer Usha Uthup's daughter Anjali bought a painting by Shashwath Ghosh, and featured him and his family on Episode 2 of her YouTube channel India Diary.[41] Usha Uthup was so impressed that she wanted to meet the artist, so when she came to Bengaluru for a performance she fixed an appointment to meet him.

Akshayee's deep, instinctive connection with kids with autism enables her to locate and tap their creative vein, and guide them towards their finest work. When Ayush's mother Preeti Bhambhani brought him to the centre, they wondered what to do with him because he was on the extreme end of the spectrum. His sensory

---

[41] 'Autism and the Spectrum – India Diary Episode 02', Sense Kaleidoscopes (a Unit of Ayathi Trust), YouTube, 2 January 2020.

difficulties made it impossible for him to hold a pen, so where was the question of his doing math or art? They tried giving him a fatter pen, but it was of no use. It was Akshayee who finally had an epiphany: instead of a thicker pen, why not give him an even thinner one than normal – a Rotring pen that architects use? Ayush took to the Rotring pen immediately. He started drawing intricately patterned illustrations, and today his paintings sell for enough to sustain a livelihood.

Anish Victor, who offers theatre classes, noticed that an almost catatonic boy would respond when music was played. Anima recalls how the boy was otherwise totally unresponsive and withdrawn, with a vacant look in his eyes. Music brought him alive. Then there are those who cannot bear sound. One boy is so disturbed by ringtones that the very instant he hears a mobile ring, he hits out at whoever is in front of him.

Shashwath has had a fixation on microphones ever since he was little; in fact his mother told Anjali that the first word he uttered was not 'Ma' but 'mike'! Microphones always enter his paintings and are often their focal point. Adarsh Shetty specializes in portraiture, Shreyas draws cartoons – every student has their own predilection.

When students from Sense Kaleidoscopes had their first ever exhibition at the Rangoli Metro Art Gallery on MG Road in Bengaluru, some parents did not want their children's art to be part of the group because they feared the stigma of the 'autism' tag. One hopes that the achievements of the unique, young artists of Sense Kaleidoscopes will dispel such misgivings in the future.

# 23

# EASING THEIR DAY-TO-DAY LIFE

WHEN WE SPEAK OF PWDS, WE OFTEN CONCENTRATE ON 'important' issues such as education, employment and entitlements, as we have done in the previous few chapters. It is now time to ask: Aren't their physical needs and desires equally important?

Average people like us tend to gloss over the right to a social life; like everyone else, PwDs too want to keep in touch with the world around them. They might wish to wander in parks, go shopping, eat at a restaurant, go on a date, travel to a tourist spot, watch plays and movies, visit museums, enjoy music and dance performances...not to mention have sex, find partners and have children.

'Recreation' has not been overlooked by the RPwD Act; in fact, it is part of the title of Chapter V. Section 29 requires the government to promote and protect the right of all PwDs to 'have a cultural life and to participate in recreational activities equally with others'. It includes 'making art accessible' to them, having Sign Language interpretation or subtitles for TV programmes, enabling them to participate in 'scouting, dancing, art classes, outdoor camps and adventure activities' and even envisions the 'establishment of a disability history museum'!

While we wait for that golden dawn to break in the horizon

when all these grand plans materialize, it will benefit us to live in a PwD's skin for a few moments. We hardly realize, as we go about our daily business, how much we take our surroundings for granted – unaware of what might be obstacles for PwDs. Sometimes, they are little things that have to be brought to our notice.

Ashwin Karthik loves to dress fashionably. The problem is that clothes and accessories in his size are only to be found in the children's section. And kiddie colours and patterns look ridiculous on a grown-up, right? Even an Extra Small for adults won't work for him. He has a form of CP that has not only immobilized his limbs but also constricted his physique. People with dwarfism also face the same predicament. Ashwin prefers a certain cut of jeans, and he covets ankle boots with zippers. But these things aren't designed for children, while the adult section doesn't carry them in his size. If there are clothes designed for Plus Size adults, why not for Minus Size?

Now try to imagine organizing your romantic evenings around the daily schedule of a third party. This is what used to happen with Anita Sharma, a wheelchair user living in Jaipur. When asked out on a date, she couldn't fix the day and time until she had checked when it would be convenient for a friend to transport her. 'My dates had to be confined to weekdays because I had to depend on someone else to take me,' she says. All that changed when she learnt driving, but we'll get to that part later.

When was the last time you saw a customer with a disability in a restaurant? In 2015, when an eatery in a mall in the nation's capital denied entry to wheelchair user Nipun Malhotra, he didn't take it lying down. He kicked up so much dust, the news reached the ears of so many influential people that the Delhi government was forced to order a magisterial inquiry into the incident. Nipun then got in touch with Zomato, the restaurant-finder and food delivery app, and suggested that they add a 'disabled-friendly' filter to the app. Zomato took it up immediately and introduced the 'wheelchair access' feature across six metros.

The problem doesn't just go away, though. Even as recently as 2019, a wheelchair user circulated an E-mail petition on Change.org about a Mumbai restaurant that blocked her entry. She surveyed other restaurants in the metro that claimed to be accessible on the Zomato app and found that they were not. The app takes the 'accessible' claims at face value and doesn't investigate whether the restaurants actually comply.

More and more PwDs in India are discovering the potential of online campaigns, and some of their causes relate to their social life. In 2019, for example, Arunima, an organization for children with autism and DD, started a campaign on Change.org for equal access for PwDs to swimming pools. The management of the pool that Arunima used for their children's swimming sessions kept rescheduling the children's slots; one of the reasons that the management had the audacity to give for doing so was that other clients were 'not comfortable' swimming with 'these people'. Another online petition was related to access to venues for films and plays. BookMyShow responded by listing wheelchair-accessible venues on its website and app.

## Online Access for PwDs

Digital technology has opened up the world for PwDs in India. There are numerous offerings on disability uploaded by PwDs on YouTube. And then there's Radio Udaan. This online radio channel for PwDs launched in 2014 is conceptualized, produced and broadcast by blind and VI persons. It has listeners in at least 115 countries.

Among websites, *Newz Hook* stands out for being both exclusive and inclusive. India's first (and to date only) website and app that exclusively carries disability-related news and features, it is also inclusive in that it is fully accessible. What this means is that it follows Web Content Accessibility Guidelines so that it can be used by persons with any kind of disability. WCAG's principles are: the user must be able to perceive the content through whichever sense they possess, navigate the site (operate the interface), understand the information and access the content as technologies advance.

The content on *Newz Hook* is written in simple English. The website supports the use of screen readers for the blind, has Sign videos in which a reporter interprets the news in ISL and allows the user to have a high-contrast view, and increase the size of the text so that senior citizens and people with low vision can read it.

*Newz Hook* was an initiative of BarrierBreak, a web accessibility company founded by Shilpi Kapoor which has been working towards inclusion since 2004. *Newz Hook* was recognized by the prestigious Zero Project as an Innovative Practice in 2018. When Shilpi founded *Newz Hook* in 2015, she reached out to Shai Venkatraman to take on the role of editor. Shai had covered public health when working for NDTV for 16 years and found that the mainstream media's coverage of disability was limited to campaigns and protests.

Shai tells us that in the beginning they were only curating stories from other sources, but as the site gained traction among PwDs, corporates, NGOs and educational institutions, and their social media presence grew, they were able to start carrying only their own exclusive stories three years ago. They have only one full-time correspondent based in Kochi who covers southern India; but story ideas and stories flow in from contributors, most of whom are PwDs. Since 2019, *Newz Hook* has struck out on its own, breaking away from BarrierBreak, under Shai's continuing editorship.

*Newz Hook* has been holding an annual one-day event in Mumbai called Inclusive, with renowned speakers sharing stories and ideas towards disability empowerment. The theme for 2020 was 'Independent Living'.

## Automative Independence

Independent living for a PwD often begins by going outdoors and travelling long distances. For most of us, hailing a taxi is as easy as pie. PwDs might get a taxi, but getting into it is another matter. If you're a wheelchair user, you will most likely find that a taxi will refuse to take you. Even if the wheelchair is foldable, the driver will trot out excuses – it won't fit into the dickey, it will ruin the covering of the rear passenger seat and so on.

Vidhya Ramasubban and her business partner Srikrish Siva started KickStart Cabs in 2016. These automobiles are specially modified to accommodate passengers on wheelchairs. The fleet of eight vehicles serves 450 customers, and it makes commuting easy for employees with disabilities.

Anyone with mobility issues, whether it's a pregnant woman or someone with disabilities caused by age or medical problems, would appreciate Anand Kutre's Turn Plus, the affordable and adjustable seat. Its swivel mechanism allows the seat to turn 90 degrees and stick out of the car door while you lift yourself off the wheelchair, sit on it and swing back into the car.

But what if you are a wheelchair user and yearn to drive your own car? This dream of independence is harboured by many a PwD, but it was Anita Sharma, founder of the driving school On My Own, who converted the dream into a reality for herself and others like her.

Anita contracted polio when she was six months old. She couldn't walk till the age of eight, and nine surgeries later she was able to progress from callipers and crutches to walking without support, although it was still difficult. Her father, a bank officer, was constantly travelling on work. His transferable job had taken the family to over 20 Indian states. So her mother conveyed her to wherever Anita needed or wanted to go. She craved independence, though. She started using a modified two-wheeler when she joined college in Jaipur in 2001, and after she had finished her MBA and started teaching in a local college, she became determined to buy a car with her savings.

Anita's parents were dubious, but she convinced them by showing them a video of the national award-winning, adventurous Navin Gulia who broke records in driving despite being paralysed from the neck down. 'I told them if he can do it, I can also do it,' she recalls. The first car she bought was a regular one with manual transmission and an accelerator, brake and clutch. She took it to a mechanic called Rajesh Sharma in Jaipur, who has retrofitted thousands of cars for PwDs (including for Navin Gulia) since 1998. All his designs for modifications have been approved by the Automobile Research Institute, Pune. He tested the scope of the functions she could perform with her legs and tweaked the mechanism accordingly. 'I understood every function of the car in 15 minutes,' she says.

After five years of teaching, in 2011, she decided to take a shot at getting into IIM and succeeded. She took her retrofitted car to the IIM Indore and taught a few PwD friends driving in it. Word spread, and when people came down from Delhi to stay for a week in Indore and learn from her, she adjusted the training sessions with her classes. By 2015, she had completed her PhD and in September that year she got a teaching job at the Thapar School of Management in Chandigarh. She continued her informal training sessions with PwDs wanting to learn to drive, and *The Tribune* carried an article about her. In 2018, when she moved to Amritsar to teach at IIM, she put out a message on the Voice of Amritsar Facebook page: a simple two-liner saying that she was a PwD, new to the city, and could teach PwDs and elderly women driving. She got a heartening and an overwhelming response, which snowballed further when news channels picked up the story. That is when On My Own had a formal beginning, in April 2018.

Anita first did a market analysis, personally calling up over

2,000 driving schools across the country. Hardly any of them taught people with mobility impairments. When she asked them why, they replied either that retrofitting technology was unavailable or, even when it was, that there was 'no market' for teaching PwDs. The school would have to be registered fit to teach in an 'invalid carriage'; why bother when there wasn't enough demand? The dice is anyway loaded against the mobility-impaired because the Regional Transport Office (RTO) will not give them a learner's licence unless they buy their own retrofitted vehicle. Since they are not confident of being able to learn, they balk at spending lakhs on buying and retrofitting a car.

It's this lack of confidence that Anita first tackles when a person with reduced mobility expresses a desire to learn. She visits their home and meets the family as well. 'We want to see the world' is the answer most wannabe learners give her when she asks them why they want to drive. Since many of them have become wheelchair users following a traffic accident, parents are generally reluctant to allow them to resume driving. Then Anita tells them, 'my journey of independence started when I started driving'.

She gives tailor-made lessons to each PwD on the manual or the automatic car depending on their disability. The level and type of mobility loss has to be assessed. For example, the training would have to vary for those affected in the left foot, right foot, left arm, right arm, both upper limbs or both lower limbs. She also teaches those with CP, for whom special seat belts can be used to restrain their involuntary movements, and spinal cord injury persons, for whom she recommends automatic transmission. First, she teaches them on her manual car which can be adjusted to each individual's disability. After the weeklong lessons, consisting of three sessions per day are over, she takes them to Rajesh Sharma to get their own cars adapted to their requirements. Those who come from out of town can rent a room in her house at a nominal ₹500 a day.

Today Anita lives independently in Jaipur, in a house designed for complete wheelchair accessibility. She is a visiting professor at IIM Indore and IIM Amritsar and also teaches at two institutions in Jaipur. She is the managing director of Inkpothub, a commercial venture in which she has invested.

## Making Shops Accessible

It beggars belief why more commercial establishments haven't realized the fundamental truth that welcoming PwD customers will only improve their business. Big Bazaar, India's first accessible retail chain, did not act from a purely commercial motive though. Vineet Saraiwala, deputy manager of the Future Group which owns the Big Bazaar chain, is visually impaired.

Over one lakh PwDs have shopped at over 140 accessible Big Bazaar stores countrywide, and of them 15,000 have been persons with autism and ID. It won the annual NCPEDP–Mphasis Universal Design Award for its store design which incorporates Accessible Design principles with accessible trial rooms and toilets, obstacle-free passages and sensitized staff.

The project to make Big Bazaar accessible, kicked off in January 2018, is named *Sabke Liye* which means 'for everyone' in Hindi. The sensitization programme is a daylong training session conducted quarterly at every single store in the country. Using the train-the-trainer methodology, which has a cascading effect, they managed to train every one of the 30,000-strong staff.

The stores have special parking places, wheelchairs on demand, Braille shopping guides, Sign language audio-visuals and so on. 'Quiet Hour' is geared towards persons with autism, with soft lighting, music turned way down, and all sounds including announcements and cash register noises eliminated or kept to a minimum. On a 'Big Day', such as Independence and Republic days, customers with disabilities are specially recognized and celebrated.

In Western countries, the built environment has yielded to the daily requirements of PwDs to a monumental degree. To cite a few shopping examples, there are supermarkets that have prices and names of products in large print for the VI, soft lighting to prevent epileptics from having a fit, and less crowded areas for people with autism. Aira makes smart glasses for the blind, which are connected to a help centre where an assistant can see what you see and guide you through a supermarket aisle – these are handy, for example, to help users choose produce.

Newer and newer tech emerges in the West every day. There are already tactile indicators in the beeping boxes at traffic signals so that the deaf-blind know when to use the pedestrian crossing. Now they're developing a Braille panel attached to signal boxes that would give the blind additional information (besides the name) about the road they're about to cross. One waits for the software that Google has developed, which converts Sign to speech, to become a smartphone application.

One may have to wait a long time for such technology to land in the hands of ordinary Indian PwDs. Meanwhile they would expect – and should vociferously demand – at least the basic level of accessibility that would see them through their everyday lives.

# 24

# LET'S NOT FORGET THE FUN SIDE

YOU MIGHT HAVE RECEIVED 'FORWARDS' ON YOUR PHONE
that show PwDs leading independent and adventurous lives
– mountain-climbing, swimming, surfing, posing against
picturesque backdrops in remote places and so forth.

What they all usually have in common is: they live abroad. Why
should this be so? Why can't PwDs in India take delight in the
great outdoors like your average Joe or Janaki? This is a question
that some thoughtful souls in India have asked. Finding no answer,
they have provided the solution themselves.

## Inclusive Tourism

'The world is your oyster' is the message that Neha Arora's
Planet Abled wants to give all PwDs. It provides accessible travel
for tourists with disabilities, arranging inclusive group trips,
customizing tours, ensuring assistance for every kind of disability,
and covering varied themes such as heritage, adventure, nature,
spirituality and so on. Unmarried couples and same-sex couples
who are PwDs are welcome to travel through Planet Abled.

Among the organization's achievements are the NCPEDP–
MPhasis Universal Design Award 2016 and the National Award for

Most Innovative and Unique Tourism Product in 2017–18. When we meet her in October 2019, the spunky 35-year-old has just returned from Sydney where she was to pick up yet another award, the Bumble Bizz prize, at the APAC Bumble Bizz Summit. 'It was the first time in my life I downloaded a dating app! I had to do it to apply for the award,' she says, explaining how Bumble (which has Priyanka Chopra and Serena Williams among its investors) instituted a $5,000 prize for women-founded businesses across the Asia-Pacific region. 'Because we are bootstrapped, wherever I see the money I apply,' she adds. Five women were chosen, of whom she was the only one from India.

Inclusive tourism has been an uphill journey for Planet Abled. Getting average people to join a group with PwDs is not easy; Neha confesses that when she organized her first inclusive trip, 20 of the average travellers were her own friends who had volunteered. There were 22 PwDs, but convincing their parents to let them go was quite a task. These were people staying in Delhi but hadn't seen the monuments situated virtually next door to them. Neha observes that many Indian parents' reaction to their disabled children's desire for a tour is: Don't waste money; save it for your future, spend it on essentials and don't fritter it away on a 'luxury'. But is a pleasure trip a luxury? Apparently it is, but only if you are a PwD.

Planet Abled gets more foreign than Indian customers, says Neha, because the kind of multi-experience tours they offer entails travelling for 20 to 30 days across half a dozen cities and not too many Indian PwDs are willing to spend that kind of time or money. Ideally, she would like her company to organize only inclusive tours, where 'disability is just another human feature like your complexion or length of your hair'.

With experience, Neha has learnt the way to ensure that the tour goes smoothly. She gets all the required permissions beforehand from the 'proper authorities' – whether ministers, bureaucrats or heads of government departments (such as the Archaeological Survey of India, for example, which is in charge of monuments and museums). 'I make a list of what needs to be done. Wherever there could be a problem, I prepare for it,' she says. In the Ooty Botanical Gardens, she gets permission for PwDs (especially the VI) to touch and smell the flowers; in museums, permission to touch some exhibits; at the Red Fort, permission for their vehicle to go right in through the special gate meant for the military; at Amber Fort in Jaipur, access through the internal special pathways made for horses and armies. 'I keep revisiting places to re-audit because things keep on changing. It's a slow process,' Neha adds.

Checking into hotels is another troublesome operation. Only hotels that are four-star and above have a room for PwDs – yes, just one room in the entire hotel! Neha comments that they reserve this room just to comply with regulations to get a higher star rating and don't bother to decorate it. So the room invariably 'looks clinical, like a hospital room'. Besides, the room is made accessible just for wheelchair users and not for those with other disabilities.

It's the familiar vicious cycle: PwDs don't travel in large numbers, so people don't bother to cater for them, and so PwDs don't travel... Neha is not ready to give up hope, though. 'It will happen,' she says. 'PwDs themselves are not ready to travel with people with disabilities other than their own! Each one thinks their challenge is the biggest.'

When India and its PwD population are fully prepared for accessible travel, maybe we will start seeing more images online of Indian PwDs posing in remote scenic locations.

## Parks for All

In 2005, Kavitha Krishnamurthy and her husband Ganesh Anantharaman had taken their three-year-old son Ananth who had developmental delays (and was later diagnosed with autism) to a local park in Bengaluru. Ganesh commented that there didn't seem to be any kids with disabilities coming to the park. That got Kavitha thinking: Why were no kids with disabilities to be seen in public spaces?

Kavitha had taken a break from work – after an MA in social work, she had been involved in child rights issues. Now she and Ganesh were taking Ananth to therapy, and while talking to other parents she realized that they too were 'caught up in the circus' of rushing their children from one therapy to another, and then to special schools. 'Where is the whole aspect of play in their lives?' she wondered. The irony was that developmental paediatricians were always emphasizing the importance of play, but there didn't seem to be any playtime for these children.

With the question of inclusive public spaces ringing in her brain, Kavitha spent four months meeting everybody she could find in the disability sector in Bengaluru. She got together a 'motley crowd' of parents and special educators to form Kilikili in 2006 (the name, in Kannada, means the warbling laughter of a child). They zeroed in on Coles Park, which had a few pieces of ramshackle play equipment. How could they turn it into the park of their dreams?

First, Kilikili took children with mobility, hearing and vision impairments to experience Coles Park firsthand. They gave them modelling clay and drawing material, with which they could design their ideal park. After a consultation with their accompanying adults, all the inputs were collated. Kavitha sat down with architect Chitra Viswanath and special educator Meena Jain to translate the wish list into a blueprint for an inclusive park.

The Bruhat Bengaluru Mahanagara Palike (BBMP)[42] commissioner readily gave them the go-ahead. They looked at

---

[42] The Bruhat Bengaluru Mahanagara Palike is the administrative body responsible for civic amenities and some infrastructure assets of the Greater Bangalore metropolitan area.

the catalogue of play equipment for Corporation parks to devise modifications. In fact it was the equipment supplier himself who suggested, and made the mould for, bucket seats which would suit those with locomotor impairments. On World Disability Day in 2016, the new play equipment was inaugurated.

Within one month, every piece of equipment was damaged. There were seven schools around the park and usage was high. So Kilikili once again went to BBMP to get it all repaired. That's when they discovered that the civic body had huge budgets for maintenance – ₹70 lakh annually for Coles Park alone! 'We said we will use your money and tell you what to do,' she recollects.

The equipment was refurbished. Kilikili hired a watchman and paid his salary, which the local community took charge of after a while. Realizing that social support should complement physical infrastructure, Kilikili got young volunteers to call up families of kids with disabilities and encourage them to come to the park every Saturday; the volunteers supervised the kids' play. On weekdays, special schools were encouraged to bring their children; and on some Saturday mornings, huge inclusive events were organized with around 200 kids from both mainstream and special schools.

The BBMP commissioner sanctioned funds for two inclusive parks in other zones of Bengaluru: the Gayathri Devi Park Extension in Rajajinagar and the M.N. Krishna Rao Park in Basavanagudi. But there was one thorn in their sides, which they couldn't remove. 'Play equipment maintenance for some strange reason is not under Horticulture but under Education,' says Kavitha. The absurdity of it is apparent as soon as you try and imagine staff of the education department going to parks armed with tools to repair swings and slides. Gardeners only take care of the greenery. Kavitha points out that the BBMP preferred to 'let it become a mess and then again re-develop it' rather than maintain it. It is no secret that when fresh contracts are awarded, 'cuts' and 'commissions' flow in.

Residents' groups in Defence Colony, Whitefield, Jeevan Bima Nagar and Koramangala were keen to develop similar parks, but projects got stalled at various stages with funds drying up – midway through construction in one case. Kilikili had been approached by people from other cities too for guidance: a determined 70-year-old woman from Mangalore got an inclusive park built there in two years, and a parent from Mumbai did a similar thing in her neighbourhood. They decided it was time to bring out a manual. 'Breaking Barriers Through Play' contains policy guidelines on making public play spaces inclusive, and exhaustive technical measurements and instructions on how to design a variety of play equipment for children with disabilities.[43]

Kavitha moved to Chennai in 2015 but soon found common ground with likeminded individuals. Parks were a major item on the agenda of Disability Rights Alliance (DRA), a loose federation of individuals and organizations working on disability issues in Chennai. DRA teamed up with the mental health organization Banyan, founded by Vandana Gopikumar and her friend Vaishnavi Jayakumar. Vaishnavi roped in Kavitha for the park project.

The Tamil Nadu government was keen to support them, because the government of India Smart Cities Mission mentioned inclusive spaces such as 'sensory parks'. The park team identified a government site strategically located next to the State Resource Centre for Special Education. Architectural and design skills came into the picture. Kavitha Selvaraj of the architectural firm Cityworks who designed it made vast improvizations based upon the basic inputs she was given. The Greater Chennai Corporation (GCC) Inclusive Park on Santhome High Road, inaugurated in 2018, was the first of its kind in Chennai. GCC plans to build at least three more in Chennai, and aims to develop 70 elsewhere in Tamil Nadu.

---

[43] Kilikili Inclusive Play Manual, Web, 2021.

Kavitha takes us around the GCC inclusive park. It has sections for different age-groups. The first as you enter is for the under 8s; next, the under 12s; and the furthest, a paved ground for teenagers that can serve as a basketball court and any other play space, along with some exercise equipment. A child in a wheelchair can go through the entire park and also enter the bathroom, which has a rubberized floor to lessen the impact of potential falls. There are benches for adults and minders to sit, and a gazebo where groups can convene. Besides Braille signage there is a herb garden at the entrance with fragrant plants for the VI to relish. For children with Sensory Integration Disorder, there are stepping stones of different heights that teach them to gauge distances, and there is a pathway paved with material of varying textures: pebbles, grass, brick, sand etc.

Equipment is adapted or designed to be accessible for varying kinds and degrees of disability. There are basketball hoops at two levels – the lower one meant for the kids who use wheelchairs; the slides with curving edges, and seesaws and swings with bucket seats, are for those with CP and locomotor disabilities; the merry-go-rounds come with a central bar that average kids can stand on and platforms onto which wheelchairs can be easily rolled and securely fastened. The raised sandpit is accessible to kids using wheelchairs, while average kids can easily climb to the top to play. Traditional board games are etched onto the surface of black granite tables. A vivid mural is comprised of elements that kids with and without disabilities can explore: some fixed and some revolving tyres of different vehicles, embossed shapes, separate letters of the word 'Chennai' cleverly concealed among the images and so on.

Kilikili also sourced equipment from others. There's a musical stone that Swaram in Auroville designed; if you moisten your hands and rub the sides vigorously, it produces a melodious note. A 'telephone' designed by Gudgudee (More on them below) – a large red funnel into which you can speak and be clearly audible in the matching funnel at the other end – reminds the older generation of the matchbox-and-string phones they used to play with.

Kavitha says state governments looking to fulfil the Smart Cities Mission have been contacting them, as have local government bodies including municipal corporations. Queries have come in from places as diverse as Kanpur, Bhubaneswar and even Guwahati. Kavitha listed Kilikili's overall goals: 'Building awareness in the local community and among other groups of children, giving a sense of solidarity and giving parents the confidence to start bringing children outside the home.'

## Inclusive Playgrounds

'One slide, two swings, a seesaw and a merry-go-round – that's what a playground usually is,' says Aditi Agrawal. 'We have developed a toolkit on how to design an inclusive playground. It's the first of its kind in the country.'

Forbes magazine wrote about Aditi Agrawal and Anjali Menon, founders of Gudgudee, in a story on 30 up-and-coming business entrepreneurs under the age of 30. Their toolkit was launched in Delhi on 1 March 2019 by the National Institute for Urban Affairs, which has started an initiative under its Smart City project called Child Friendly Smart Cities. Using simple language and easy-to-grasp illustrations, the kit lays down every step in building an inclusive playground. It explains the requisite location, size, landscaping, types of building material for different areas of the park, types of hedges, trees and flowering plants and so on. 'We have to include adults too,' Aditi points out. 'Parents needn't just sit around on benches while their kids play.'

The play equipment is accessible to those with mobility, vision, hearing and sensory disabilities. The interactive wall, for instance, is made up of shapes that invite the child to play with it in different ways: it has raised patterns that a blind and VI child can feel, bells they can hear and sections that they can climb, step across or crawl through. Children with unsteady movements can safely sit inside a Basket Spinner and whirl around, while a child using a wheelchair can board the Floor-Level Spinner, grab onto the circular railing and enjoy the same sensation. Upright coloured lollipops, each transparent disc in a different colour, give you a view of the world through tinted glasses, as it were. The VI can bang away at cuboidal drums and cymbal mushrooms, or produce music from the freestanding xylophone and tembos.

Aditi and Anjali were classmates at the National Institute of Design (NID) in Ahmedabad when they embarked on a project that resulted in Gudgudee (which means 'tickling' in Hindi). They had both chosen a module on design for special needs, as part of which they visited the Blind People Association (BPA). They noticed that the kids were active indoors but had never gone outdoors to play; this was because the equipment in the neighbourhood park was not disabled-friendly and the public would pass insensitive comments about them. When the two mooted the idea of designing inclusive play equipment, the BPA administration 'loved it' and found donors for them.

They spoke to teachers, researchers, child psychologists and occupational therapists, and came to realize that playthings don't just develop the child physically but help them learn cognitive and social skills, and use their imagination. They immersed themselves in the project; marks and attendance were the least of their priorities. 'We used recycled material; we physically built the playground,' says Aditi, recalling the joy with which they returned each day to their project armed with fresh ideas they had thrashed out the night before. Aditi is quick to thank her professor Praveen Nahar for encouraging them and adds that she is grateful that the NID curriculum allowed for such ventures.

In 2011, their design for the BPA campus won them the iF Concept Design Award in Hamburg. The jury was impressed by their use of local and recycled materials, and the play space being not just safe and innovative but also inclusive. After graduating in 2012, both took up jobs – Anjali in Mumbai, where she still lives, and Aditi in Bengaluru. After a year and a half, they quit their respective jobs to form Gudgudee. They have been working together from different cities all along.

Gudgudee's clients include apartment complexes in Mumbai, a school in Rajkot and builders who have begun to realize that an inclusive playground can be a selling point when they advertise 'outdoor facilities' as part of the amenities they offer. In Panchkula, Haryana, they designed an inclusive playground in collaboration with the Reliance Foundation. Ideas constantly bubble up in the minds of these young women. The inclusive indoor playscape they designed in Indore includes a miniature cooking unit with kitchen utensils and the shell of an old car they found in a junkyard. Kids can sit inside the car and steer, change the tyres and number plates, and even fill 'fuel'!

All of Gudgudee's ideas are founded on the central truth that 'the playground is nature's way of developing the brain'. And there's no better way for every kind of brain to develop than by playing together harmoniously in an all-embracing environment.

# 25

# TIME TO STOP SKIRTING
# THE TOPIC OF SEX

THE 1973 COMEDY FILM *NO SEX PLEASE, WE'RE BRITISH* would become a tragedy if you replaced the last word with 'Indians'. We're serious. Sex being a taboo in India often leads to tragic consequences. Associated as it is with procreation and not pleasure, sex is also cloaked in shame and misinformation – which provides easy scope for exploitation and violence.

How on earth can we in India then have frank conversations about the sexual lives of PwDs?

Ashwin Karthik is one of the rare members of the PwD community who is not afraid to speak his mind on the subject. 'For years I have been puzzling over why nobody wants to talk about this crucial part of our lives,' he tells us. Why does Indian society, and especially the ultra-prudish middle class, simply blank out the notion of sex for PwDs? We too are intrigued, and we can only speculate about the reasons.

Most Indian parents fall over themselves to look for partners for their children of 'marriageable age'. Not the parents of children with moderate to severe disabilities, though. They have entirely given up hope of finding someone willing to take on the 'burden of caring for' their offspring – yes, the partner's primary purpose is presumed to be 'caring for' their son or daughter with disabilities and sex is firmly relegated to the background. Paradoxically, many Indians cling to the myth that marriage can 'cure' those with mental disabilities. And in such cases, their idea of marriage not only includes sexual intercourse but prioritizes it as being the supposed cure for the disability.

Indian society takes a wholly utilitarian approach to the delicate subject of the physiology of PwDs. Do their relevant organs and appendages function efficiently enough to produce a child? If so, they gain a certain 'market value'. The rest are doomed to celibacy.

Of course there are people – not just PwDs – who are asexual. And sexual experience cannot be narrowed down to penetrative sex. Disability rights activist Dhanya Ravi writes in a guest column on *Newz Hook* that social connection and intimacy are hardly acknowledged as a basic need, and that PwDs desire intimacy just like everyone else – not just physical but also social and emotional. In her words, 'Who would not like having friends with whom they can share their heart out? Who would not like the warmth of a loving touch, hug and a kiss?'[44]

Erotic impulses might awaken in a paraplegic body or an intellectually disabled mind. Given the tendency of Indian parents to infantilize their children with ID and take unilateral decisions on their behalf, obliterating their sexual identity is the easy way out. But an adult with ID may feel sexual desire and be unable to verbally express it; a person with a physical disability might experience a strong sexual urge and be helpless to fulfil it. Isn't it strange how even a loving caregiver dismisses this possibility outright?

We spoke to a few PwDs of what is usually deemed to be marriageable age for average people, who agreed to speak

---

[44] Dhanya Ravi, 'We Need More Than Just Food, Clothing and Shelter!', *Newz Hook*, 11 May 2020.

anonymously. These were intelligent, articulate men who were highly dependent on their caregivers for their daily needs. Words like 'frustration' and 'fear' recurred in our conversations with them. Their predicaments moved us deeply.

Imagine the frustration of being unable to even masturbate, because someone would have to assist them. And who can they ask? Not their parents or siblings, surely. They fear rejection if they dare to confess they're sexually attracted to someone. A total lack of privacy means they live in fear of being caught watching porn or of the phone sex app they've downloaded being found. When other avenues of sexual gratification are denied, isn't it wholly natural for them to seek it vicariously? And yet, they say, they fear that a hypocritical society will judge them as 'perverts' for doing something that millions of non-disabled people do in secret. As victims of 'inspiration porn', they often feel obliged to keep up the self-image that others have built for them. 'You're so courageous, how I admire you! What? You want sex? *Che-che*, don't be disgusting. You're supposed to just think noble thoughts and inspire me by your actions.'

A young man narrates how he was watching a popular Sharon Stone movie on his phone when his parents told him, you shouldn't be watching 'films like this'. The mind must remain pure as virgin snow, you see; it mustn't be exposed to anything that might stimulate or titillate.

A wheelchair user with paraplegia tells us, 'When I was 14 or 15, I started having these feelings that a teenager normally has. Just imagine, for 20 years I've been bottling it up!' He wistfully describes the films in the Inclusion section that he has watched online during the Bengaluru International Short Film Festival (BISFF) 2020. Jonay García's Spanish film *The Beds of Others*, in particular, shook him to the core: 'I'll never forget that movie my whole life.' Sofia Primavera plays a sexual assistant for men and women with severe disabilities. We agree that not in a hundred years would a film like that be made in India. *The Wagon* by Gayle Knutson features a woman with DS who has a job and is sexually active – another scenario that sounds farfetched in the Indian context.

Women with disabilities in India are doubly disadvantaged. Society has woven peculiar myths around them that paint them as being either asexual or hypersexual. Dhanya Ravi points out in her aforementioned column that the absence of social connections coupled with the lack of sexual and emotional literacy exposes them to sexual exploitation. Those with mental disabilities are especially vulnerable to predation and assault. In institutions in India, until very recently it was considered par for the course for the wombs of 'MR girls' (women with ID) to be removed for their 'protection' – read 'to prevent pregnancy', whether it occurred through consent or rape. Clearly, men too were subjected to medical interventions to render them 'infertile', because the RPwD Act refers to these practices.

The Act says on Rights and Entitlements that 'No person with disability shall be subject to any medical procedure which leads to infertility without his or her free and informed consent.'[45] On Offences and Penalties, the Act stipulates punishment – six months to five-years-with-fine in prison – for terminating the pregnancy of a woman with disabilities without her express consent (besides humiliating PwDs or sexually exploiting women with disabilities).[46]

Human Rights Watch brought out a 61-page report in 2018 on sexual violence against women with disabilities in India after investigating 17 cases of rape and gang rape from eight Indian states. The report found that despite The Criminal Law (Amendment) Act 2013 having included several provisions to safeguard the rights of women with disabilities, PwD survivors of rape faced

---

[45] RPwD Act, Chapter II, Section 10(2).
[46] RPwD Act, Chapter XVI, Section 92.

tremendous barriers to access the justice system. Women and girls with disabilities face challenges right through the justice process, from reporting abuse and getting appropriate medical care to getting compensation. Those with ID may be unaware that non-consensual sex is a crime, the deaf and HI may find it difficult to communicate the abuse, and those with physical disabilities may be unable to escape a violent situation. Police and judicial officers utterly lack the sensitivity and training needed to handle such cases and provide an enabling, supportive environment.

Sex education is a hot potato. When average children themselves have no legitimate access to knowledge about sex, children with disabilities are surely left completely in the dark. 'We're working with adolescents and sexuality,' says Gitanjali Sarangan of the Snehadhara care centre for those with developmental disabilities. 'Sex is not spoken of at home, so we're educating the adults now, [and] giving sexuality advice for parents.' She says that a boy of 17 was turned away from five or six special schools because he was masturbating and they said he was a bad influence on the others, who would learn his 'bad behaviour'.

The staff members of Snehadhara are well apprised of the kids' sexual needs. One of them narrates an incident: A young female intern at the centre wanted to use one of the toilets. It was occupied and a staff member waiting outside the door told her calmly to come back later because he's masturbating. She rushed, bug-eyed, back to her seat – much to the amusement of the others who explain that any child in obvious need of urgent sexual release is led to the toilet. Gitanjali too recalls an instance of a boy who was in agony because he didn't know how to climax. She explained the problem to his parents and 'we don't know what they said or did but we found out that he had figured out how'.

A prepubescent girl with DS in the Special Ed. department of Deens Academy loves to hug and kiss others, and had to be told it's not always appropriate. Children with DS are typically quite physically demonstrative. Mini Menon of Endeavor ELS, which runs the department, describes how the girl kissed her male classmate on the lips, and when chided she asked innocently, 'Why ma'am? But I like him so much.' How do you teach a kid with DS that you have to wait till you're grown up before you seek consent and kiss someone on the lips? Later, an attendant spotted a drawing the girl had made of a male and a female figure kissing, and handed it over to Mini. Making it clear to the little artist that she wasn't annoyed, Mini asked her casually, 'Did you draw this today or yesterday?' Today, she replied. Mini asked, 'Did you see anyone kissing in school or at home or anywhere else?' She'd seen it on the Romedy Now TV channel, she said, much to Mini's relief.

Janaki Narayan was told by doctors that her autistic son Sid 'may not have sexual needs'. Now that both her daughter and her younger son were looking for life partners, Sid had questions about his own marriage. 'I think he is looking at all the attention and presents that marriage brings,' says Janaki. 'We have been talking to him time and again that marriage is a lot of responsibility; one should look after the other person, not all people need to marry, etc.'

## Personal Essays on Sexuality

That women with disabilities are sexual beings, just like anyone else, was the premise on which two women's groups came together to start a website called sexualityanddisability.org. Bishakha Datta, founder of the Mumbai-based women's empowerment non-profit Point of View, and the New Delhi-based feminist human rights organization Creating Resources for Empowerment in Action (CREA) got together in April 2012 to launch this pioneering website – the first ever to address the concerns and sexuality of women with disabilities. The website was designed as a series of questions these women may have about their bodies, sex, intimacy, relationships, marriage, parenting and violence.

Point of View hired Shreya Ila Anasuya in 2016 as a part-time editor to give shape to its sporadically written blog. This was transformed into *Skin Stories*,[47] a digital publication launched in 2017 that carries engrossing personal essays of the multifarious experiences of women with disabilities. Shreya, who was its managing editor till December 2019 and is a consultant now, speaks to us about the 'criminal silence around sexuality' in India, which gets progressively worse when it comes to those with disability, women and the LGBTQIA+ community.

Describing how *Skin Stories* was compiled, Shreya says that the writers pitched ideas to her or else she commissioned stories, 'They're in charge of the narrative; we don't want to be appropriative.' After offering suggestions for their first draft there would be some back-and-forth, and the final edited playback version would be sent to them for approval.

She has known many examples of disability in her own family, including an uncle who 'had an intellectual disability and lived his entire life without being able to form intimate relations with anyone'. She herself has a debilitating condition, which she writes about in one of the essays in the book. Describing the 'chronic fatigue and pain' from endometriosis, a gynaecological condition that has no known cause or cure and for which she has consulted countless medical professionals, she writes: 'The only thing almost every doctor I have ever seen...has been concerned about is whether I want to have children, because it can also make you infertile. And what use am I, as a womb-haver, if I don't push out at least a child or two from my body?'

The riveting, profoundly intimate essays on body politics are grouped under sections, the titles of which are self-revelatory:

---

[47] 'Looking Back: "Skin Stories" in 2017', *Medium*, 27 December 2017.

Mind, Body, Romance, Friendship, Sex, Work, Violence, Marriage, Self, Children, Discrimination and Myths. Some women have contributed to two or three sections, as they share different aspects of their personal lives, and very few have chosen to be anonymous.

A rainbow shines across these pages and the voices get under your skin as you soak in a wide variety of experiences – of being queer, bipolar, Dalit, deaf, blind, non-binary, or pregnant; of child abuse, abusive relationships, living with Obsessive Compulsive Disorder (OCD), depression, and borderline personality disorder. And also of embracing one's 'imperfect' body, dating, trekking, mountain-climbing, being part of a community and finding love and support.

These days, Tinder has come to the rescue of many a PwD. Tony Kurian literally goes on a blind date after he declares his visual impairment online: 'By creating a Tinder profile and mentioning my disability on it, I was making a statement...that I was worth dating.'[48] Although his dates end in coffee and conversations, he writes that he is still hoping to find a match.

Antara Telang, who was also on Tinder until she met someone offline, renders an upbeat account of the kind of men she's dated 'as a one-legged girl in Mumbai' (she is a below-the-knee amputee). There was this sci-fi enthusiast who became intensely excited at the prospect that he could be dating a cyborg, and a banker who made Excel spreadsheets categorizing the women he met on Tinder. The piece de resistance – a guy who wanted to confirm that her crucial body-parts were in working order: 'It's just one foot, right? All the rest is there na?'[49]

Parvathy Gopakumar narrates her journey towards accepting

---

[48] Tony Kurian, 'What it means to be on Tinder as a person with an identifiable disability' in *Skin Stories*, ed. Shreya Ila Anasuya, Mumbai: Point of View, 2017, p. 84.

[49] Antara Telang, 'Tindering as a one-legged girl in Mumbai' in *Skin Stories*, ed. Shreya Ila Anasuya, Mumbai: Point of View, 2017, p. 92.

her amputation and her prosthetic hand, 'In the initial years of being a disabled person, all I wanted was to prove that I wasn't one.'[50] Hiding her amputation meant she was unable to ask for help when she needed it. She would wear full-sleeved tops and avoid full-length mirrors; it took years for her to embrace her true self. 'The hollow part of my prosthetic arm is where I hoard chocolate at times, and I love applying nail polish on the silicon fingernails these days, because why not?'[51] she says. However, her disability still looms large in the minds of others. 'People compliment me on my wit, my sense of humour, my "cute" face and even my sense of style. But when it comes to dating, my most dominant feature seems to be my prosthetic hand,'[52] she says in another essay in the book.

Among these women writers, a few have been written about. Such as Malini Chib who has CP and is the inspiration behind the film *Margarita with a Straw* made by her cousin Shonali Bose, Aditi Verma who runs a restaurant in Mumbai and has DS and Nidhi Goyal – the blind stand-up comic who, incidentally, reveals her 'other' disability of having a hypersensitive stomach and digestive system that reacts violently and unexpectedly to unfamiliar foods.

Unmana Datta, who suffered extreme food allergies for years before it was discovered, speaks of how she came to terms with her body once she encountered the concepts of 'temporary disability' and 'invisible disability'. 'The idea of "temporary disability" led me to the idea that bodies cannot be conveniently categorized into able

---

[50] Parvathy Gopakumar, '"Fake it till you make it": Surviving the terrifying loneliness of being a young person with an amputation' in *Skin Stories*, ed. Shreya Ila Anasuya, Mumbai: Point of View, 2017, p. 45.

[51] Ibid.

[52] Parvathy Gopakumar, '"My most dominant feature seems to be my prosthetic hand": Dating as a woman with a disability' in *Skin Stories*, ed. Shreya Ila Anasuya, Mumbai: Point of View, 2017, p. 88.

and disabled. That abilities can ebb and flow, morph and disappear and reappear... None of us is impervious,' she says.[53]

In the last essay, Preeti Singh who has CP refers to how PwDs are either pitied or looked up to as 'inspiring' objects: 'Whether we are being pushed away because we are pitied or pushed forward because we are used as objects of "inspiration", both ways, our common humanity is denied. Let us be who we are: complex, capable of many things, both good and bad. Realize that the most extraordinary thing about us is that we are ordinary.'[54]

Point of View has been teaming up with NGOs to hold workshops across the country that enable women with disabilities to learn about their bodies. These workshops also provide them with essential information about their sexual and reproductive health. Their website contains vital information that answers a range of questions women with disabilities may have – on how to stay healthy and enjoy their bodies, about the mechanics and dynamics of having sex, the complexities of being in an intimate relationship or having children, and the fears or experiences of encountering abuse and violence.

We can only hope that their pioneering efforts are replicated, bringing to a wider audience a subject that has been kept under wraps for far too long and rarely finds mention in the disability discourse.

[53] Unmana Datta, 'Dealing with my intolerance to certain foods helped me to reject the judgment that had followed me all my life' in *Skin Stories*, ed. Shreya Ila Anasuya, Mumbai: Point of View, 2017, p. 63.

[54] Preeti Singh, 'As a woman with a disability I'm either seen as "helpless" or "heroic"' in *Skin Stories*, ed. Shreya Ila Anasuya, Mumbai: Point of View, 2017, p. 243.

## Inclusive Matchmaking

Matrimonial ads and websites cater to every known caste and creed in our country. So why can't we have a sort of shaadi.com for PwDs?

An unusual project provided an outlet for Kalyani Khosla's natural bent for social advocacy after she graduated from college in Mumbai in 2013. She was aware that PwDs used many online avenues for dating and companionship, but they had none that offered traditional matchmaking involving the parents/community.

Kalyani was clear, when she started building the project in 2014, that it would be inclusive. People with and without disabilities, people from the LGBTQIA+ community, acid attack survivors – everybody should be able to find a life partner. When her attempt at crowd-sourcing proved successful, she knew she was on the right track; within a month the project had garnered $10,000. The Inclov app was built in 2015. Angel investors came forward to fund it and it was launched in January 2016.

The app took off with a bang. Then, those using the app expressed a wish to convert the chats into meetings, but accessibility was a problem. The Inclov team began to host meet-ups, first in smaller towns and cities such as Baroda and Jaipur, and then in other 'safe spaces' generously provided by hotel chains such as Lemontree and Lalit. Parents would come to the meets and many matches were arranged. Kalyani recalls that in just 15 months from 2018 to 2019, they had arranged no less than 150 meet-ups.

Unfortunately, Inclov had to shut down when the funds dried up. Even today people contact them asking: When's the next meet? There are many videos online that people have uploaded on how they found their partners through Inclov. 'A lot of them have had babies,' says Kalyani, recounting a memorable instance of what appeared to be, at first glance, an unlikely match. A 35-year-old wheelchair user from a village in Sultanpur near Lucknow used the

Inclov app to meet a non-disabled 28-year-old man from Delhi, an out and out 'city boy' who had his own YouTube channel. When Shweta and Alok met face to face, they clicked, got hitched and became parents as well.

We eagerly hope to see more enterprises that assist PwDs in their search for satisfying relationships and actively support their right to emotional and sexual contentment. If the world spins on the axis of love, why should it stop turning for those with disabilities?

# 26

# HELPING THEM LIVE THEIR WAY

A LOVING PARTNER, A STABLE RELATIONSHIP, A FRUITFUL domestic life…this is what parents fervently crave for the future of their children with disabilities. And if their hopes begin to fade, the 'after me what?' question gives them recurring nightmares. But this question is being answered, ever so slowly, in stages. The Indian government has taken baby steps to ensure the right of persons with any sort of disability to live amidst the wider community, instead of being set apart as they have tended to be.

The RPwD Act chapter on rights and entitlements states that PwDs have the right to live in the community, are 'not obliged to live in any particular living arrangement', and must be 'given access to a range of in-house, residential and other community support services, including personal assistance necessary to support living'.[55]

The cold hard reality is that 'homes' for single PwDs in India often make headlines when their pathetic living conditions are brought to light. Many of their 'inmates' are those with ID and DD who had been wandering the streets, abandoned by their

---

[55] RPwD Act, Chapter II, Section 5.

families. Persons with ID are commonly herded into institutions where they live like virtual prisoners – confined to a compound with locked gates, wearing ill-fitting uniforms, with their heads shaved for easier 'maintenance', and subject to a strict timetable for eating and sleeping. In short, they have no individual identity. The timeworn misconception that adults with ID are 'children' who cannot think for themselves has yet to be erased from the Indian consciousness.

When Poonam Natarajan of Vidya Sagar was chairperson of the National Trust (for persons with autism, CP, ID and multiple disabilities), she had chaired an expert committee set up by the Kerala government to prepare a project report on assisted living for adults with ID and DD. In the preface of the report, which was submitted in 2013, she had noted that institutions for PwDs in many states were 'getting a very bad reputation for neglect, abuse and over-crowding'.

The report described several existing models of assisted living programmes – including homes run by PwDs or by parents of PwDs, and those on the lines of the National Trust schemes that Poonam had conceived, Gharaunda and Samarth. The committee also developed a pilot model. It featured units of a dozen or so residents each, with varying disabilities, living with three caregivers, and accessing the services of a part-time social worker and visiting therapists. The model visualized the PwDs living in a home-like environment where decisions were taken individually or as a group. They would go out to work in the community and follow individual short- and long-term plans.

## Centre for Interdependent Living

Poonam hasn't checked whether the Kerala government acted on the committee report of 2013 because she is too busy planning her own project, which would be 'one of a kind in the country': BLISS, or Begin to Live Interdependently with Support Systems, a resource centre she envisions for PwDs to help them live interdependently in the community.

Poonam explains that while the West is closing down institutions and has progressed to community-based living, what is currently available in India is basically 'a hostel'. She says that even the better ones, whether run by the government or NGOs, are merely a smaller version of the same old 'institution'. The current models of assisted living are 'following a top-down approach which doesn't give you autonomy or self-determination, or help you find your strengths or build your personality or live a life in the community'. They exercise a great degree of control over the daily regimen, entertainment and work life of the PwD in exchange for care and protection. 'If I were disabled that's not what I would want as an adult,' she says. 'PwDs have a right to autonomy, to make choices, have a dream and work towards it.'

BLISS will be a pathfinder that demonstrates how PwDs can live in the community, says Poonam. 'Human beings live in a connected way. Interdependence does not mean lack of independence.'

She then lists the nine 'pillars' on which the centre will rest:

*Advisory:* BLISS will not rely purely on the PwD's medical diagnosis but will use Person-Centred Planning (PCP) through the method of PATH (Planning Alternative Tomorrows with Hope) to help them plan how to fulfil their dream. The plan will be periodically revisited to incorporate changes.

Even as they enter the centre, those with locomotor disabilities will benefit from a seating clinic, which is a novel idea for India. In our country, they are often consigned to a one-size-fits-all wheelchair, instead of one that is specific to their shape, size and disability. At BLISS, experts from all relevant fields will assess the individual's body and posture, take measurements, and fit them for a wheelchair 'like being fitted for trousers, custom made'.[56]

*Employment:* Besides skill training, specialists will guide PwDs on ways to find employment of their own choice and help with placement. Experts will guide them on entrepreneurship.

*Manpower Development:* Poonam points out that there is no manpower in India for working with adults with disabilities – although there are people working with children. BLISS will train people for four key professions: caregiver, job coach, independent travel trainer (a person who trains the PwD to travel independently) and group home manager. She plans to offer these training curricula to the RCI, universities and the government's Skill India Mission so that enough manpower can be created for the country.

*Maintenance Therapy:* Poonam tracks 100 of Vidya Sagar's 30,000 alumni who have been out of school for nearly 10 years to find out the main barriers they faced. Therapy is one of the areas of concern and, once again, the focus thus far only has been on children; what therapy exists for adults with disabilities is inappropriate.

The maintenance therapy department will be a hub for body maintenance. For instance, a wheelchair user sitting for hours at a stretch needs a massage, and to swim or exercise at a gym; a foot care unit will take care of issues with their feet, which tend to get bent out of shape; and the spine too needs regular, diligent attention. Grooming is equally important.

*Leisure:* A variety of activities will be offered, such as art, music, dance, yoga and storytelling.

---

[56] Incidentally, Jo Chopra of the Latika Roy Memorial Foundation wrote a stinging article in the *Wire* on how they received adult wheelchairs for children as a donation from the chief minister on his birthday. Jo Chopra, 'Not All Wheelchairs Are the Same. Our Politicians Need to Recognise That', *Wire*, 17 September 2020.

*Team for Accessibility and Reasonable Accommodation (TARA):* Access audits are being done in India but only for public spaces. 'It should be done for personal spaces and workplaces,' says Poonam. TARA will spearhead the accessibility project, designing living spaces for accessibility and providing disabled-friendly vehicles through its Get Going initiative, as well as assistive devices through Sambhav, its centre for assistive technology.

*TED-S:* Trust Enabled Decision-Making with Support System (for details, see Chapter 6 of this book, 'Guidelines for Parents') will tackle the 'after me what?' problem. BLISS will employ a chartered accountant who will oversee and audit the trust to ensure PwDs' money is spent correctly.

*Swayam*: A sudden move to independent living after the parents die is difficult for an adult with a disability who has leaned on them all along. Swayam is a stepping stone to independent living. It envisions flats where they can live for a week or so to practice how to live independently; there will be a carer for every two or three PwDs, and a group home manager who will be in charge of quality control, checking that hygiene and food are okay, and resolving conflicts that might arise.

*Peer counsellors*: There will be a special training programme for PwDs as peer counsellors. Counsellors with disabilities will be able to understand and empathize better since they have faced the same barriers and similar experiences as those whom they're counselling.

## Independent Living for Those With ID

A group home that fostered independent living of women with intellectual disabilities, that too in a housing colony among mainstream society, was an utterly radical concept in India in 1991. But Manjula Kalyan, armed with a master's degree in ID from the University of Pittsburgh, broke new ground when she took up a house on rent for women and girls with varying levels of ID. It was the birth of Swayamkrushi (own effort /self-reliance in Sanskrit).

Manjula's qualifications attracted NIMH, which was being set up in Hyderabad, and she worked there for six years. When her husband retired from the air force prematurely and took up a well-paying job, he offered his air force pension to her to do what she pleased with it. That's when Manjula put her novel plan into action.

She conceived the idea of a group of eight 'girls' (as this 77-year-old still calls them, whatever their age) living together in a home, like the average Indian joint family. Of the eight, she envisioned that three could have mild ID, four moderate and one severe; the one with severe ID would be looked after by the seven. The three with mild ID would be trained to perform the basic functions of running a household, such as grocery shopping, cooking and managing the budget. The four moderate ones would be trained in sweeping, mopping, cleaning, making beds, etc. The initial 24-hour supervision of the women and girls would be reduced as they grew more self-reliant and would eventually be replaced by caregivers functioning in shifts. Although Manjula did lay down house rules for the women and girls, there was to be no signboard or security guard because they had to live like regular residents.

But before Manjula could rent the house, there was a critical barrier she had to cross: convincing the colony residents to accept the women and girls in their midst. Her method for each house or flat she subsequently rented was the same: go to the colony or apartment complex, inform the residents what she planned to do and invite them to have a cup of tea with her. Of the 25 or so residents, perhaps two or three would attend and get sensitized; they would then convince the rest to wait and watch.

A survey done six months into the experiment showed that everything was running smoothly. So Swayamkrushi rented two homes in Secunderabad, close to the office premises. 'In seven years we were running eight houses! After a while people would come and tell me, "Aunty, there is a house vacant, do you want it?" That was the [level of] change,' she recalls.

Since the houses were in different locations, she could sensitize a greater number of neighbourhood communities. Raising public awareness was her mission, and she was doing it singlehanded alongside trying to raise funds. 'I was like a one-man army, I was much younger then!' she tells us. She would go to schools and speak in the assembly. Even as she did so, she would garner resources in the most basic way, accepting donations in kind which would reduce domestic expenses. In one school she would tell the students: Tomorrow each of you should bring one onion. In another it would be one tube of toothpaste, and so on. Awareness was also generated during the social gatherings they organized on festivals such as the *bommala koluvu* (doll festival, celebrated in the south) when the capabilities of the women and girls would be showcased through the dolls and decorations that they had made and arranged.

When it came to employment, Manjula's ideas were 'all out-of-the-box'. She says, 'I never did any chalk-piece making, [or] candle making,' referring to the staple of special schools. Instead, she looked at the local environment and identified what would satisfy the community's needs. She contacted working women who were eager to buy the chopped vegetables and idli-dosa batter the women and girls provided. Women and girls with severe ID would earn by peeling 25 to 30 kilos of sambar onions each day and supplying them to two or three hotels. Similarly, Manjula identified a contractor supplying cardboard for packing electric fans, got a sub contract for the women and girls to package fans and finally approached the fan manufacturing company directly.

'My girls have worked in [the luxury hotel] Krishna Oberoi,' she says with a touch of pride. 'In Housekeeping, the severely challenged girls would separate towels and the mildly challenged would fold them into three. They devised a jig to do it, which the other staff also started following! Speed was important since productivity is measured and so they would practice with stopwatches.'

Swayamkrushi's programme is continuously reviewed: data sheets are scrupulously maintained, lesson plans revised where needed and individual progress monitored. Manjula's work has earned her public recognition as well as appreciation from unexpected quarters. She mentions a recent letter she received from a man who said he'd met her although she doesn't recall where. He wrote that in his daughter's wedding invitation he had printed: 'No presents please, but donations to Swayamkrushi welcome.' The numerous awards she has won take the backseat in her scheme of things. She converts the expensive shawls with which she is honoured at functions into 'nice skirts for my girls'!

Swayamkrushi's new five-acre campus is underway. Built for 200, and with a small but fully equipped medical intervention unit, most of the women and girls being admitted have severe disabilities, and are either orphans or with a single parent. They come from many states across India, and the hope is that once they return they can be integrated into their social environment, leading their lives with self-reliance and self-respect.

## Assisted Living for Persons With Autism

Merry Barua, whose son Neeraj was born in 1981, reminisces about the notions that prevailed about assisted living 20-odd years ago: 'There was a group of us five friends who were parents of kids with disabilities: three had kids with DS, I had Neeraj with autism, and one had a kid with intellectual impairment. We got together to talk about assisted living. Our kids were in their early teens. We thought we'd take an apartment, have a car for them to travel since they can't travel on their own. And that, to my mind, is what assisted living was about. Twenty years ago it was all working out to ₹35 lakh a month! I couldn't afford it.'

In the intervening years, Merry, who pioneered the autism movement in India, has gained vast experience and knowledge both about autism and assisted living. 'Assisted living is not only about a person having a comfortable place to stay and food to eat and clothes to wear,' she says. 'It is about dignity, and leading the best possible lives that their potential will allow.'

Over the years, she kept looking for an apartment or a house somebody would donate so that she could start an assisted living programme for adults with autism. Eventually other members of the AFA board said: Let's look for a piece of land outside the city. And that's what eventually transpired. The Haryana government donated 10 acres in a village outside Delhi, and Ananda – a residential centre for adults with autism and other conditions – was set up in 2018. Equipped with trained support staff, it provides a space for adults with autism to live and work in an ambience of dignity and respect.

Ananda has full-time residents with high support needs but it also accommodates those who stay for a short respite during times of crisis. Parents are not allowed to stay at Ananda along with their children. Merry says that most parents optimistically believe they could all move in there too, and that when one set of parents died the others would look after their child. 'Does it really work?' she asked the parents. When AFA was set up in Delhi in 1991, there were parents who had moved into apartments nearby. 'I asked them: "How many of you went out of your way to take another's child to live with you?"' she remembers.

AFA is training the support staff to shed the 'I'm doing charity' mindset. For example, one professional who was forcing a child to eat, leading to challenging behaviours, 'got it' suddenly during training. He realized that what he was doing was wrong and learnt how not to over-instruct, to give instructions in a clear manner and give the children time to process it. The dignity of the individual is always front and centre. Merry is sharply critical of the kind of 'homes' that have CCTV cameras everywhere in the name of safety. Some even go so far as to install cameras in the bedrooms – a gross violation of privacy.

The workplace is in a separate building, clearly distinguished from the living space. People can work for as many hours as they wish, and there are those who don't want to work too. Ananda makes it a point to involve the rural community in its activities and not give the impression of being an isolated unit cut off from its surroundings. For instance, it holds health camps for people from the surrounding villages and educational programmes for their children.

It is worth noting that way back in the 1960s students with disabilities on college and university campuses in the United States initiated measures towards assisted living, and the notion of independent living took firm root in that country by the 1970s. India has just about begun acknowledging the need. Initiatives like the ones we've described must be replicated if we are to effectively tackle the niggling 'after me what?' problem. We need to spread 'bliss' and 'ananda' (joy) across the country to make every PwD swayamkrushi (self-reliant) !

# 27

# THE STATE'S ROLE IN MASS AWARENESS

WE HOPE BY NOW YOU ARE FULLY ACQUAINTED WITH THE cradle-to-grave approach to disability that covers everything from early intervention to assisted living. But merely helping PwDs to be self-sufficient is not enough. The ultimate goal is not integration into society but inclusion. And for a society to be inclusive it must first become aware about disability.

Educating the public and raising mass awareness about disability is best done by the government, which has stupendous reach and manpower. But has the government achieved the best results? Sure, awareness programmes find a place in the old PwD Act as well as the National Trust Act later. India's First Country Report to the UNCRPD (due in 2009 but submitted only in 2015) listed the various measures taken under these two Acts. The primary focus was on detection and early prevention of impairments. The Report states that post the CRPD, the country shifted the focus from prevention to rights.

The actions of the Indian government have a familiar ring to them; it took a predictably bureaucratic approach. It increased the number of national awards given on the International Day of

Persons with Disabilities, brought out commemorative coins and a stamp on Louis Braille's bicentenary, started funding (through the 'Badthe Kadam' campaign) those who organize activities to promote awareness of the UNCRPD and the National Trust, and continues to support the 'We Care' international festival of documentary films on disability. Keeping pace with digital technology, the RCI has an interactive web portal, punarbhava.in, with disability-related information, so that PwDs can be apprised of the latest government schemes for them.

All well and good, but disability is just one of the myriad social concerns of the Indian government, amid the ceaseless battle it has been waging against the seemingly immortal spectres of poverty and hunger. Its public service ad campaigns, for example, have covered family planning, breastfeeding, drunk driving, pulse polio, diabetes, communal harmony, saving water, eye donation, child labour and female foeticide – to name a random selection of the staggering range of topics. Disability can get drowned out by the many issues that are simultaneously crying for attention.

But haven't we said before that disability affects us all? Therefore, shouldn't our country of 1.36 billion (and counting) be made aware of it?

## Awareness Within Government

Before we get to the 1.36 billion, it is pertinent to ask whether the hydra-headed government is itself aware of what it seeks to create awareness about. In a classic case of 'the right hand doesn't know what the left hand is doing', *most government ministries and departments have little knowledge of the RPwD Act.*

'Disability inclusion is an issue spearheaded by the Ministry of Social Justice and Empowerment but has not been addressed in a cross-sectoral manner,' states the Alternate Country Report submitted to the CRPD in February 2019 in response to the

India Report. Arman Ali, director of the advocacy organization NCPEDP, echoes this important point: 'Disability has been made an issue only where the MSJE is involved. There is no awareness about disability among other departments, so health, education, transport, etc. don't make provisions for them. The framers of the Draft National Education Policy 2019 didn't even consult our nodal agency, the DEPD!"

The wheels of government turn ponderously. The information about RPwD Act has to trickle down to the various states.

According to Section 101 (1) of the RPwD Act, state governments are required to notify the State Rules within six months from the date of commencement of the Act. Notifying State Rules is the first step towards implementing the Act in the state. The Rules provide the manner in which the disability committees/boards have to be constituted and the procedures for their meetings; the salaries and allowances of disability commissioners and staff and other members, and several other aspects.

A joint report by NCPEDP and two other organizations in 2018 notes that even two years after the Act was passed, most states hadn't notified the Rules. The report was based on a questionnaire sent to the states and union territories to assess their administrative machinery for implementing the Act. The findings revealed that most states were falling behind. They hadn't yet appointed officials, hadn't constituted committees, boards and special courts, hadn't constituted a disability fund, and so on. Also, the central government, which was supposed to have translated the Act into the other Indian languages, had only done it in two: Odiya and Hindi. NCPEDP, however, had jumped the gun and already translated it into 10 languages, including Sign.

Disability awareness can never be achieved unless the letter and spirit of the RPwD Act and the CRPD first percolates to the influencers, lawmakers and law enforcers, and then right down to the lowest functionary of every department.

Towards this aim, the RPwD Act (in Chapter VIII) asks the state governments to:

(*a*) mandate training on disability rights in all courses for the Panchayati Raj members, legislators, administrators, police officials, judges and lawyers;

(*b*) induct disability as a component for all educational courses for schools, colleges and university teachers, doctors, nurses, para-medical personnel, social welfare officers, rural development officers, ASHA and Anganwadi workers, engineers, architects, other professionals, and community workers.

While the ponderous wheels of government machinery are creaking along, fund allocation for awareness-raising is actually showing a downward trend, and there are vast funds for disability lying unused by the centre and the states.

Taking an essential step that was long overdue, the central government launched a Unique Disability Identity project in 2015 to compile a national database of PwDs. It would issue UDID cards to every PwD so that they could easily avail of benefits related to scholarships, inclusive education, skill training, rail travel, rehabilitation and pension. As part of the scheme, it would issue Disability Certificates to those with the newer disabilities of the 21 mentioned in the RPwD Act (the PwD Act having named only seven).

Five years on, the government of India has barely scratched the surface of the UDID project. Till mid 2019, cards had been issued to only a third of the over 61 lakh PwDs who had applied, and there were lakhs more who weren't aware of the scheme. 'The UDID process is only 25 per cent complete,' states Dr Himangshu Das, director of the National Institute for Empowerment of Persons with Multiple Disabilities (NIEPMD) in August 2019 in Bengaluru. He is speaking at the National Conference on Assistive Technology for All by 2030 organized by Mobility India. 'Many states are yet to start, or else they've achieved 10 per cent, or they're half way,' he adds. One cannot expect significant progress to have been made till date.

There is a fundamental question that remains unanswered, though, before we speak of a national database. Do we have the right numbers?

Even as the Indian government continues to take a 'charity approach' in the words of the Alternate Country Report, construing rights more as entitlements, it has *no reliable, disaggregated data*. It cannot effectively make policies and allocate resources for disability if it doesn't even know the answer to the simple question: *How many PwDs are there in India?*

## Disability Census

The colonial administration started counting PwDs – or, in the terminology of that era, those who were 'idiots', 'insane,' and 'lepers' – in 1872. The practice was discontinued after the 1931 census. The government of India briefly reverted to measuring disability in the 1981 census because the UN had declared it the International Year of the Disabled. This token acknowledgement of the disabled population by counting the number of 'totally blind, totally crippled and/or totally dumb' resulted in an unconvincing statistic of 0.16 per cent as the PwD population. PwDs were not counted in the 1991 census, and nearly wouldn't have been in 2001 as well if not for the agitations by NGOs and Disabled People's Organizations (DPOs).

When NCPEDP came to know that even after the PwD Act of 1995 was passed, the government had no intention of measuring the disabled population, it swung into action. An advocacy campaign was carried out in New Delhi under the banner of the Disabled Rights Group (DRG), an informal cross disability advocacy network of organizations based in and around the national capital. NCPEDP had set up a national network of NGOs and DPOs in 1999 called the National Disability Network (NDN). DRG members wrote to organizations and PwDs across the country, and NCPEDP called on its NDN partners to bring pressure on the government. Hundreds of letters and faxes poured into the Census Commission office, and top ministers and political parties were addressed as well.

When the Census officials stubbornly stuck to their decision, NCPEDP and its fellow-campaigners decided to switch from a persuasive to a confrontational mode. They held a huge rally in the capital on 7 March 2000. Just two days before they were to organize a massive sit-in in April, the Home Ministry made overtures to them. Several meetings and two months later, the government officially announced that a question on disability would be included in the 2001 census. It was question number 15 in a list of 23, and it asked whether the person was disabled 'in seeing, in speech, in hearing, in movement, mental' with code numbers for each category.

NCPEDP and its NDN partners raced to beat the clock; they had less than six months to spread awareness among PwDs and their families to step up and be counted. They held regional workshops, mobilized the media and created awareness materials that were translated into *desi* languages. However, they didn't have time to train the enumerators in a structured way, which was crucial since they would be the ones going door to door contacting PwDs directly. It later transpired that many enumerators had skipped question 15 altogether. The final figure of 2.1 per cent of the total population was well below the conservative estimate of 5 per cent, but at least it was better than the 1981 figure of 0.16 per cent.

When it was time for the 2011 census, NCPEDP and its partners started preparations a year in advance. Met by a supportive Census Commissioner, they got cracking on framing the disability question. Generally, countries ask disability questions that are impairment-based or activity-based: either naming the disability, or describing what activities one can or cannot do and to what degree.

The Washington Group on Disability Statistics, which was formed as a result of the UN International Seminar on Measurement of Disability in New York in June 2001, suggested questions that focus on some basic/core activities designed to capture the bulk of adults with disabilities. The questions ask about difficulties one may have doing certain activities because of a 'health problem', or difficulty in the following areas: seeing, even if wearing glasses; hearing, even if using a hearing aid; walking or climbing steps; remembering or concentrating; self-care; and understanding or being understood by others. The optional responses to each of these questions – no difficulty, some difficulty, a lot of difficulty or can't do it at all – would capture the full spectrum of functioning from mild to severe.

To decide the nature of the 2011 disability question, a two-day Round Table Consultation was organized in collaboration with the Census Commission. Participants rejected the WG's model, which they felt wouldn't suit the Indian context. Since the census questions were generally answered by the head of the family, it would be culturally insensitive to ask questions about other members' ability to wash or dress themselves. Also, questions were felt to be so general or vague that they might lose their purpose in the Indian context. It was unanimously decided to have separate categories for mental illness and mental retardation, and to add the options of Multiple Disabilities and Any Other (since it was not possible to list all impairments).

The disability question was advanced to number 9 of a total 29. NCPEDP and its partners conducted far-reaching awareness activities and undertook a multi-stage training of enumerators as well. They were deeply disappointed when the 2011 census results came out though. It showed only a marginal increase in the disabled population: from 2.1 per cent in the previous census to 2.2 per cent. Enumerators were still clearly chary of asking families about their members with disabilities; they felt it was too sensitive or even offensive to do so.

It just goes to show you how difficult it is to remove the stigma around disability and how much more needs to be done to dispel ignorance. To accelerate those lumbering wheels, to ratchet up awareness, private players must wield their heft. Every little bit helps.

# 28

# PRIVATE EFFORTS TOWARDS
# PUBLIC AWARENESS

WHILE THE GOVERNMENT SHOULD IDEALLY TAKE THE LEAD in spreading awareness, some private efforts have been truly commendable. One such individual who has made a significant contribution is Prarthana Kaul.

Prarthana noticed something peculiar going on. Many deaf and HI women in their first pregnancy were delivering stillborn babies. The experience of one such woman provided a rare insight. Who would have imagined that disability awareness could mean the difference between life and death?

When a pregnant deaf woman goes to a hospital, she can barely communicate with any of the doctors, nurses or other paramedical staff because none of them know Sign. Through gestures and lip-reading, she gains half-baked knowledge about how to bring her baby to term. Perhaps she has gathered that she has to return to the hospital for regular check-ups. But nobody has told her about the possibility that her amniotic sac could rupture. And that water breaking is a sign that the baby is ready to be born.

A woman who was HI told Prarthana, 'I was carrying a baby, and in my ninth month the water burst. I was not aware I had to rush to hospital.' She thought the pain she felt was normal, and when she went to the hospital the next day her baby was born dead. 'These cases happen with hearing impaired women almost every other day,' Prarthana tells us. 'Even these basics are not communicated. So when it comes to the next level, illness or disease, who will make them understand?'

Prateek and Prarthana Kaul saw the urgent need to spread awareness and the message of inclusion when they set up GiftAbled, which began as 'inclusive gifting' of products made by PwDs. Currently based in Pune, they are working out of a rented building in Bengaluru when we meet them in 2019. One of their major victories had been sensitization in police stations and hospitals, where they held awareness sessions. Teaching traffic police the right way to help the VI cross the road was one of the small but key lessons they imparted. A gynaecologist who attended one of their hospital sessions went with the GiftAbled team to rural areas to conduct sessions on women's health. One such hour-long session in Bengaluru stretched to four hours, because the 53 VI and HI girls who attended from various neighbourhoods in the city had never had access to a doctor before.

Prarthana, who is 'the mother ship' in Prateek's words, had been intimately involved with the NGO sector even before he met her. She had quit IBM and joined iVolunteer, the leading organization promoting volunteerism in India. As the national head of programmes, 5,000+ volunteers from across India had reported to her. Prateek was working for Target India as the lead of Community Relations in his technology team. His company was associated with NAB at the time, and they were thinking of gifting something to the students there when he asked Prarthana for suggestions. They put their heads together...which later brought their lives together.

GiftAbled places a special emphasis on creating awareness about disability, and they have 'added the volunteer flavour to it'. Prarthana learnt Sign a decade ago, and the couple have been extensively working with the deaf. They started with four or five Sign workshops a month in Bengaluru and attracted volunteers, some of whom became Sign trainers. This has grown exponentially, and especially during the Covid-19 lockdown volunteers could hardly wait to join the flurry of online Sign workshops that GiftAbled held. They also gained volunteers who wished to read to the blind and trained them in how to do so. Obviously, the greater the number of volunteers, the more the overall awareness of disability grows.

Sensitizing the corporate world is no cakewalk. GiftAbled holds customized workshops for corporates but this alone cannot adequately drive home the message. 'When we show the impact, sensitization automatically happens,' says Prarthana, citing an example of a corporate in Bengaluru. The contact person, eager to spend the company's CSR funds and seeking a conveniently located beneficiary he could monitor, had asked her, 'Can you find me a deaf school within 3 km (from the office)?' Hiding her amusement, she replied that even if a city had a deaf school, there would be just one or two.

GiftAbled got the corporate to fund around 15 hearing aids for kids in Gadag in northern Karnataka, but they didn't stop at that. They picked volunteers with a theatre background and asked them to teach mime to deaf kids of two local orphanages. At first the ad hoc troupe enacted their mime act at the Forum Mall signal in Bengaluru to spread awareness about disability. Then the Kauls asked the corporate whether the kids could do mime on their premises. They said: 'Why not during our Family Day?'

The employees and their family members numbering almost 1,000 watched the kids' mime in St. John's Auditorium and gave them a standing ovation. At the end of the performance, GiftAbled announced that the kids were HI. And the number of hearing aids the corporate funded in Gadag then went up from 15 to 300.

'Now funds are going to rural areas. From 3 km to 300 km!' says Prarthana.

The following year on Family Day, the company wanted a repeat performance but this time GiftAbled sourced the deaf kids from Gadag. Volunteers went to Gadag and stayed there to teach mime to deaf kids. Ten of them came to Bengaluru, some of whom had received hearing aids from the corporate. Employees and their families remembered GiftAbled from the previous year. Prarthana explains that those kids had been from Bengaluru, whereas these had come from 300 km away because of the company's support. Clearly, this endeavour created a far more widespread and powerful impact than if the corporate had just written a fat cheque to some invisible recipients.

GiftAbled is spreading its wings across different segments of the population: inhabitants of the most remote areas and people from various age groups. Children, who Prarthana playfully refers to as 'the *bacha* (kids) party', are an important target. Prateek concludes: 'If children are sensitized today, in the initial schooling years, then you don't require organizations like us; 20 years down the line you'll have a society which is inclusive.'

He states their goal: 'By 2035 disability should no longer remain a cause in India, period.'

## Educating through Stories

The child who is sensitive to PwDs will grow up to be an adult for whom inclusion comes naturally. There is no better way to make a child aware of disability than through storytelling. And the earlier you attract them the better.

Karadi Tales is an independent publishing house based in Chennai, which focuses on picture books and audio books. In 2013, *Little Vinayak* won the Outstanding Books for Young People with Disabilities award instituted by the International Board on Books for Young People (IBBY). Karadi Tales co-founder and publishing director Shobha Viswanath explains what drove her to write the story: 'The impetus behind *Little Vinayak* was to tell a story about someone who was different, but not resolving it through magic or granting him/her an undiscovered talent, but by bringing to light the fact that many times, a disability simply has to be managed or worked around.'

Other books from the Karadi Tales stable centred on disability are *The Bookworm*, which is about a boy with a stammer, and *Thukpa for All*, about a blind child in Ladakh.

---

How many parents in India would buy their children a disabled doll?

A young couple in Delhi came up with a radical idea that is perhaps ahead of its time in our disabled-unfriendly country. Jamal Siddiqui and his wife Shweta Verma, both social work professionals, are particularly keen to home in on children when spreading their message of inclusion and diversity. They created Ginny, a doll who wears thick glasses because she has low vision; she wears a brace on her 'radial club' right arm which is shorter than her left and is curled at the wrist; and she has only nine fingers. They gave her a whole planet to live on, too! A planet where nobody is the odd one out – where diversity is the norm.

Shweta and Jamal founded Ginny's Planet in 2019, with plans to bring out a whole range of dolls and action figures that showcase human diversity. They also want to publish books that feature Ginny and the fun adventures she has with average kids on her planet. In fact they have already published the first book, written by Shweta, simply titled *Ginny*.

The inspiration for Ginny came from their son. Soham Meer was born in 2016, premature, with multiple medical complications.

Weighing 1.7 kilos at seven months, he had a hole in the heart and a radial club arm with a hand that had four fingers. The hole in the heart had side-effects that necessitated continuing medication even after surgery, and the arm had to be corrected through multiple bone surgeries. The hospital clock was ticking, and the medical insurance money would come in only months later (just 70 per cent was reimbursed in the end). The hefty hospital bill almost broke the backs of this young couple. The costs for the room, surgeries and medicines had to be met as down payments or even in advance. 'We had exhausted all our money,' says Jamal, 'and I started borrowing from friends for day-to-day expenses.'

In 2018 he took up an assignment with the humanitarian organization Mercy Corps. He was the head of their youth programmes, which dealt with child protection, livelihoods and psychosocial support. The posting was in Iraq, in Erbil, the heart of the Iraqi-Kurdish conflict. It was a deliberate choice, says Jamal, 'Actually I hoped I would die there so my family could get the insurance money.' There was every chance he would be killed in a shooting or explosion in Erbil or in any of the other cities his job took him to. The insurance money would clear his debts and meet his son's considerable medical expenses for the future.

In the event, his desperate wish was not granted. Jamal returned alive to resume his uphill journey. His 'Why did this happen to me?' and 'Why do I have to watch my child suffer?' questions were answered by Shweta: 'He [God] chose us. He chose us as parents because he knew we would love and care for him better than anyone else.' Soham is used to hospital visits now, and will have to take medicines all his life, but he is thriving. His name, after all, is Soham ('I am [an] Eternal') Meer ('leader').

Ginny's Planet offers 'empathy and diversity' training sessions for children aged seven and above, using a combination of stories, toys, games, reflections and action. Adults aren't left out either: there is disability awareness training in the form of short orientation sessions for employees of organizations.

## A Lifeline for Caregivers

Prachi Deo had enough and more on her plate in 2015, but that didn't stop her from deciding to set up Nayi Disha, a website that provides information on ID and DD. She had literally forced her reluctant parents to move from Mumbai to her home in Hyderabad, because her father had had his first heart attack and her mother had early onset Alzheimer's, and they couldn't be expected to take sole care of her brother Pranjan who has DS.

Prachi had a minor epiphany when her daughter was born in 2006. As she tended to her eight-month-old she realized that whatever she was doing for her daughter her parents had been doing for Pranjan for the past 38 years. And they would continue doing it for the rest of their lives, while her daughter would soon grow to be independent. This realization stayed with her, prompting her to think of other parents like her's who were facing the same situation, perhaps unassisted.

Prachi abandoned her dream of building 'this amazing special school' and started volunteering at the vocational centre she had found for Pranjan in Hyderabad. When her friend Sudarsana Kundu suggested she start a centre for ID persons, Prachi knew it would be too much to handle. Then she thought: Why not do something for parents? She and Sudarsana went about meeting parents of children with ID, phoning them, interviewing them in schools and holding focus group discussions. And they found almost everyone wandering in the dark.

'One of the parents said, "For the first two years, I felt like I was in a jungle and I didn't know where to go,"' says Prachi. 'Another said, "I was in a haze; I didn't know what was happening." Till now I have met only two or three parents who said I knew about the condition.' An educated friend of hers whose child was diagnosed with DS even asked the doctor whether there was any medicine for it.

She and Sudarsana co-founded Nayi Disha with Reema Gupta. It has three pillars: a service directory, verified information resources and a parent support group.

The directory is a painstakingly collated countrywide list of contacts for every kind of service a parent of a child with ID or DD might need – education, diagnosis, intervention, therapy, you name it. The contacts are not only of services related to the child's medical condition but also to their daily life; it could be a music teacher or a swimming coach who is willing to teach a child with autism, an advocate who will take care of guardianship, or a financial adviser to help with planning. Parents can rate and review service providers anonymously if need be.

Under 'information resources', they share relevant audios, videos, infographics and slide shows 'instead of long articles that nobody is going to read'. For example, what's the difference between ADHD and autism, what are the health conditions to look out for in DS, or what is the first aid for epilepsy? Subject matter experts vet this vast repository of information that guides parents through different stages of the child's life. New parents would want basic information about the child's condition – including what it means and what are the various therapies needed. Then it's time to look for schools. When the kid hits puberty the parents might seek information on behaviour issues such as how to bring down aggression. Open schooling and options for vocations come next. Older parents can find answers to the 'after me what?' question: How do we plan for our children's future and make them as independent as possible?

The support group is where parents find a safe space to share their ups and downs. It started in 2015 with Prachi creating a homegrown website with 10 parents. The last we checked, the website had attracted over 1,20,000 unique visitors and around

700 to 800 visitors every day. Nayi Disha merely plays the role of facilitator or enabler. 'Parents themselves are the experts; they have so much experience and they have suggestions on what to do, so they help other parents,' Prachi explains. A discussion among the group can lead to Nayi Disha bringing in a subject expert who conducts a workshop for 30 to 40 parents, which benefits thousands more when a recording of it or an infographic about it is uploaded online.

In May 2019, Nayi Disha started a helpline. Parents and caregivers call in from all corners of the country and wherever possible, they are put in touch with support groups within easy reach. Nayi Disha has formed links with doctors and hospitals, which refer parents to them for further guidance. Next, they plan to provide information on stress and depression, as requested by many parents.

Nayi Disha has seven people from varied backgrounds working on it at the moment, besides several volunteers, freelancers and more than 50 partners who play various roles from disseminating information to contributing content. They want to target Tier Three and smaller towns, and translate content not just on the website but also as printed material to be distributed in public places. They have already made a start with Hindi and Telugu.

'We have grown brick by brick,' says Prachi. The structure they've built stands firm today, sheltering those who had been groping in the dark.

## Mental Disability, Most Misunderstood

The least understood and most misunderstood disabilities are those of the mind. As mentioned earlier, most of our population has only the most rudimentary knowledge of mental illness or disorders. One young woman intends to tackle this monumental ignorance head-on, through action on a national and a global scale.

Neha Kirpal, the World Economic Forum's Young Global Leader, says she has been looking at the mental health sector for the past 30-odd years. This might seem a long period, given that she is below 40, but her interest grew from her own personal experiences dealing with mental disability and seeing the fragmented nature of the care system in India in the 1980s and 1990s; she was barely six when her mother started showing symptoms of schizophrenia and, although fully rehabilitated today, she went untreated for 25 years. Turnaround stories like these must make us believe that those with these difficult conditions are certainly treatable, and can return to a degree of 'normalcy and functioning if the right help is sought at the right time. As a society we must find faith in a care system that understands the biological and psychosocial aspects of these diseases, and aims to address them collectively for best outcomes and with long-term rehabilitation. But not all stories end happily. Sadly, Neha lost her younger brother to suicide last year as he succumbed to a long battle with depression, reminding us of the impact untreated mental illnesses have on the entire family and especially the next generation.

Neha shares some alarming statistics: *India has one-third of the world's cases (and that's one-third of each of the following) of depression, alcoholism and suicides.* Where mental health should rightfully take up 10 per cent of a country's health care budget, in India it is a mere 0.6 per cent. In our defence, the rest of the world too has come rather late to the table. 'Globally, mental health is a new issue,' she says. 'Only in the last decade or so there has been organized interest in and committed capital around mental health.'

As mental health is one of the UN's SDGs, and as it gains the increasing attention of the World Health Assembly, there is a push in private philanthropy as well as by the government for more investments in mental health, she says. 'Data, research and reporting play a key part, to show the scale of the problem and its multidimensional aspect.' Together with Dr Vikram Patel, who set up Sangath in Goa, and Dr Shekhar Saxena, who was heading Mental Health at the WHO and is now at Harvard – both of them distinguished professors – Neha co-founded a global think-tank on mental health called Librum. The think-tank works with governments and developmental agencies globally on systemic solutions for global mental health issues, particularly in low-resource settings.

Spreading awareness about mental health is also the mission of the White Swan Foundation. Although it is winding down for lack of funds as we go to print, its portal[57] remains active. The website is a knowledge repository on mental health, arming people with the right knowledge so they can take the right course of action. Apart from helping people browse and seek knowledge on mental health, it is also a platform for them to share their personal stories of hope, struggle and success. 'It is a bridge between psychiatric counsellors and the public,' says Pavithra Jayaram, head of content.

Operating in six languages, the website has been seeing a 25 per cent spike each quarter over the last six to eight quarters, Manoj Chandran tells us in early 2019. More people were reading in *desi* languages than in English – a hopeful sign of wider reach. Manoj reports to us in 2021 that 'the portal receives more than 7 lakh users in a year, a large part of who come from smaller towns'.

White Swan aims to change public perceptions about mental health not only through the website but also through physical outreach programmes and social media campaigns. The outreach programmes have covered schools and colleges, professionals and, most crucially, those who work in rural areas – especially Anganwadi and ASHA workers.

They tried out an interesting format in Bengaluru – storytelling sessions. In September and October 2017, they got professional storytellers to interact with the public by telling stories in public

---

[57] White Swan Foundation, 2021, Web, 10 August 2021.

spaces such as parks, malls and restaurants. These stories based on real life experiences of people with mental disabilities would start a conversation with members of the public who happened to be passing by and who stopped to listen and stayed on for a discussion.

Could they reach out to 10,000 people in a single month? This was their ambitious Mission 10K in October 2018 when they trained 200 people during that month for four hours on aspects of mental health. Participants – called Mental Health Champions – were a diverse set including students, teachers, managers in start-ups, human resources teams and people from the development sector. Each of these people in turn had to commit to hold 90-minute conversations on mental health with (ideally) groups of 50, with as many sessions as possible during the month. Nearly 90 of them actually had these conversations with groups of 30 to 40 and reported on their experiences on the login page. That's a sizeable number even though it falls below the Mission 10K target.

Manoj says they witnessed a difference in how men and women use the portal. Women tend to seek help, while men tend to look for medical information on mental health. Guided by this insight, they conducted two social media campaigns separately addressing each group. A Women's mental health campaign titled 'Not just hormones' was launched to discuss subjects such as the after-effects of street harassment and the impact of nutrition on mental health; the campaign on Men's mental health included discussions on 'toxic masculinity' and how it influences help-seeking.

Predictably, after the lockdown was announced in March 2020 following the outbreak of the coronavirus pandemic, White Swan noticed an increase in cases of emotional distress. Stress and anxiety were the common issues, says Manoj, and domestic abuse cases spiked. Immediately, they shifted their focus to knowledge around coping with the 'new normal' and arranged several webinars with experts on topics such as loneliness, working from home, relationship issues, managing anxiety and managing addiction.

White Swan has brought out e-books too – on topics such as pregnancy and mental health, managing exam stress, understanding a teacher's role in student mental health and a special LGBTQIA+ edition on mental health. Their e-book on mental health in the workplace is based on a survey they conducted in 2019, with 829 online and offline respondents whose average age was 30 – most of whom had full-time jobs. To the question on whether they had an mental health issue – anything from worry and stress to diagnosed illnesses such as anxiety and depression – one in two people answered yes. Two out of three said they knew someone at their workplace with an mental health issue; however, most of them said there were few or no discussions about mental health at their workplace.

Although this survey was limited to a thin segment of an urban and educated population, it is the first step pointing to the need for an in-depth survey of a large and diverse pool of employees. Employers are not aware that their employees' mental health has a direct bearing on productivity and attrition rates. 'A report by the WHO estimates that depression and anxiety disorders cost the world economy US$ 1 trillion annually in lost productivity,' says the e-book. 'The costs of mental health issues among employees are significant, and the benefits of addressing them even more so.'

But disability awareness cannot and should not be seen merely in terms of profit and loss. Besides making (as we have seen) the difference between life and death, it can open the doors to a new way of perceiving the world.

# 29

# DISABILITY THROUGH
# THE MEDIA LENS

ONE OF THOSE WHO BELIEVE THAT THERE HAVE BEEN 'major changes' in the disability sector after the RPwD Act was passed is Christy Abraham of APD. APD has been working in the sector for over 60 years, impacting over 5,00,000 lives through its various programmes. Speaking from a historical standpoint, Christy says that she has seen increasing awareness 'at least in urban centres', and a growth in Special Ed.

Part of this awareness can be linked to the news media's coverage of disability.

## Disability in the News

While it is true that mainstream media wallows in 'inspiration porn', the space it devotes to para sports does contribute to heightening public awareness. Christy observes that 'The Paralympics have helped in a big way to bring disability centrestage, although we have yet to identify drivers of change such as brand ambassadors to campaign for this sector.' Paralympic events always snag press coverage, as a result of which physical disability, at the very least, has entered the public consciousness. Indians have won 31 medals so far at the international Paralympic Games.

An individual who has perhaps grabbed as much news coverage as our Paralympians have is India's first blade runner Major Devender Pal Singh.[58] Initially a solo marathoner, DP began to inspire other amputees to join him. The trust that he formed in 2011, The Challenging Ones (TCO), is a loose conglomerate of over 2,000 amputees – many of whom have gained the confidence and the strength to become marathoners and para athletes.

The aim of TCO marathoners: 'Change the mindset of society wherever we run'.

DP, as we may remember from an early chapter in this book, persuades his fellow marathoners to reveal their prostheses to the world and not hide them behind trousers. This public display of their disability will not only make the world aware of what they can do, but also encourage them to accept their disability and boost their own self-confidence. TCO started including wheel runners (wheelchair users who race).

Then one day, DP realized that they were mostly running in metros. 'What about the interior, how will we change their mindset?' he pondered. This propelled DP's SwachchAbility Movement where he organized an event across seven cities. In each city, any of the local citizens could register for the run; although it was open to all, children were the main target of the organizers. They chose one school in each city as the venues; the schools had to have a running route and a dirty area around it, because after the run they would pick up brooms and start cleaning the dirty area. Over 12,000 people with and without disabilities took part.

SwachchAbility Runs were then held in eight other cities over 2016, 2017 and 2018, culminating with a special event in

---

[58] His life story has been captured in the graphic novel *Grit: The Major Story*. Major D.P. Singh, V.R. Ferose and Sriram Jagannathan, *Grit: The Major Story* (Gurugram: Hachette India, 2019).

Kanpur – the head office of their sponsor, JK Cement. Altogether the movement had 55,000 participants, including 30,000 children and 2,500 PwDs. And that certainly adds up to a lot of awareness.

Christy Abraham's point about brand ambassadors is worth noting. They are an ideal way to spur disability campaigns. Unfortunately, we haven't been able to identify sportspersons with disabilities who have ignited the mass imagination and could lend their faces to the disability movement. There are stars in wheelchair basketball, wheelchair badminton and so on, but why are their names not imprinted on our minds? In film-crazy India, the only stars are those on the silver screen and the very term 'brand ambassador' brings to mind celebrities from the film world.

## Disability in Popular Cinema

In 2015, by publicly revealing her ongoing battle with depression, film actor Deepika Padukone brought the subject of mental illness to the forefront. She subsequently started the Live Love Laugh Foundation to spread awareness about mental health, reduce the stigma around it and support those seeking mental health care. Actor Aamir Khan addressed disability in his popular TV series *Satyameva Jayate*. Hrithik Roshan, also from the same industry, has often described how debilitating his stammering was during childhood and how he struggled to overcome it through therapy and determination; he has also played characters with disabilities in three films. Film director Sriram Raghavan too had a stutter; during his talk at the India Inclusion Summit 2019 he described how he tried to conquer it and managed to succeed only when he was around the age of 40.

Cinema exerts such a powerful influence on the mind and behaviour of the Indian public that it would seem natural to think of using it as a medium to bring about awareness and change. But representations of disability in popular Indian cinema have been far from satisfactory. Academic papers have been written about films with characters having disabilities – including Tamil, Telugu, Kannada, Malayalam and Hindi cinema of the past and present.

In the past, crude caricatures of PwDs have appeared in films, and disability has often been portrayed as being pitiable, laughable, evil, or punishment for wrongdoing. The comic sidekick with dwarfism, the hero as a blind singing beggar, the villain with a handicap that 'deforms' his body, the 'cured' disability as a happy ending – the demeaning stereotypes were numerous. Depictions of people with mental illnesses or intellectual disabilities have been especially problematic.

In the 1970s and 1980s, there were a handful of films that moved away from marginalized and formulaic to more realistic depictions of disability. Some of these were Gulzar's *Koshish* (1972) about a deaf couple, Sai Paranjpy's *Sparsh* (1984) about the blind, and Singeetam Srinivasa Rao's *Mayuri* (1985) about the real-to-reel story of Bharatanatyam dancer Sudha Chandran (who played herself) who lost her leg after a traffic accident but continued dancing with a (prosthetic) 'Jaipur Foot'.

The twenty-first century saw a spate of mainstream movies (mainly Hindi, but also in Malayalam) featuring all sorts of disabilities. Some disabilities that made it to the screen were CP, DD, OCD, Alzheimer's, Asperger's, dwarfism, autism, deaf-blindness, dyslexia, progeria and paraplegia. Cynics would say that stars deliberately seek roles of characters with disabilities because it's a sure-fire method of winning a national award.

PwDs have a fundamental question for filmmakers, though – a question that always leaves them fumbling for an answer: Why don't they choose PwDs for the roles of characters with disabilities?

Instead of Kalki Koechlin playing a woman with CP in *Margarita with a Straw*, Hrithik Roshan as a paraplegic in *Guzaarish*, Priyanka Chopra botching up the role of a person with autism in *Barfi!* or VFX being used to give Shahrukh Khan dwarfism in *Zero*, couldn't the directors have cast PwDs instead?

Since we haven't got any straight answers from them yet, we can only hazard a few guesses and put words into their mouths. One: There are no PwDs among the acting fraternity. (Even if true, whose fault is that?) Two: Stars guarantee box office success. Three: A producer would never fund a movie starring an unknown person with a disability and even if they did, the public would reject it.

Perhaps these filmmakers haven't looked hard enough. It is more convenient to reach for a popular name than to hunt for a PwD who might not only fit the role but also play it admirably. Lavish praise is heaped on the star for her ability to 'become' a person with CP, for example, but we must remember that she has full control over the muscles and movements of her body and face, and is more easily able to fine-tune her performance to suit the requirements of the director. Perhaps audition-calls for PwDs should state: No Severe or Moderate, only Mild cases need apply! It's the tyranny of the 'normal' all over again.

Nagesh Kukunoor chose a different route when making *Iqbal* and *Dhanak*. He spoke at the India Inclusion Summit 2017 about treading the fine line between not overtly bringing disability to the forefront, and yet introducing a subtle message. His characters were not defined by their disability; they just happened to have it. *Iqbal* was a film about cricket, not deafness; *Dhanak* was about the adventurous journey of a boy and his sister, not about blindness. And naturally, he wasn't interested in creating tearjerkers, coaxing sympathy from the audience through maudlin scenes.

There's a Kannada movie currently in the making that promises to be unique when it is completed. *Arabbie* will be a mainstream feature film with a PwD as the hero. Kannada director Rajkumar, who has worked in the film industry for 15 years, saw Vishwas K.S. three years ago in a dance programme and decided to make this film about him. He followed Vishwas for three years, intending to make a biopic on the swimming champion and dancer who lost both arms in a childhood accident.

To trace his life's journey on film – from the accident to his education, search for a job, dance performances and international swimming competitions – would entail a budget of ₹3 crore, a sum that no producer was willing to pony up. They would also have to find a young boy with no arms to play his role as a child. Further, they would have to shoot at the international venues of competitions. Instead, Rajkumar decided to embark on an even more radical venture, which would be only one-third the cost: a feature film starring Vishwas in the lead role. Vishwas said he was going to learn how to act, the same way he learnt other skills that nobody dreamt he could – swimming, kung-fu and dance.

Rajkumar was finally able to find a producer and shooting started in December 2019. The *muhurt* (first shot) of the film was scheduled for World Disabled Day (December 3), but since Tuesday is considered inauspicious in southern India it was put off by a day. The Covid-19 pandemic disrupted the shooting schedule further in 2020. Since the wrap-up is going to be delayed, we'll have to wait a little longer for the premiere. But surely, it will be worth the wait!

## Documentaries on Disability

Unfortunately, feature films attract far greater numbers of viewers than do documentaries in India. Pavitra Chalam is a young, award-winning filmmaker who has been making documentary films on disability, among other subjects.

In 2012, DSFI commissioned her company Curley Street to create a film titled *Indelible* about seven people with DS in India. It won the Asia Pacific Screen Awards for Outstanding Documentary

Filmmaking in 2014 at the DocWeek film festival in Adelaide, Australia, and received critical acclaim across the international festival circuit. The film also introduces the chairperson and co-founder of DSFI, Dr Surekha Ramachandran, whose daughter Babli has DS.

*Rooting for Roona* (available on Netflix) is a film that captures the story of Roona Begum, a baby born with hydrocephalus, a birth defect that results in a massive swelling of the head caused by a build-up of fluid in the brain. Roona's head was 36 inches in diameter. Her young parents Abdul (17) and Fatema (22), who lead a hand-to-mouth existence, tried in vain to get her treated at government hospitals in their home state of Tripura. Her fate changed when a local photo-journalist took a photo of her that went viral globally overnight. It triggered a chain of events that eventually resulted in Roona's admission into one of India's premier private hospitals in New Delhi. Headlines across the world celebrated her journey and the media frenzy peaked, but soon abated.

The world moved on but the Curley Street team remained with her. They followed her story for six years, standing by her as she completed a string of surgeries from which she seemed to emerge stronger than ever. In May 2017, when they took Roona to Delhi for a final medical assessment, her doctor scheduled her last surgery for mid-July. He was highly optimistic about her progress and said she would soon be walking.

On 18 June, however, Curley Street received a sorrowful call from Fatema. Roona had developed unexpected breathing issues and died at home. Pavitra and her team were shattered. But they pushed forward and managed to complete the film.

*Rooting for Roona* has held deep personal meaning for Pavitra. A few months after Roona's death, Pavitra found out that she was pregnant. 'The edit of the film took place through my pregnancy and this gave me a certain strength and conviction I have never experienced before,' she writes to us. 'My dream was to bring both babies to life in the best way I could: Roona to the screen and my own little one into a better world – one that would fight for children like Roona.'

# 30

# TOWARDS A NATIONWIDE MOVEMENT

IT BEARS REPEATING THAT INDIA IS OVER HALF A CENTURY behind the West in its attempts to include PwDs in our society. Our recent progressive laws on disability will have to be translated into action on the ground. As we have seen, there is a tremendous deficit in social awareness of disability. There is little or no accessibility, as a result of which PwDs are denied educational and job opportunities. There are practically no support systems for their productive, routine living.

But we have also seen laudable examples of individuals and institutions who're plugging away at their task of creating an inclusive nation. Unless their efforts are multiplied a thousandfold, change will only come in dribs and drabs.

Yes, we need nothing less than an uprising – a powerful, overarching, countrywide disability rights movement that brings together persons with every kind of disability and fights for total inclusion.

## Be Visible, Be Vocal

Christy Abraham makes an acute observation about the main reason for the lack of steam in organizing for disability rights: 'There hasn't been enough anger to spur activism and generate a disability movement, as in other rights discourses. When fighting injustice against women and transgenders, the target or the enemy is clear, the perpetrators are clear. But in disability, although there is injustice, who do they fight against? Who do they blame? Society is too vague a target. There is sadness. Anger or frustration is not there.'

Christy also cites another pertinent reason. International pressure groups often determine a country's priorities, and NGOs in India (and other developing countries no doubt) follow in their path. In the 1980s, Community-Based Rehabilitation was in the forefront until the HIV discourse dominated the global arena and disability receded into the background. After HIV, it was violence against women, women's rights and transgender rights. 'Disability got lost among these agendas,' she says. 'It's like a trend or a wave, the way NGOs function or focus.'

Whatever may be the prevailing trend, PwDs in India should take ownership of the well-recognized motto of the global disability rights movement: 'Nothing about us without us'.

Of course there is widepsread societal indifference and rejection. G. Vijayaraghavan, founder of The Autism School in Kerala and former member of the Central Advisory Board on Disability, says, 'If you look at reforms in the disability sector they're all court-driven. It should be society-driven.' Society is not empathetic enough, he says, and is weighed down by stigmas, taboos and prejudices.

But PwDs cannot wait for society to change its mindset. They should be self-advocates. Lead from the front. Demand their rights.

## Rights, Not Charity

Arman Ali, head of the NCPEDP, says, 'PwDs should move from the role of beneficiary to a leadership role.' One of the biggest problems is that the disability community itself lacks an understanding and awareness of its rights, he says. 'PwDs still play the pity card. What happens the day pity runs out? The discourse of disability from the human rights perspective is missing.'

Christy observes that 'entitlements, not rights' predominate. 'Even today, it's a welfaristic (sic) agenda that the government pursues. Disability has not become a development agenda.' Sympathy is the operating principle, so the government concentrates on pensions and other things it can give away, she says.

The NCPEDP keeps a sharp eye on potential rights violations. When the Indian government took the absurd step of attempting to delete the RPwD Act provision that metes out punishment for those who humiliate or abuse PwDs, there was such a strong pushback from the NCPEDP and other disability organizations that the government hastily backed off.

In recent years we have seen sporadic instances of individuals or small groups of PwDs in India taking up cudgels for disability rights. These have usually taken the form of online petitions or protests on specific issues.

Some members of the Deaf community started a signature campaign complaining about the bad quality of Sign interpreters on TV news. For the hearing, a Signer in a corner of the screen is just something to be ignored, but for the Deaf it can literally make a difference between life and death. For example, imagine an impending catastrophe like a flood or a cyclone being announced on TV and the Deaf not being able to understand the warnings issued.

Demonetization was another catastrophe for certain PwD

communities. When the sizes of the currency notes changed, the Blind could no longer make out their denominations. They started an online petition for notes to have Braille indicators. Perhaps in response to their demands, the Indian government launched a mobile phone app called MANI (Mobile-Aided Note Identifier), which can be downloaded for free on any smartphone. Instructions for use are audio-based. All one has to do is point the mobile at the note and the denomination will be read out. But MANI is of no use to those from the Blind community who can't afford smartphones; Braille indicators on notes would serve them best.

Sometimes the issues that PwDs protest about have been personal, but they've ended up having spin-offs for the wider community. A restaurant denying entry to a wheelchair user or a swimming pool excluding members with intellectual disabilities would become a rallying point for others with the same disability. Commercial outfits have started taking such complaints seriously, for obvious reasons. It makes economic sense for food delivery services to make their websites accessible to the Blind.

This slow awakening in fits and starts must gather a steady momentum. Disparate efforts must coalesce.

## Need for Cohesion

Disability organizations need to come together on a common platform. Now, each works and fights for the narrow, specific disability that they are championing. It's a scarcity mindset that prevails, with each guarding what they believe is their own share of the pie. NCPEDP is the country's only cross-disability advocacy organization.

'The disability movement is scattered,' Arman Ali observes. Rati Misra of the government's DEPD adds, 'Everything is held so close to the chest that there is no sharing that happens.' Javed *bhai*'s unique achievement was how he got other rights groups –

human rights, women's rights, workers' rights, etc. – involved in the protest to get the disability bill passed.

Christy sees the need for coordination and collaboration among disability organizations, for multiple organizations of varied disabilities to work together. Pankajam Sreedevi, a long-time champion of diversity in industry and currently managing director of the Commonwealth Bank of Australia in India, says: 'NGOs have conflicting priorities. If everyone works together it can become a movement.'

## Secure Political Space

Obviously, if PwDs have to move to leadership roles, more disability organizations need to be headed by them. Disability rights activist Nipun Malhotra believes that they should also start occupying the political arena. He says, 'In order for the government to take the disability rights movement seriously, PwDs need to start talking to politicians as equals.'

Nipun questions why political parties don't have a disability wing: 'They have a "cell" for everything and everyone, for Dalit, minorities, etc. So why not a disability cell?' Part humorously, Nipun starts spitballing names for various party cells: Akhil Bhartiya Divyang Parishad for the BJP, All India Disability Congress for INC, Aam Disabled Cell for AAP... 'Unfortunately PwDs have not been looked at as part of the political vote bank,' he remarks.

But perhaps politicians are slowly beginning to acknowledge this reality. Tarit Datta of the Indian Association of Assistive Technology, speaking at the 2019 national conference on AT for All in Bengaluru, points out that some political parties have released accessible election manifestos, including videos in Sign and closed captioning.

G. Vijayaraghavan has a persuasive argument for the parliamentarians he meets: 'I tell them there are three per cent

PwDs in India. If you take in parents and at least one sibling, that's 12 per cent of the people who're directly impacted. But those parents have parents; so counting grandparents, 15 to 20 per cent of people in the country are directly connected to PwDs. I tell them, think of the votes!'

## Change in the Periphery

'When the remotest village becomes disability friendly, when a disabled child is able to go to a neighbourhood school in the village, then the change will happen,' says Arman Ali. 'The change in the disability movement will come when the fight starts from a district or a block or a village. It is not going to happen in Delhi.' He points to a discrepancy in the disability sector: 'There is an Us and Them – those who are articulate and well-connected, and those who are poor and can't speak for themselves.'

Ummul Kher is particularly scathing when she remarks on some of the glitzy seminars held in metros that merely pay lip service to disability. 'These are the stage shows of privileged people, a waste of time and money,' she says. 'My observation has been, we invite four or five already well established disability activists, the same people you see every year in national and international conferences. They come, they speak, talk to each other what they already know, and then they go. This is not making any difference in the lives of people who require intervention. Nobody dares invite PwDs who are begging, people at the grassroots, a person who had polio and runs an e-rickshaw for example.' Ummul believes that awareness programmes on disability held in remote areas will be far more effective and productive, besides being far less expensive. 'I hope in my official capacity [the] Almighty will give me the chance to organize such programmes,' says this young assistant commissioner in the Indian Revenue Service.

## A Disability University

In 2014, Mohan Sundaram of Artilab wrote a strategy paper for the disability sector, in which he came up with two ideas: infuse technology into the sector, and start an institution for disability studies. 'Every other industry has one section focussing on a body of knowledge for that particular industry – petroleum, mining, etc. There's nothing for disability,' he says. 'There is no body of knowledge accumulated over time for good decision-making or policies.'

This is a suggestion echoed by several people in the sector. G. Vijayaraghavan speaks of the importance of setting up a national university exclusively for disability studies. Many speakers at the 2019 national conference on AT for All, including the chief guest, vice chancellor of the Rajiv Gandhi University of Health Sciences (RGUHS) Dr S. Sacchidanand, voiced the need for a disability university. Tarit Datta says, 'Not enough research is carried out in India on disability.'

———

The disability movement should send out a resounding demand for total inclusion. While society's apathy towards, if not outright rejection of, PwDs stands in the way of their goal, there are some serious drawbacks that need the urgent attention of the state:

- **No accessibility:** The appalling absence of (both physical and digital) accessibility in every sphere of life is the number one area of concern. How can PwDs be visible and vocal if they cannot step out of their homes onto the street? How can they hope for academic and professional careers if their very first step is blocked by a wall of exclusion?
- **No data:** If appropriate policies – for education, employment and daily living – are to be framed and measures taken

for different disabilities, accurate and disaggregated data is a prerequisite. The numbers of PwDs are heavily under-reported and hence underestimated. A reliable and comprehensive disability census is of vital importance.

- **Lack of services:** The disability census can give us an idea of the types and magnitude of services that should reach PwDs. But there is a crippling shortage of professionals who can provide these services. There aren't enough occupational therapists, speech therapists, Special Ed. teachers, rehabilitation professionals... The list goes on. Mental health care is severely under-funded and there is a yawning gap in service delivery.

- **Stuck in red tape:** Everybody in the sector says with one voice: 'Great law, poor implementation'. Although notification of the rules by each state was supposed to be done within six months of the RPwD Act being passed, even years later the process has not been completed.

Also, only those departments directly connected to disability are aware of the requirements laid down in the Act. All government departments should be apprised of the Act and be required to act on it.

The National Building Code 2016 stipulates that all public and private buildings – repeat *all* public and private buildings – must be made accessible. A wonderful move. But the building bye-laws of each and every state have to be suitably amended to incorporate the latest NBC standards.

## Thoughts on Inclusion

Changemakers in the disability space are cautiously optimistic, by and large, about the prospect of an inclusive India. They know it's a long trek but they can see where the road is leading to.

Arman Ali is conscious of carrying forward Javed *bhai*'s legacy, of having been mentored in a way that inculcated a sense of responsibility in him for the sector and helped him find his own path. 'I'm not going to fill his shoes because I have my own shoes to fill, a different style and size!' he says, adding that although the goal of inclusion may not be achieved in his lifetime, he believes it will be as long as everybody pitches in. 'I have a role to play as a PwD myself and also the position which I am in. I have to continue the work. For any movement you just continue the fight, you carry forward that hope,' he concludes.

Major D.P. Singh loves talking to children because he believes they are at the right age for him to work on them, and get them used to disability and the idea of inclusion. For the country to become inclusive 'it will take a generation', he feels.

Prateek Kaul sounds the most upbeat of all, and is confident of being able to scale greater heights faster, even as he admits that 'there's a lot of work to be done'. GiftAbled has been ramping up its efforts exponentially, connecting with smaller organizations in remote areas and reaching out to volunteers, networking with corporates. 'Inclusion may not happen in five or 10 years, but we have to hand over the baton to someone else. Whoever is next in line will have to complete it,' he says.

Given the nature of autism, self-advocacy among persons with autism is rare anywhere in the world, and even more so in India. But Action For Austism has been persevering at this 'daunting task'. On the prospect of inclusion, AFA founder Merry Barua is quite forthright. Indian society is inherently exclusive, she says. 'We constantly divide [ourselves] on the basis of colour, religion, caste, everything.' If we want to make India inclusive we have to consider PwDs who are poor and belong to a minority community or belong to the oppressed castes. 'Inclusion is a process and I believe we will get there, but it will take longer. We will get there, maybe not in my lifetime,' says Merry.

Nipun Malhotra's mode of self-advocacy doesn't only take the form of litigation. He makes effective use of humour as well. He says he can't be a stand-up comic because, well, he can't stand up! So he does what he calls 'sit-down comedy'. There is a growing number of disabled stand-up comics in India who speak about their experiences and, although they often don't set out to become self-advocates, end up spreading awareness of disability among their audiences.

Shanti Raghavan of Enable India points out that all of us, even the so-called non-disabled, have inabilities to perform certain functions: 'You have both ability and inability, but you reject your inability. To me inclusion is when you can value both parts of yourself.'

The outspoken Jo Chopra of the Latika Roy Foundation in Dehradun projects a slide, in her talk at the India Inclusion Summit 2019, displaying the words: 'F*** inclusion' (with censored letters). Jo says emphatically, 'I am sick of the word "inclusion". It presupposes a power relationship.' It implies that PwDs are outside society and are 'permitted' to come inside. 'Stop asking for favours. Stop raising awareness,' she tells the audience. 'Be a little more badass, a little less grateful.'

## The Three C's

Here is where we strike a personal, partisan note and talk about an initiative that co-author and disability evangelist V.R. Ferose spearheaded a decade ago. To further the cause of disability in India, he conceived a set of programmes around the concept: 'Celebrate, Connect, Catalyse'.

Celebrate disability, connect the right people, catalyse entrepreneurship.

The India Inclusion Summit, which has been taking place every November since 2012, is a wholehearted celebration of disability. A Friend-Raising Evening on the eve of India Inclusion Summit brings people in the disability sector together, giving them opportunities to connect and strengthen each other's efforts. The Inclusion Fellowship, which was kicked off in 2016, is a mentorship programme for entrepreneurs working on innovative solutions for PwDs.

'We cannot build a movement through a traditional organizational structure,' says V.R. Ferose. 'We need the empathy of an NGO, the professionalism and agility of a corporate, and the scale of government.'

India Inclusion Summit is a free and entirely volunteer-driven event with the central theme: 'Everyone is Good at Something'. Thousands attend it in person and hundreds of thousands watch it online. Physical attendance is deliberately tailored to a ratio of 49:51 – 51 per cent of the participants are PwDs and 49 per cent are average, so that the 'minority' tag is stripped from the PwDs, and they become the majority here. Besides providing PwDs an accessible environment (both physical and digital), a buddy is assigned to each of them to offer whatever assistance they might ask for. The day-long programme is broken up into segments, hosted by PwDs, and alternates between talks and performances so that the atmosphere in the hall is kept live and bubbling. There are celebrity speakers from fields such as the arts, sports, science, technology and business, as well as respected figures from the academic, social and disability sectors.

You can read all about India Inclusion Summit on its website.[59] Find out what novel projects the Inclusion Fellows (some of whom are featured in this book) are working on to improve the lives of PwDs. Take a look at the magnificent works that the Art for Inclusion Fellows – all artists with disabilities – are creating.

But building a movement is not the work of a single person

---

[59] https://indiainclusionsummit.com

or entity. You know what they say about many grains of sand coming together to make a mighty land. Nothing stops you, for example, from passing on gleanings from this book to another person, teaching them some of the ABCs of disability. All the changemakers we've written about, and hundreds more out there whom we haven't mentioned, are pitching in mightily.

'How much impact do they all have?' the pessimists among you might ask. Will we ever live in an inclusive India? Can we really bring down the stone wall of indifference and exclusion, and admit everyone into the same social space? Well, there's no point measuring the size of the wall before we attempt to break it down. We have to keep hammering away at it.

That wall will not begin to crumble until there are enough of us pounding on it. But beyond that wall, we assure you, a space will open up before us that is vast enough to accommodate us all – irrespective of gender, caste, creed or ability – so that not a single person is left behind.

# MESSAGE

I convey my appreciation to V.R. Ferose and C.K. Meena, the authors of this book, *The Invisible Majority*, for having provided an excellent panoramic perspective on India's disability sector.

The book uses our country's progressive Rights of Persons with Disabilities Act 2016 as a focal point from which to expand into every aspect of the subject, from awareness to advocacy, diagnosis to early intervention, education to employment, lifestyle, assistive technology and assisted living.

The book is enriched by diverse and authentic voices of divyangjans as well as their caregivers. I am sure this well researched and deeply engaging book will help policymakers and practitioners to serve the cause of divyangjans more effectively.

**(M. Venkaiah Naidu)**

New Delhi
16 June 2021

# APPENDICES

## APPENDIX ONE

# WHAT THE STATE MUST DO

We have discussed extensively the role the state must play to make the lives of Persons with Disabilities truly comfortable and productive. Here, in brief, are the action points that must necessarily be addressed for India to become an unquestionably inclusive nation.

1.  Ensure that every PwD is included in the 2022 Census of India and that a detailed breakdown of data on disability is available.
2.  Make every public space and building accessible to all (from pavements, playgrounds, schools, colleges and banks to bus stands, railway stations, airports, etc.).
3.  Update the building by-laws of each state to conform to the National Building Code of India 2016, which mandates that every new construction must be accessible to all.
4.  Ensure that every government department and ministry takes disability into account when planning and budgeting for the future.
5.  Introduce disability as a subject in every educational and professional course.
6.  Remove the Goods and Services Tax (GST) levied on all assistive devices.

7.  Provide affordable health insurance for PwDs as part of universal health coverage policies for all.
8.  Promote the concept of Universal Design for all consumer products and services.
9.  Conduct disability awareness campaigns among all stakeholders, and training sessions for those working at every level of the judiciary, executive and legislative.
10. Model the proposed university for disability studies in Assam on similar disability-friendly universities abroad.

# APPENDIX TWO

# TEN VITAL FACTS ABOUT
# THE RPwD ACT

1.  In the earlier PwD Act of 1995, only seven kinds of disabilities were mentioned. In the RPwD Act, 21 disabilities are mentioned. Some of the new ones are Dwarfism, Parkinson's Disease, Autism Spectrum Disorder, Thalassaemia, Haemophilia, Sickle Cell Disease and Leprosy-cured.

2.  If you are 40 per cent disabled or more, you have a 'benchmark disability'. You can apply for a disability certificate, which entitles you to benefits such as free travel in state transport buses, concessional rail and air fare, scholarships for students with disabilities and bank loans. The government is also issuing a pan-India unique ID card for PwDs called the UDID.

3.  Every PwD between the ages of 6 and 18 has the right to free education in a neighbourhood school or a special school of their choice.

4.  Of the total number of government job vacancies every year, four per cent is reserved for those with benchmark disabilities. Of this, one per cent is reserved for the blind and visually impaired and one per cent for the deaf and hearing impaired. One per cent is for those with mobility impairment. This category also includes those with cerebral palsy, MD and

dwarfism, the leprosy-cured and survivors of acid attacks. The remaining one per cent is for those with multiple disabilities, autism, intellectual and learning disabilities, and mental illness.

5. No government establishment should discriminate against PwDs in employment. It should give them 'reasonable accommodation' in the workplace – that is, provide them a barrier-free, conducive environment.

6. You will be imprisoned for six months to five years and punished with fine if you insult or humiliate a PwD, if you forcibly sterilize a man or woman with disabilities, or forcibly terminate the pregnancy of a woman with disabilities.

7. PwDs who are being abused or exploited can report the matter to the local magistrate, who will have to give orders to rescue or protect them. Anyone who comes to know of such abuse can pass on the information to the magistrate.

8. All public buildings must be made accessible. 'Public' includes whatever is used by the public for education, work, leisure, medical, legal, commercial or religious purposes. In effect this means everything from schools, hospitals, banks, courts and police stations to shops, gyms, theatres, parks, polling booths, places of worship, bus stands, railway stations and airports.

9. All forms of public transport must be made accessible. This includes autos and cycle-rickshaws. Roads must also be made accessible.

10. The disabled have the right to live within the community and must be given a choice of housing options.

Go to https://legislative.gov.in/sites/default/files/A2016-49_1.pdf to download the 36-page pdf of the complete RPwD Act.

# APPENDIX THREE

# LIST OF INTERVIEWS

Christy Abraham. Personal Interview. 13 May 2019.

Aditi Agrawal. Personal Interview. 11 February 2019.

Arman Ali. Personal Interview. 15 October 2019.

Shreya Ila Anasuya. Telephonic Interview. 8 July 2020.

Neha Arora. Personal Interview. 14 October 2019.

Mohammed Asheel. Personal Interview. 15 February 2019.

Shashaank Awasthi. Personal Interview. 20 August 2019.

Avantika Bahl. Personal Interview. 26 November 2018.

Richa Bansal. Personal Interview. 11 October 2019.

Merry Barua. Personal Interview. 10 October 2019.

Pancham Cajla. Telephonic Interview. 20 July 2020.

Meena Cariappa. Personal Interview. 9 July 2019.

Pavitra Chalam. Message to V.R. Ferose. 13 June 2020. E-mail.

Gagandeep Singh Chandok. Personal Interview. 7 December 2019.

Manoj Chandran. Personal Interview. 5 December 2018.

Manoj Chandran. Messages to C.K. Meena. 13 January 2021 and
    26 July 2021. E-mail.

Prachi Deo. Personal Interview. 19 December 2019.

Pavithra Y.S. Personal Interview. 5 April 2019.

Rajesh H.R. Personal Interview. 9 July 2019.

Siddharth V. Jayakumar. Personal Interview. 6 August 2019.

Manjula Kalyan. Personal Interview. 19 December 2019.

Shravya Kanithi. Personal Interview. 19 December 2019.

Sujatha Kanithi. Personal Interview. 19 December 2019.

Ashwin Karthik. Personal Interview. 16 November 2019.

Ashwin Karthik. Telephonic Interview. 28 August 2020.

Ummul Kher. Personal Interview. 12 October 2019.

Kalyani Khona. Telephonic Interview. 5 September 2020.

Neha Kirpal. Personal Interview. 14 June 2019.

Kavitha Krishnamurthy. Personal Interview. 21 August 2019.

Vishwas K.S. Personal Interview. 3 December 2019.

Satheesh Kumar. Personal Interview. 15 February 2019.

Aditya K.V. Personal Interview. 10 October 2019.

Nipun Malhotra. Personal Interview. 11 October 2019.

Ganesh Mani. Personal Interview. 9 April 2019.

Suja Mathew. Personal Interview. 15 February 2019.

Mini Menon. Personal Interview. 7 January 2019.

Ramya S. Moorthy. Personal Interview. 21 August 2019.

Anima Nair. Personal Interview. 22 March 2019.

Mahima Nair. Personal Interview. 18 April 2019.

Janaki Narayan. Personal Interview. 21 March 2019.

Janaki Narayan. Telephonic Interview. 22 April 2019.

Poonam Natarajan. Personal Interview. 20 August 2019.

Shanti Raghavan. Personal Interview. 3 April 2019.

P. Rajasekharan. Personal Interview. 20 August 2019.

Aditya Rajesh. Personal Interview. 23 March 2019.

Smrithy Rajesh. Personal Interview. 23 March 2019.

Vidhya Ramasubban. Personal Interview. 14 August 2019.

Dhanya Ravi. Personal Interview. 5 September 2019.

Gitanjali Sarangan. Personal Interview. 16 May 2019.

Parag Shah. Telephonic Interview. 7 July 2020.

Saumitra Shah. Telephonic Interview. 6 December 2020.

Meera Shenoy. Personal Interview. 20 December 2019.

Jamal Siddiqui. Personal Interview. 18 November 2019.

Jamal Siddiqui. Telephonic Interview. 23 November 2019.

D.P. Singh. Personal Interview. 9 October 2019.

Thorkil Sonne. Personal Interview. 16 November 2019.

Pankajam Sreedevi. Personal Interview. 8 August 2019.

Geetha Sridhar. Personal Interview. 9 July 2019.

Aman Srivastava. Personal Interview. 5 June 2019.

Mohan Sundaram. Personal Interviews. 3 June 2019 and 20 September 2019.

Uma Tuli. Personal Interview. 9 October 2019.

Suresh Vaidyanathan. Telephonic Interview. 3 December 2020.

Shai Venkatraman. Telephonic Interview. 25 April 2020.

G. Vijayaraghavan. Personal Interview. 14 February 2019.

Shobha Viswanath. Email message to C.K. Meena. 25 October 2019. E-mail.

# ACKNOWLEDGEMENTS

*From Ferose*

To Vivaan, the enlightened soul
For making me a better person.

To Deepali, my love
For being my friend forever.

To my parents, brother and in-laws
For their unconditional love.

To Arun and Denise
For being my invisible pillar.

To everyone
who continues to fight for inclusion.

*From Meena*

To my nephew Rahul, prime motivator.

And to Ferose, for persuading me to take up this project. If not for him I wouldn't have measured the full breadth of the disability spectrum or been illuminated by the human rainbow that spans these pages.

*From both authors*

To Poulomi Chatterjee, editor par excellence, for shaping our book with her eagle eye and skilful hand.

# ABOUT THE AUTHORS

A science graduate from Kerala who fled to her adoptive city of Bangalore for her post-graduation in English, C.K. Meena strayed into journalism and later branched out into writing fiction. She has been on the staff of *Deccan Herald* and is a columnist for *The Hindu*. She is also a founding member of the Asian College of Journalism in Bangalore, and has three published novels and innumerable features and columns to her credit. A card-carrying Luddite, she has never been remotely tempted to tweet or blog, but she has succumbed to the lure of her rarely used Kindle during the pandemic and is wondering what horrors await her.

V.R. Ferose is a senior vice president at SAP SE and the head of SAP Academy for Engineering. He is the founder of the India Inclusion Foundation, a non-profit organization that aims to bring the topic of inclusion to the forefront in India. Ferose has co-authored *Gifted: Inspiring Stories of People with Disabilities*, a best-selling book on people with disabilities, which has been translated into six Indian regional languages and whose Kannada edition has won the prestigious Karnataka Sahitya Academy Award. Among his other published work as a co-author are *Innovating the World: The Globalization Advantage* and *Grit: The Major Story*. Ferose teaches Personal Leadership at Columbia University, New York, and is a columnist for *Forbes*, *New Indian Express* and *Mint*.